Digital Personae
and Profiles in Law

Protecting Individuals' Rights
in Online Contexts

Arnold Roosendaal

Digital Personae and Profiles in Law
Protecting Individuals' Rights in Online Contexts

Arnold Roosendaal

ISBN: 978-90-5850-989-5

Fotografie omslag:
Tobias Groenland
http://www.tobiasgroenland.nl
+31614669030

Published by:
Wolf Legal Publishers (WLP)
PO Box 313
5060 AH Oisterwijk
The Netherlands
E-Mail: info@wolfpublishers.nl
www.wolfpublishers.com

Digital Personae and Profiles in Law

Protecting Individuals' Rights in Online Contexts

Proefschrift ter verkrijging van de graad van doctor aan
Tilburg University op gezag van de rector magnificus,
prof.dr. Ph. Eijlander, in het openbaar te verdedigen ten overstaan
van een door het college voor promoties aangewezen commissie in
de aula van de Universiteit op dinsdag 21 mei 2013 om 16.15 uur
door Arnold Petrus Christiaan Roosendaal,
geboren op 18 april 1979 te Halsteren

Promotores:
prof.dr. R.E. Leenes
prof.dr. E.J. Koops

Commissieleden:
prof.mr.dr. M. Hildebrandt
prof.dr.ir. W. Kraaij
prof.dr. E.G. Smit
prof.dr. P. de Hert

Table of Contents

Part III
Protection of Digital Personae

Abbreviations

CNIL	La Commission Nationale de l'Informatique et des Libertés (French DPA)
DCC	Dutch Civil Code
DNT	DoNotTrack
DPA	Data Protection Authorities
DPD	Data Protection Directive (95/46/EC)
EC	European Commission
ECHR	European Convention on Human Rights and Fundamental Freedoms
ECtHR	European Court on Human Rights
FCC	Federal Communications Commission
FTC	Federal Trade Commission
GDPR	General Data Protection Regulation (Proposal)
OBA	Online Behavioral Advertising
SNS	Social Networking Site(s)
W3C	World Wide Web Consortium

Preface

The chance to write a PhD thesis is a wonderful privilege. It requires effort, lots of effort, but also a good working environment. An environment with high academic standards and culture, which consists not only of the physical surroundings but also, perhaps even more importantly, of people who support and contribute to your own academic development. I found this environment at the Tilburg Institute for Law, Technology, and Society (TILT) at Tilburg University. I am grateful to those who created this environment for me and trusted me in writing and completing this thesis. Special thanks should go to my supervisors, Professor Ronald Leenes and Professor Bert-Jaap Koops, and to my M706 office mate, Martin Pekárek.

Doing my research and presenting the interim results gave me the opportunity to meet all kinds of people. This was a great pleasure and very inspiring, it also strengthened my ability to communicate my research and its societal relevance to the outside world.

Finally, nothing is possible without a good home. Thanks to my lovely family and their unlimited support by creating room for my work and by giving love and understanding. I dedicate this book especially to my beloved children: Jetske and Tjabbe.

Chapter 1
Introduction

"We are programmed to receive.
You can checkout any time you like, but you can never leave!"

(The Eagles, Hotel California, 1977)

1. Setting the stage

"Personal data is the new oil of the Internet and the new currency of the digital world."[1] This statement by the European Consumer Commissioner pinpoints the importance of personal data in contemporary society. Over the last decade, society has become an information society, with information and knowledge as key assets for development. Currently, we are heading towards a data society,[2] in which the collection and processing of data is at the heart of the economy.

A specific type of data that is frequently processed is personal data. Processing of personal data leads to tensions concerning control and power. Commercial organizations try to leverage data to create value, while individuals have perceptions of harm and powerlessness concerning the use and protection of their data.[3] The personal data of customers have become a major asset for commercial companies. Together with technological developments in the field of ICT and internet services, this implies that personal data about every individual are collected, further processed, and analyzed for commercial purposes by numerous businesses.

The massive use of personal data also leads to concern among individuals. "Three out of four Europeans accept that revealing personal data is part of everyday life, but they are also worried about how companies – including search engines and social networks – use their information."[4] People are concerned about lack of control and lack of transparency. Individuals have

---

[1] Meglena Kuneva, European Consumer Commissioner, March 2009.
[2] Van Lieshout et al. 2012, p. 20.
[3] World Economic Forum 2012.
[4] European Commission. Data Protection: Europeans share data online, but privacy concerns remain – new survey. Press release IP/11/742, Brussels, 16 June 2011, on survey results of the Eurobarometer on "Attitudes on Data Protection and Electronic Identity in the European Union": <http://ec.europa.eu/public_opinion/archives/eb_special_359_340_en.htm#359>.

few means to prevent their data from being processed, while at the same time they have no clear view of the purposes of the processing. The impact the processing may have on the individual is even more opaque.

1.1. Digital Interactions

In everyday life, individuals present themselves in interactions with others and with institutions. They make all kinds of decisions concerning themselves and choose for specific (re)presentations in specific contexts. However, nowadays everyone also has an online life in the form of digital personae. These digital personae are digital representations of the individual. For instance, social networking sites (SNS) such as Facebook[5] provide a platform for individuals to create a personal profile page which can contain all kinds of information, from name, age and gender to personal interests, videos and photos, and blogs. Other entities create digital personae as well in the form of detailed records, based on (personal) data from individuals, to make certain decisions, such as excluding someone from an offer. Thus, these decisions do affect the individuals. Next to digital personae, numerous data sets are created to represent individuals who are unknown to the creating entity. These are called profiles and are in a web context typically constituted from data concerning, for instance, browsing behavior of an individual.

Human beings are protected with rights such as privacy, integrity and dignity, as laid down, for example, in the European Convention on Human Rights and Fundamental Freedoms (ECHR). The function of these rights is to protect individuals in their everyday life against infringements against or violations of their body or personality. The rights enable individuals to live an autonomous life. For digital personae and profiles, rights or other forms of protection do not exist for obvious reasons as rights concern individuals, not tangible nor intangible goods such as information. Nevertheless, digital personae and profiles increasingly, certainly metaphorically, lead their own (digital) life. However, they are closely connected to the individuals they represent, even though some of the characteristics of the digital representation may not conform to reality.

The way individuals are represented in data and the way decisions based on these data affect individuals has an influence on identity. On the one hand, companies decide on how to create a representation and what models to use to that end. According to Turow, personalized advertising has the effect of social and consumer discrimination, which results from three converging developments: "advertising practitioners' infatuation with data about online audiences, the rise of companies that can provide that data in a

---

[5] See <http://www.facebook.com>.

readily accessible form, and the growth of technologies that can selectively serve advertising to individuals based on the data associated with them."[6] Commercial interests make that individuals are seen as "targets or waste".[7] Nevertheless, "the version of you being constructed [by others] is probably not who you think you are."[8] Companies often claim that the data they process is anonymous. However, even when no directly identifying information is available in the data set, as is the case with profiles, based on the data and specific links, such as cookie identifiers, they can reach and somehow affect this individual: "If a company can follow and interact with you in the digital environment […] its claim that you are anonymous is meaningless, particularly when firms intermittently add offline information to the online data and then simply strip the name and address to make it 'anonymous'."[9]

On the other hand, individuals can, if they are aware of the models, feel the need to modify their identity. As Lanier indicates: "[W]e are beginning to design ourselves to suit digital models of us."[10] In this respect, it is important to realize that the models are not objective. Commercial companies create these models with a commercial interest in mind. The decisions based on the models can be double-biased: first there is the model, which is a form of representation as chosen by the company, and, second, there is the decision which is biased by the commercial interest or the philosophy of the company. For instance, search results on Google are based on the digital persona Google has of the individual who enters the search term, and, even though Google's mission is to organize the world's information and make it universally accessible and useful,[11] the displayed results are based on opinions of Google that are implemented in the search algorithms.[12]

Because the data of the digital representation can be used to affect an individual by taking decisions based on the data that constitute the digital persona or the profile, the rights of the individual are at stake. This has triggered the present research, which explores whether protecting digital personae can help to protect the privacy of individuals. Profiles, as closely related to digital personae, are taken into account along this study as well, and the exact differences between digital personae and profiles, and what these differences mean for the individual, will be discussed extensively. Digital personae will be used as a red thread and where relevant differences with profiles appear, these will be addressed explicitly.

---

[6] Turow 2011, p. 90.
[7] Turow 2011, p. 89.
[8] Rosen 2000.
[9] Turow 2011, p. 190.
[10] Lanier 2010, p. 39.
[11] See: <http://www.google.com/intl/en/about/index.html>.
[12] Metz 2010.

Technological development in the field of digital personae and profiles brings new challenges for privacy and data protection. Besides, the debate on the importance of privacy, in particular in relation to the Internet, is livelier than ever. This was also recognized in an OECD report on Personhood and Digital Identity, which stated: "[G]iven the importance of these issues for the future information society, more investigation is needed into how to address gaps in international data protection in light of the emergent identity infrastructure".[13] This research takes a strategic approach towards privacy protection in a digital environment.

1.2. Digital personae

Digital personae are (digital) representations of individuals. This is, however, still a vague definition which needs further explanation. For this study the starting point will be the definition of digital personae given by Roger Clarke: *"The digital persona is a model of an individual's public personality based on data and maintained by transactions, and intended for use as a proxy for the individual"*.[14] This definition clearly reflects the issue of representation. Furthermore, Clarke makes a distinction between projected digital personae and imposed digital personae. A projected digital persona is created by the individual and is strictly related to the way this individual wants to present himself. A personal web page is a good example of this form. In contrast, the imposed digital persona is created by institutions based on the information they collect(ed) about the individual, and this persona has a certain function related to the goals of the institution. Based on digital representations, decisions are made, some of them unknown to the individuals affected. However, the link between the digital persona and the individual is clear and the decisions clearly have an influence on these persons. This may affect the privacy and autonomy of the individual and result in unreasonable constraints on the construction of identity.

With regard to the projected persona and the imposed persona, Clarke states: "The individual has some degree of control over a **projected persona**, but it is harder to influence **imposed personae** created by others. Each observer is likely to gather a different set of data about each individual they deal with, and hence to have a different gestalt impression of that person."[15] In this study, a third form of digital persona is presented which is more prevalent in contemporary practice: the **hybrid persona**, which is a combination

---

[13]   OECD 2007.
[14]   See: <http://www.anu.edu.au/people/Roger.Clarke/DV/DigPersona.html>. Last accessed: May 18, 2008.
[15]   See: <http://www.anu.edu.au/people/Roger.Clarke/DV/DigPersona.html>. Last accessed: May 18, 2008.

of projected and imposed elements. In this form, the individual provides certain information, which is combined with information by another entity. For instance, when an individual creates a profile page on Facebook, the information posted on the page is a projected element. Facebook combines this information with data concerning web browsing behavior and analyses of data provided by other members of the SNS. The result is an enriched data set that forms a digital persona of the individual.

A distinction between digital representations and software agents can be made. Software agents perform certain actions on behalf of an individual or company and may thus also function as a representation. We have skipped the question whether intelligent agents should be able (or in fact allowed) to perform transactions and to make decisions. They already can. In this light, it should be taken into account that in the near future the capabilities of digital personae may be extended. However, this study primarily focuses on the passive digital persona.

Another form of passive data sets are profiles. These are closely related to digital personae, with the main difference that profiles concern individuals who cannot be identified, whereas digital personae represent known individuals. Enriching data sets by means of monitoring and profiling, or with processes of data mining, occurs in both governmental contexts (e.g. surveillance for security purposes) and in commercial contexts (e.g. profiling for the purpose of targeted advertising). In this study, the focus will be on the use of digital personae and profiles in commercial contexts. The processing of data concerning individuals can have implications for privacy and is subject to data protection legislation.

1.3. Privacy and data protection legislation

The European Directive on the protection of personal data (Directive 95/46/EC,[16] DPD) regulates the processing of personal data. Article 2(a) of this Directive gives a definition of personal data: "'personal data' shall mean any information relating to an identified or identifiable natural person ('data subject'); an identifiable person is one who can be identified, directly or indirectly, in particular by reference to an identification number or to one or more factors specific to his physical, physiological, mental, economic, cultural or social identity". Examples are name and address. The Directive is applicable if personal data are being processed.

---

[16] Directive 95/46/EC of the European Parliament and of the Council of 24 October 1995 on the protection of individuals with regard to the processing of personal data and on the free movement of such data, OJ L 281.

Given the need for clarification of the notion "personal data" in various contexts, the Article 29 Working Party adopted an opinion on the concept of personal data. The Working Party argued that the technological state of the art at the time of the processing, as well as the future technological possibilities during the period for which the data will be processed, have to be considered. More specifically, the Article 29 Working Party stated that "if [the data] are intended to be kept for 10 years, the controller should consider the possibility of identification that may occur also in the ninth year of their lifetime, and which make them personal data at that moment".[17] Since technology is developing rapidly, in many cases it will not be possible for the controller to "guess" the means that might be used within a few years time. Trying to foresee the possibility of identification after 10 years can be extremely difficult for a controller and therefore the question arises whether data protection legislation must be applied in all relevant applications, following a "just-in-case" model.[18] In this light, the distinction between digital personae and profiles is important. Similarities and differences between the two[19] will be used throughout this study to clarify the use and impact of data sets concerning individuals.

It is important to distinguish between privacy and data protection. "[T]he vast bulk of continental Europe actually subscribed to privacy as a fundamental Human Right in terms of Art. 8 of the European Convention on Human Rights and viewed data protection as hierarchically one step below that, a kind of enabling right which exists to protect the hierarchically one step higher fundamental right to 'private and family life'."[20] Data protection is necessary in order to enjoy informational privacy. This implies that personal data which are a part of digital representations also need to be protected. Following Joel Reidenberg's suggestion of a Lex Informatica,[21] there currently is a plea for a Lex Personalitatis,[22] which, next to personality rights, also encompasses such concepts as the right to a guarantee of confidentiality and integrity in information-technology systems. In essence, this approach is an elaboration of data protection to current technological developments.

Social and technological developments have put the sustainability of the current Data Protection Directive (95/46/EC) under pressure. "[T]he Directive is becoming increasingly out-dated, is not sufficiently clear in its objectives, is more bureaucratic and burdensome than it needs to be and is out

---

[17] Article 29 Working Party 2007.
[18] Cf. Fischer-Hübner & Hedbom 2007. They proposed this model in relation to RFID technologies.
[19] See Chapter 2, section 4.
[20] Cannataci 2008.
[21] Reidenberg 1978.
[22] Cannataci 2008.

of step with good regulatory practice."[23] An evaluation of the Directive was needed.[24] In January 2012, the European Commission presented a proposal for a General Data Protection Regulation (GDPR) which is to replace the current DPD. The aim of this proposal is to update data protection regulation to meet current technologies and practices and to reinforce the rights of the individual provided for by the DPD, while at the same time improving legal certainty for data controllers as regards the applicability of the DPD.

1.4. An alternative approach

Because it can be difficult to foresee what information will be revealed by certain data in the future, the question is whether it is sufficient to look at bits of data as such, as is now the case in data protection legislation, or whether protection of complete digital personae, including personal data and data that may become personal data, is a viable alternative. Holistic digital representations are increasingly created from separate data. Data are connected, so even data which are not considered to be personal data yet, because they cannot directly or indirectly be connected to an individual, have a link to a person via the representation. Digital representations are conglomerates of data. The background for data protection legislation is, among other things, to enable privacy protection. By focusing on privacy as a whole, taking an alternative approach by protecting digital personae might lead to a similar or even better result. This alternative approach might include providing protection for digital personae, which may also make it easier, or more legitimate, to set certain rules and basic requirements for the creation and use of digital personae. As a result, it will become easier to balance rights and duties. In this study, the possibilities for protecting digital personae, possibly by embedding them as a new concept in the legal system, will be explored.

2. Aim of the study

The aim of this study is to investigate whether privacy and autonomy of individuals can be better protected by implementing the concept of the digital persona in law. The use of digital personae and profiles clearly has an effect on the rights of individuals. These effects will be described from a multidisciplinary perspective. When the effects and related rights of individuals that need to be protected are set out, an analysis will be made of possible ways to implement the digital persona in law. First, the concept will be analyzed from the perspective of existing legal constructs and then a proposal for a new implementation will be presented.

---

[23] Information Commissioner UK, 'Invitation to Tender – Review of EU Data Protection Law', 14 April 2008.
[24] See, for instance, EDPS 2007.

The main research question to be answered in this study is the following:

Can the (legal) protection of digital personae as coherent data sets, taking into account that they are used by businesses as a basis for making decisions that affect real-world individuals, improve the protection of privacy and autonomy of the individuals represented by these digital personae?

In order to answer this question, the following subquestions are relevant:
- What are digital personae?
- How are digital personae used?
- How are individuals affected by decisions based on digital personae?
- What rights of the individual are at stake?
- How are these rights protected?
- Are these rights adequately protected in view of digital personae?
- If not, how can the protection of these rights be improved?

These sub questions will be answered step by step throughout this study.

The research is carried out from a European perspective, in the sense that EU legislation forms the regulatory framework for this study. Furthermore, the study is particularly focused on the commercial domain, so the use of digital personae by governmental institutions is excluded. This limitation is related to the major differences that appear between the governmental/ administrative and commercial purposes, as well as the legal safeguards that apply to these contexts. Moreover, the type of impact related to the use of digital personae by governments may significantly differ from the impact resulting from commercial use.

3. Methodology

Although this study was mainly executed from a legal perspective, sociology and ethics were also relevant disciplines. The questions on the representation of individuals in the form of digital personae and profiles include societal issues that are central to the debate on Internet and ICT development, as well as privacy and data protection. In addition, a technological component is included to make data collection and use in an internet context more concrete.

The author does not have a degree in all disciplines, so obviously the research and findings related to the non-legal field may show limitations. Nevertheless, based on a literature study and conversations with experts in the relevant fields, the descriptions should be appropriate for the purposes of this study. Several research methods were used in this study. Most of the work is based on desk research. With the author having a background in law, the research concerning other disciplines, such as sociology and philosophy, was based on handbooks and key literature in these disciplines. For the legal and technical work, a great deal of literature on the subjects was consulted.

This research contains a case study on Facebook's tracking practices,[25] which required technical experiments. These tests were performed by the author himself. The findings have been confirmed by Facebook, and have been reproduced by researchers from German and Dutch Data Protection Authorities and the Wall Street Journal, amongst others. Discussions on the findings took place with Facebook engineers, in particular Gregg Stefancik, and with Ulrich Kühn of the Datenschutzbeauftragte Hamburg, Germany. More general in-depth discussions on the technical details and workings took place with Ashkan Soltani and Chris Hoofnagle. Additional findings and comments on the Facebook case study were derived from qualitative interviews with Luc Delany, Facebook's European Policy Manager, and Gregg Stefancik.

For the case study on Google, several documents and communications, in particular between Google and the CNIL, were analyzed. A third case study concerns real-time web personalization and the combination of online and offline data. This study is based on literature and six semi-structured qualitative interviews with representatives of companies who are involved in these activities. One interview was telephone-based, the other five were face-to-face interviews. The interviewees of this case study have expressed their will to remain anonymous, which is respected. Amongst the interviewees two persons are active in the credit rating and finance industry and two persons are working at an insurance company that uses the described technologies. One interviewee works as a tracking technology provider. The telephone interview concerned a representative from an EU advertising branch organization.

Furthermore, interim results have been presented at several (inter)national conferences and summer schools and received feedback from participants as well as informal talks have been very valuable for collecting information and getting ideas in the right direction.

4. Outline of the study

This study is divided into three parts: (1) Theory and Abstract Level; (2) Practice and Concrete Level, and; (3) Protecting Digital Personae. In Part 1, "Theory and Abstract Level", the theoretical background of the study will be described. Digital personae and profiles are representations of individuals and can be seen as digital identities, so a first step is to look what identity and representation actually mean (Chapter 2). Identity will be discussed

---

[25]   Chapter 5, section 4.1.

from the perspective of sociology, philosophy, and media theory. In Chapter 3, the concept of the digital persona will be discussed. First, the step from presentation and representation to digital presentation and representation will be made and the digital persona will be compared to profiles. In this study, the focus is not on the process of profiling (including machine learning and correlations), but on profiles as coherent data sets resulting from data collection practices.[26] Second, the specific forms of digital personae will be assessed, including reasons for the creation of digital personae.

In Chapter 4, the legal background of the study will be presented. Autonomy and privacy will be discussed as the main value and right to be protected. They are related to the human dignity, identity, informational self-determination, and contextual integrity. Subsequently, the general level of the legal implementation of these values and rights at a European level will be described, followed by the more specific level of data protection regulation.

Part 2 of the study, "Practice and Concrete Level", starts with a description of the use of digital personae (Chapter 5). First, a short fairy tale will be told to sketch the 'life' of a digital persona. Second, the events in the fairy tale will be explained by describing the technical processes of web interactions and cookie use. The Chapter will end with two case studies on large web companies that create and use digital personae: Facebook and Google, and a case study on the combination of online and offline data sources and real-time web personalization. In Chapter 6, shortcomings in current data protection regulation observed in the previous chapters will be described. Here, the way in which the use of digital personae affects the rights of individuals will also be discussed. On the basis of all this, at the end of Chapter 6, the overall problem definition of this study will be presented.

In Part 3, "Protecting Digital Personae", a solution is sought for the problem thus presented. In Chapter 7, an assessment will be made of existing legal constructs that may offer opportunities to protect digital personae. This will show advantages and drawbacks and allow focusing on the exact difficulties that have to be taken into account when implementing the concept of the digital persona in law. Finally, in Chapter 8, a proposal will be presented for embedding the digital persona in law. The limitations of the proposal will also be discussed and a final conclusion will be drawn, including the answer to the main research question of this study.

---

[26] Compare Custers, Calders, Schermer & Zarsky 2013, p. 4.

Part I

Theory and Abstract Level

Chapter 2
Identity and Representation

1. Introduction

For the purpose of this study, several disciplines need to be combined, or at least interrelated, since the topic of digital personae and the privacy protection of individuals is inherently an interdisciplinary one. In, this chapter, the theoretical framework of this study will be presented, in order to clarify the terms used (e.g. digital persona, individual, representation, profile, identity) and to validate the choices made in defining these terms. The interpretation of these terms depends to a large extent on the disciplinary view that is taken. Not only will the different disciplinary viewpoints be described, but also how the terms themselves relate to each other. A number of theories will be described and the relations between these theories will be discussed. The aim of this chapter is not to give an extensive overview of and insight in all identity and representation theories, so a selection has been made of a number of theories and authors to be discussed. The selected theories and their authors are generally accepted as the main contributors to the relevant concepts in their disciplines. The primary sources have been used as a starting point, supplemented with secondary literature.

Presentation and representation are important terms in relation to identity theory and in relation to how digital personae function as proxies for individuals. These terms are briefly introduced in section 2. In section 3, the concept of identity is described with a focus on sociological (3.1), philosophical (3.2), and media theory (3.3) perspectives. Next, the link to the digital environment is made by looking at digital presentation and representation (4). Subsequently, there is a description of digital personae (4.1) and of profiles (4.2), and a description of how a profile can transform into a digital persona (4.3), followed by a comparison between the two (4.4). In the comparison, use is made of semiotics to analyse how digital personae and profiles acquire meaning and how they relate to each other. Finally, in section 5, a synthesis is presented in which the main findings and relations from the chapter are briefly summarized.

2. Presentation and representation

A number of issues are relevant to be able to describe the impact and value of digital personae. The digital persona is a form of a digital representation of an individual. Obviously, representation is closely related to presentation.

In short, it can be said that a presentation is the direct and active form of presenting something, whereas representation is more indirect. "Representation means a presenting again, a presenting of something not present, which may take a linguistic as well as a visual form."[27] Nevertheless, the terms are somewhat confusing, since presenting an object to an audience, whether or not in real time, leads to a representation of the object concerned. The way of presenting always includes the interpretation of the presenter, thereby distinguishing the presentation from the original object. In addition, the audience interprets the presentation, thereby creating a follow-up representation. For each cycle of representation, a relationship between three terms is involved; "an object[28] is a representation of something for some information-processing device."[29] This triadic relationship will be elaborated in section 4.4 below. In the context of this study, it is useful to note that the information-processing device can be a human being or a machine. Traditionally, humans have made interpretations of the objects concerned whereas nowadays 'interpretation' often takes place through automatic devices.

Representation is a central issue and is strongly related to identity. Identity can relate to an object or to an entity (subject or person). In the context of this study, identity is discussed in relation to natural persons, which I will call entities.[30] In order to gain more insight into the concept of identity and its relation to presentation and representation, this phenomenon will be described in detail in the following sections, using different disciplinary approaches. Special attention will be paid to the sociological and philosophical approaches, because they are more specifically related to individuals and their (re)presentations.

3. The concept of identity

Identity is a complex phenomenon: its meaning depends on the disciplinary approach that is taken. In general, identity is related to sameness or difference, i.e. something is the same as it was under different conditions, or something diverges from another thing to which it is compared. It has to do with being identical. In mathematical terms, identity can be defined as $A = A$ (sameness), but $A \neq B$ (difference). Gottfried Leibniz[31] held that $x = y$ if

---

27 Goody 1997, p. 31.
28 Note that the terminology is used differently by different authors. For C.S. Peirce, for instance, the object here is the interpretant, whereas 'object' in his terminology is the original (the something that is represented). See also section 4.4 below.
29 Goody 1997, p. 32.
30 Cf. Clarke 2003.
31 Leibniz 1969, p. 308.

and only if every predicate true of x is true of y as well and if every predicate true of y is true of x as well. This theory is commonly known as Leibniz's law. If any concession is necessary to conclude that $x = y$, the theory does not apply.[32] Logic describes this as $x = y$ if x is the same thing as y.

It becomes more complicated when the aspect of time (or a different conditional factor) is introduced. The question whether a table is the same table as it was a year ago can be answered positively, notwithstanding the fact that the table might now have some scratches or may have changed colour a little because it has been in the sun. However, it can not be claimed to be identical in mathematical terms, given the different characteristics. Similar problems arise with regard to individual persons. I am still the same person as I was ten years ago, but in a different sense, taking into account physical and mental changes, I am not. In this context, specifications of identity in personal, sociological, and cultural identity can apply. The focus of the concept of identity then shifts from 'being identical' towards 'identification' in the meaning of 'identifying as' or 'identifying with'. 'Identifying as' has to do with identifying an individual as George, a specific individual, whereas 'identifying with' has to do with connecting someone to a group, such as heavy-metal music lovers.

Another quite common approach towards identity is to use the term 'identity' to refer to an 'identifier' or a token for identification.[33] Identity, then, means any set of attributes that individuates an individual within a group. In some cases, one single attribute can be sufficient, for instance, a genetic profile or a unique identification number. Or the combination of a password and a username to access a certain web service is called an identity. This approach is problematic, since the terms 'identity' and 'identifier' are used as exact synonyms while they are not. A distinction can be made between types of (digital) identities, with a focus on their richness. An extensive set of data can form a rich identity of an individual, whereas a small set can form a poor identity. A unique identifier, which refers to an individual but does not contain any further information concerning the individual, can be called a super poor identity. However, unique identification numbers exist which are constructed in a way that they contain information such as age, gender, and region. For instance, in Belgium, the INSZ-number is used as an identification number for social security services. The number's composition is: YY.MM. DD XXX-XX, where YY.MM.DD signifies the date of birth of the holder and XXX-XX is a serial number.[34]

---

[32] Margolis 1971, p. 217.
[33] See for instance: Nabeth & Hildebrandt 2005; Hildebrandt, Koops & de Vries 2008.
[34] Roosendaal, Steinbrecher, Leenes & Buitelaar 2009.

Having described these general approaches towards identity, presentation and representation can be introduced. An individual, George, can take a picture of himself, taking a specific pose, and thereby presenting himself; the picture is a representation. Another person can look at the picture and identify the individual on the picture as George. Here, George is identified. The George on the picture, however, is not George, but a representation of George, since the picture shows an image of George and is not identical to the physical person George.

In order to give more detailed insight into the relation between identity, presentation, and representation, the concept of identity will be elaborated on below from the disciplinary perspectives of sociology, philosophy, and media theory.

3.1. Identity in sociology

In sociology, several theories concerning identity have been developed. The importance of identity is related to people's need for interaction. Social life is based on interaction and saturated with a myriad of implicit and explicit behavioral codes and concepts. Which kind of behaviour is expected from an individual is strongly connected to the social role of the individual and the social context in which the interaction takes place. The role a person plays gives clues about the expected behavior. This is also the reason why people find it important to pigeon-hole others; it provides a frame of reference and gives clues on how interaction should take place. Whether a person complies with the social rules or not is part of self-expression and can give opportunities to individuals to change their (perceived) role and the way they are perceived by others.

Another important aspect is audience segregation. People let their behavior depend on the presence of other people: the audience. For instance, an individual behaves differently in a family context than in an employment context. This all has to do with identity construction.

Three of the main contributors to sociological identity theories are George Herbert Mead, Erving Goffman, and Anthony Giddens. Their theories will be discussed below.

Mead is the founder of the symbolic interactionism which is described in his standard work *Mind, Self, and Society*.[35] According to Mead, the self is active and creative, and he stresses people's ability, through the mechanism of self-interaction, to form and guide their own conduct. People can influence their

---

[35]   Mead 1934.

own behaviour, based on reflections on themselves. People try to estimate their (public) presence by assuming what others think of their conduct. Mead explains that communication is a process whereby each person 'takes the role of the other'; that is, each person 'assumes the attitude of the other individual as well as calling it out in the other', which would be impossible without self-interaction. As Elliott[36] puts it: "The self for Mead is at once individuality and generality, agent and recipient, sameness and difference" which means that "the self is the agency through which individuals experience themselves in relation to others, but also an object or fact dealt with by its individual owner as he or she sees fit."

Mead makes a specific distinction between the 'I' and the 'me'. "The 'I' is the response of the organism to the attitudes of the others; the 'me' is the organized set of attitudes of others assumed by a person. The attitudes of the others constitute the organized 'me', and then the person reacts to that as an 'I'."[37] So, the attitudes of others are seen by an individual and make the individual aware of himself. This self a person is aware of is called the 'me'. The individual responds on the basis of this self-consciousness. This response is given by the 'I', as an "action over against that social situation within his own conduct,"[38] and this is what constitutes the 'I'. The 'I' is that with which individuals identify themselves. After an action has taken place, the action becomes part of the past experiences of the individual and thus becomes part of the 'me'.

The individual wants to present himself to others in a way that is assumed to be appropriate for the given situation. As a result of this situation-oriented behavior, "in different social contexts various aspects of the complete self are more evident."[39] In order to achieve this appropriate presentation, the individual creates an image of himself in his own mind, which reflects the way in which the individual thinks others look at him. This image is a representation of the assumed interpretation (also a representation) by others.

An even more direct link between identity and presentation is made by Erving Goffman in his book *The Presentation of Self in Everyday Life*.[40] "The self consists for Goffman in an awareness of the multiplicity of roles that are performed in various situated contexts [...] [P]ublic identity is thus performed for an audience, and the private self knows that such performances are

---

[36] Elliott 2001, p. 26.
[37] Mead 1934, p. 175.
[38] Mead 1934, p. 175.
[39] Turner, Beeghley & Powers 1998, p. 357.
[40] Goffman 1959.

essential to identity and to the maintenance of respect and trust in routine social interaction."[41] Goffman clarifies the distinction between self and identity in the sense that an identity is performed and the self is the effect of the scene that comes off. The performed identity is dependent on the context in which the individual interacts. In this respect, the roles an individual can play can be referred to as partial identities.

With regard to the role performance, a performer (an individual) tries to engender in his audience the belief that there is a specific relation to them. According to Goffman[42] "[f]irst, individuals often foster the impression that the routine they are presently performing is their only routine or at least their most essential one. (…) Secondly, performers tend to foster the impression that their current performance of their routine and their relationship to their current audience have something special and unique about them." Relating a role or performance to a specific audience and keeping the presentation of the self restricted to the attributes and characteristics that fit this role is essential in social life. Goffman calls this 'audience segregation' and states that "by audience segregation the individual ensures that those before whom he plays one of his parts will not be the same individuals before whom he plays a different part in another setting."[43] The self consists of several partial identities which are each related to a specific context. Thus, an individual is always known by his audience as the identity that is shown in the specific context. There is "no such thing as a 'core self', but rather an evolving network of various relational roles."[44]

A late-modern approach is taken by Giddens, who states that "[t]he self is seen as a reflexive project, for which the individual is responsible. We are, not what we are, but what we make of ourselves."[45] In this view, the individual has the main control over the development of his self and identity. Identity development is less dependent on roles and more related to social acceptance.

The development of personal identity is a relatively young phenomenon. "Through the Middle Ages, identity was largely equated with the visible person."[46] Identity depended on social rank and gender, which could immediately be seen because of dress codes, and people were mostly seen by people who knew them anyway, due to the lack of social and geographical mobility and the stability of social groups. The contact of people with

---

[41] Elliott 2001, pp. 31-32.
[42] Goffman 1959, pp. 48-49.
[43] Goffman 1959, p. 49.
[44] Van den Berg 2009, p. 42.
[45] Giddens 1991, p. 75.
[46] Baumeister & Muraven 1996.

strangers increased with the advent of urbanization. People's rank in society became changeable because of social mobility, and people began to try to pass for their betters.[47] The idea of the existence of an inner identity as an important and large part of the self continued to grow. "In short, changes in social relations and the progressive questioning of self-knowledge have removed identity from the realm of the obviously visible. Adapting to these changes, identity has come to be understood as an inner, hidden identity that is only indirectly known, such as by being expressed in one's actions or roles."[48]

Riesman[49] has formulated a personality framework describing the development of personality in the pre-modern, the early-modern, and the late-modern eras. In the pre-modern era, personality could be characterized as tradition-directed. Relationships were based on what young people learned from their parents; they were controlled by etiquette and developed before adulthood. Pre-modern personality was heteronomous, and due to this minimal range of choice "the apparent social need for an individuated type of character [was] minimal."[50] This started to change in early-modern societies. Personality was more inner-directed, meaning that individuals are steered into a specific direction by the elders towards destined goals. A person self-governs his career, but based on the patterns set earlier. In late-modern society, the inner-directed personality was replaced by the other-directed character type. This type of character was "sensitive to others – to their opinions and their approval."[51] Individuals take account of what the current standards of behaviour are when they decide, for example, on their consumption patterns.

The process of identity development is closely related to cultural developments. The social structure and personality are two interrelated concepts. Côté[52] makes the link by using Riesman's framework. In terms of social-identity formation, the three described eras relate to ascribed (pre-modern), achieved (early-modern), and managed (late-modern) social identity, respectively. Gecas and Burke define these terms as follows: " '[A] scribed' means assigned on the basis of some inherited status; 'achieved' is used in the sociological sense by which social position is to be accomplished on one's own; and 'managed' means reflexively and strategically fitting oneself into a community of 'strangers' by meeting their approval through

---

47 Baumeister & Muraven 1996.
48 Baumeister & Muraven 1996.
49 Riesman 1950.
50 Riesman 1950, p. 12.
51 Côté 1996.
52 Côté 1996.

the creation of the right impressions."[53]

3.2. Identity in philosophy

In philosophy, there are different identity theories, and the main difference with the sociological approach is that identity in a philosophical sense can also refer to objects/things instead of only individuals/people.

One theory is 'reference theory'.[54] In this theory, statements that refer to a person can fulfil the function of a reference depending on certain conditions. For instance, stating that 'the French ambassador is ill' says something about the French ambassador (has meaning) to a person who knows the ambassador or has a certain relationship to this ambassador (an appointment). However, stating in the same context that 'Mr. Renaud is ill' only makes sense to people who know that Mr. Renaud is the French ambassador. It is also possible that in another context someone who is more closely related to Mr. Renaud gets informed. Whether an indication to a person serves as a reference depends on the audience's knowledge of and relation to this person. It depends on whether the information in the reference is connected to the correct individual and makes sense to the audience.

A distinction can be made between reference and pure reference. "An expression is being used in a purely referential fashion if its sole purpose is to indicate, for the hearer, a particular mental file, or 'pigeon hole', which he is assumed to possess on a certain individual. Where the hearer is assumed to have more than one such file on an individual being referred to, it will not be legitimate, on the present view, to replace one expression by another which, although it refers to the same individual, cannot be expected to indicate, for the hearer, the same file."[55]

Reference is based on attributes (properties) and is aimed at pointing at a specific individual (identification). Attribution can be risky in the sense that bodies and persons can easily be equated. "An identity (the so-called 'physicalist study') that holds that a person, with all his psychological attributes, is nothing over and above his body, with all its physical attributes, attributes properties to physical bodies and to persons in the same sense of 'attribute'."[56] Thus, a description of a person can refer to the person (as identity) or to his body (physical) and, depending on the attribute, to both. For instance, the height of a person is an indication of the body as well as of

---

[53] Cf. Gecas & Burke 1995, cited in Côté 1996.
[54] Compare Lockwood 1971, p. 210.
[55] Lockwood 1971, p. 210.
[56] Margolis 1971, p. 225.

the person as a whole. However, X has pain in his tooth refers to a physical condition by referring to a mental condition of the person (having pain). Thus, attributes can refer to individuals, but, depending on the kind of attribute, they can refer to the body or to the person (an identity) as well.[57]

Ricoeur[58] relates the 'person' to identifying reference. In his opinion, "[t]o identify something is to be able to make apparent to others, amid a range of particular things of the same type, of *which* one we intend to speak. (…) [Here,] identifying is not yet identifying oneself but identifying 'something'."[59] We can speak about 'things'. Individuals, as entities that make up the world, can be spoken about as 'things' of a particular type.[60] A specific focus of personal identity relates to the *temporal* dimension of the self. Individuals "have a history, are their own history."[61]

A distinction Ricoeur makes, and which can be problematic in relation to the permanence in time, is the distinction between *idem* identity (sameness) and *ipse* identity (selfhood). *Idem*-identity ("*What* am I?"[62]) is "the bundle of our experiences of how we are identified and mirrored by others as being the *same*: sameness in time ("I am still the same as I was yesterday") and sameness with others ("I belong to the category of Swedish academics"). However, although Ricoeur does not propose that there is anything *outside* this *idem*-identity, he shows nevertheless how *idem*-identity gives at the same time rise to also a more existential experience ("*Who* am I?"), which he calls *ipse*-identity."[63]

The *idem*-identity can, thus, be connected to an identifier; it refers to an inference of what is *idem* about a certain person from a third-person perspective, whereas *ipse*-identity is connected to identity as a sense of self (a first-person perspective). The two forms are closely interrelated, because the 'I' can take a third-person perspective on himself.

3.3. Identity in media theory

The way of presenting and representing individuals is to a large extent dependent on the technical means available. It must be possible to distribute information, whether this is in written text, an image, or spoken words. Obviously, the more sophisticated means are available, the more sophisticated

---

[57]   Margolis 1971, p. 225.
[58]   Ricoeur 1992.
[59]   Ricoeur 1992, p. 27.
[60]   Ricoeur 1992, p. 32.
[61]   Ricoeur 1992, p. 113.
[62]   Ricoeur 1992, p. 122.
[63]   Hildebrandt, Koops & de Vries 2008, p. 22.

the (re)presentation will be, since a combined set of applications can lead to a very 'realistic' image of an individual. In a sense, the public 'sees' the individual before it.

In the context of media theory, a more technical approach towards identity can be taken. Identity is then closely related to identification: the possibility to single out a specific individual in a group. "An *identity* is any subset of attributes of an individual person which sufficiently identifies this individual person within any set of persons. So usually there is no such thing as 'the identity', but several of them"[64] The several identities qualify as partial identities. In a digital environment, a partial identity can have an identifier, such as an e-mail address or username. The identifier singles out the individual in the group of users in the specific context. An important point is that here identification is used in the sense of being able to single out an individual. The connection to a name of an offline individual is not necessary.

Traditional interaction via the Internet used to be solely text-based. E-mail, BBSs, MUDs, and IRCs are the best known examples.[65] However, even between these four types, differences occur with regard to the form of communication and the audience addressed by the messages. E-mail is a typical form which combines elements of written and spoken communication. Messages are delivered at the personal account of the recipients. The number of recipients is usually limited, except in the case of spam or chain mail, and replies can be sent to the e-mail account of the sender. This form of communication is rather private. Since e-mail was costly in its early days, the messages were often formal and short, without disclosing too much personal information. The only personal detail that was always disclosed was the e-mail address of the sender. A variant on e-mail is a BBS (Bulletin Board System), which is also text-based, but "distinguished by the size of the audience it attempts to reach and the technological manner in which messages are read"[66] Messages are sent to a single computer address where they are posted and can be read or replied to by the visitors of the website. Replies have the form of a thread, a succession of the original message and all related reactions. For specific topics, newsgroups were started with people interested in the particular field of the conversations. The messages posted on the BBS are visible to all visitors of the website.

IRC stands for Internet Relay Chat and is the first form of written communication that occurs in real time. The messages posted by the people participating in the conversation become immediately visible. All messages are shown in inverse

---

[64] Pfitzmann & Hansen 2008.
[65] Cf.: Wood & Smith 2005.
[66] Wood & Smith 2005.

chronological order, so there is not always a clustered conversation of two people communicating visible on the screen, but it is interrupted with posts of others which were sent in the meantime between the post and the reply. A last typical form of internet interaction is via MUDs (Multi-User Domains, also called Dungeons). These are virtual environments (worlds) used for role-playing games. Interaction exists because usually more users are connected at any given time. The users steer their 'characters' by typing various commands. "As players participate, they become authors not only of text but of themselves, constructing new selves through social interaction."[67]

The World Wide Web (WWW) has increasingly become a portal to various forms of communication and interaction and for the presentation of any topic via websites. Next to ordinary text, it is now possible to share or display pictures and videos, and to play sounds. People create extensive profiles on social network sites (SNSs), where they present themselves, share personal information, and try to establish a network of connections which is shown to the others in the network.[68]

The MUDs described above were typical game environments. As Turkle[69] indicated, the users constructed new selves through the social interaction in these games. This insight already points towards identity construction. The trend of identity construction and the presentation of self has continued over time and has gained an impulse with the advent of SNS and related kinds of websites and it has more and more become a key issue for users to know and influence how they are perceived by others. Obviously, presenting yourself including pictures or videos and a visible network of connections has more impact on individuals and their identity than a presentation merely in text, often even restricted to a specific area of interest or discussion topic. The interactive construction of content is the typical feature of Web 2.0 applications. The term 'prosumer' appears regularly in this context,[70] to indicate the active role of consumers as producers of content. This also has implications for the identity of individuals. "In the online environment, where a person is '@', where she can 'go' and what she can 'get' are more significant, in terms of identity, than where she is, or where she is from."[71]

From the different forms of online communication described above, it can be concluded that context and technical means influence the way in which an

---

[67] Turkle 1995, p. 12.
[68] boyd & Ellison 2007.
[69] Turkle 1995.
[70] For instance: Kotler 1986; Ritzer 2010; Ritzer & Jurgenson 2010, and specifically in relation to Web 2.0: Bruns 2009.
[71] Barney 2004, p. 152.

individual is represented. When applications become more sophisticated, more diverse data concerning individuals can be disclosed or distributed. Sets of these data can form a representation of individuals in a digital form, a digital persona.

4. Digital presentation and representation

In this section, the concepts of presentation and representation will be discussed in the context of the digital environment.

4.1. Digital personae

A digital persona is a representation of an individual, identifiable[72] by the one who creates and/or uses the data set. The concept of the digital persona was introduced by Roger Clarke, who defined it as: "a model of an individual's public personality based on data and maintained by transactions, and intended for use as a proxy for the individual."[73] The representational capacity is a key element. It follows from the definition that functioning as a proxy for a specific individual is intended, so the representations that qualify as a digital persona are limited to those data sets which contain an identifying link to an entity. Solove, however, takes a much broader perspective when he talks about a digital person. He states that "it is ever more possible to create an electronic collage that covers much of a person's life – a life captured in records, a digital person composed in the collective computer networks of the world."[74] His digital person includes digital personae as well as profiles, which will be discussed later on, and other data sets. In the case of a digital persona, the purpose of its creation is known beforehand, and therefore the data that are needed to form the representation are also known, at least to a certain extent. This implies that creating a digital persona can be compared to filling out a template since it is known which attributes the creator needs.

Clarke distinguishes between projected personae and imposed personae. A projected digital persona is "an image of one's self that an individual conveys to others by means of data," for instance, by creating a personal page on a social network site, whereas the imposed digital persona is "an identity projected onto a person by means of data, by outside agencies such as corporations and government agencies,"[75] for instance, a record created by a credit rating agency. A combined form is also possible, for instance, when an electronic patient record (usually called a 'profile') is created. The individual concerned is closely involved in the creation and provides a major part of the data. The health care

---

[72] Identifiability can take different forms. See below, section 4.3.
[73] Clarke 1994.
[74] Solove 2004, p. 1.
[75] Clarke 1994.

provider stores the data and adds personal interpretations and other data (e.g. diagnoses and personal observations). The creation and maintenance of the digital persona is based on transactions, which can be any kind of interaction between the individual concerned and persons or technical devices.

The data that form a digital persona can function as or are a representation of an individual's partial identity. A partial identity is a subset of attributes of a complete identity, where a complete identity is the union of all attributes of all identities of this person.[76] Usually, a digital persona is created for use in a specific context, so the data that are relevant for the purpose are limited to this context. For instance, data concerning the income and taxation of an individual are not relevant for a medical file, so they should not be included. Even though the represented individual is aware of the existence of digital personae, he does not always know what its exact contents are. In particular in the case of imposed personae, the individual may be aware of part of the data, mainly those data that are included as a matter of course, such as name and address and specific context-related data, but the individual may not know which additional data are part of the representation (e.g., a medical diagnosis).

4.2. Profiles

Another form of digital representations of individuals are profiles. They are the result of an automated process where large data sets are processed in order to compose (a set of) characteristics which can be used as a basis for decision making. A profile is a set of correlated data,[77] which is created with the use of profiling technologies, a set of technologies with as a common characteristic the use of algorithms or other techniques to create, discover or construct knowledge from huge sets of data. Profiling can be defined as "[t]he process of 'discovering' correlations between data in databases that can be used to identify and represent a human or nonhuman subject (individual or group) and/or the application of profiles (sets of correlated data) to individuate and represent a subject or to identify a subject as a member of a group or category"[78] or the creation of a representation based on automated monitoring of individual behavior. The data can be aggregated from different sources. In first instance, there is no direct connection to an entity, so individuals who may be affected later on are not necessarily aware of the data collection.

---

[76] Pfitzmann & Hansen 2008.
[77] Hildebrandt & Gutwirth 2008, p. 19.
[78] Hildebrandt & Gutwirth 2008, p. 19.

Profiles concern groups or individuals. Group profiles describe a set of attributes concerning a group of people and are created with a data mining process. The group can be a group because of its public manifestation, like a group of students or family members, showing the connection between the individuals or the members of the group can think of themselves as a community. The group profile can also be based on categorisation if the members share an attribute and are put into a category because of this characteristic. Thus, the starting point for a group profile can be an existing group of which a profile is made. Another way to create a group profile is to aggregate personal profiles.

Group profiles can be distributive or non-distributive. In the case of a distributive group profile, the attributes of the group are also the attributes of all the members of the group. For instance, the attribute of 'not being married' for a group of bachelors also counts for each individual member of the group. For non-distributive group profiles, matters are more complicated. Consider again the group of bachelors, and suppose an indication is added that this group has a higher risk of getting a liver disease. This higher risk applies to the group, but not to each individual, e.g., because other factors, like drinking behaviour, are also relevant. The association is statistical rather than determinate. The information contained in the profile envisages individuals as members of groups; it does not envisage the individuals as such.[79]

A personal profile is a property or a collection of properties[80] of a particular individual.[81] This individual does not have to be identified or identifiable yet when data is added to the profile, but only recognized, for instance, based on a cookie. The profile is created based on monitoring behavior of the individual concerned. Whether an individual fits a profile depends on the realization of the related characteristics. With the help of a personal profile, individuals can be recognized and identified because their behavior conforms to their past behaviour. Conversely, correlations between data provide a kind of prediction based on past behavior (probability).[82] In this respect, a distinction can be made between an inductive and a deductive approach to profiling. Inductive profiling focuses on identifying behavior, whereas the latter is related to monitoring behavior.[83]

---

[79] Vedder 2004.
[80] Note that property, characteristic or attribute are used as synonyms here.
[81] Custers 2004, p. 52.
[82] Hildebrandt & Gutwirth 2008, p. 18.
[83] Canhoto & Backhouse 2008, p. 49.

Profiling is not just about data, but about inferred knowledge. Hildebrandt[84] gives two reasons why this can be worrying: "1) non-distributive group profiles are based on probabilities, which means that the group profile does not automatically apply to each member of the group, 2) profiles may reveal sophisticated knowledge about a person that is more intimate than sensitive personal data." These worries indicate that the use of profiles in relation to individuals is relevant to pay attention to as well. There are important differences between digital personae and profiles, in particular in relation to the identifiability of the concerned individual. Along this study, it is important to keep an eye on the differences between profiles and digital personae.

The table below gives an overview of the main characteristics of digital personae and profiles. As shown, the main differences between the two concern the way in which they are created and the extent to which the represented individual is aware of content/existence of the data set. A profile can be connected to an individual later on, while a digital persona and an individual are linked from the start.

Characteristics	Digital Persona		Profile	
Creation	Collection of attributes in 'template'	Projected persona	Result of profiling technologies: automated process	Distributive profile
		Imposed persona		Non-distributive profile
				Individual profile
Awareness	Individual is often aware		Individual is not usually aware	
Connection to individual	Beforehand		Can be connected/applied to a specific individual later on	

Table 1. Characteristics of digital personae and profiles.

4.3. From profile to digital persona

Even though there is no direct connection to a specific entity, a profile can be connected to or applied to an individual later on. The connection to an individual can be made based on the identification of an individual as having one or more attributes contained in the profile. Leenes[85] distinguishes different forms of identifiability. Depending on the data in the data set, in his terms, the identifiability can be L-identifiability for Look-up identifiability

---

[84] Hildebrandt 2006.
[85] Leenes 2008.

or R-identifiability for Recognition identifiability. L-identifiability means that there is a register or table that provides the connection between an identifier and an individual, such as a phone directory which links phone numbers to names. In case of a digital persona, the data set always contains an L-identifier, like a name or a passport number. This implies that there is a direct connection to an individual and that data protection legislation applies.

Profiles do not contain L-identifiers, but they connect to individuals in an indirect manner. As shown above, an individual profile may contain an R-identifier, such as a cookie, which facilitates the recognition of the individual when he returns to the site of the profiling entity (e.g. Amazon). A group profile refers to a number of people. People who share a certain behavior or attribute that is in the profile can be identified as belonging to a certain class. After recognition as a member of a group, an identifier can be issued to enable R-identification in the future. According to Leenes,[86] the typical procedure will be: after the group profile is instantiated to the individual, an R-identifier (e.g., a cookie) is issued to the individual to maintain the link. The group profile is now an individual profile. It is important to note that at this point (R-ID in profile), there is no link to an identified or identifiable entity.

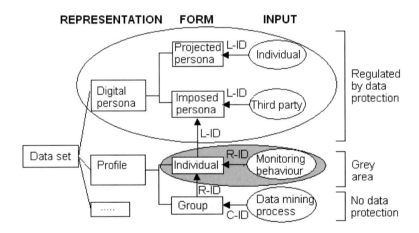

Figure 1. The relation between digital personae and profiles. The C-ID is a non-individual identifier belonging to a class that applies to all individuals in the group.

An individual profile can become a digital persona if an L-identifier is added. For instance, an individual at a certain point in time gives identifying information, or the information is obtained from another source. The L-identifier makes the connection between the individual profile and an

---

[86]   Leenes 2008.

offline individual. Since the data in the profile is provided by a third party, it takes the form of an imposed digital persona. With regard to data protection, group profiles are excluded. Individual profiles, however, are in a grey area, because there can be discussion on whether an R-Identifier can indirectly identify an individual. An example of such a discussion can be found in IP-addresses.[87] Figure 1 gives a schematic overview of the relation between profiles and digital personae.

4.4. Comparing digital personae and profiles

Digital representations of individuals consist of sets of digital data. These data can be in text, images, video, and so on. They represent the individual in the sense that they present an image of the individual without the individual himself being necessarily (physically) present. Presenting something in text or images is always a form of representation, since it refers to an original (absent) object. How this representation works can be explained with the help of semiotics, in particular, the theory of the 'triad of meaning' as developed by C.S. Peirce. His triad is a model of how things acquire meaning.[88] The process of ascribing meaning to a certain object is always an interactive process between three things: the object, the sign, and the interpretant. The object is the thing to which a certain meaning, the knowledge of the object at a specific moment (the interpretant[89]), is ascribed. This object can be anything, physical as well as virtual. The only precondition is that the receiver of information that leads to the interpretant is able to have an idea about the object, for instance, based on past experiences. The sign is something that stands for the object, since it is impossible to have knowledge of an object in a direct manner. "The sign is an instruction for interpretation, a mechanism which starts from an initial stimulus and leads to all its illative[90] consequences."[91] This implies that, for every person, the interpretant can be different, since the sign is interpreted and this interpretation can lead to different outcomes.

To clarify this, consider the following example. A table is a thing and an object. The word 'table' is a sign that stands for an object with a flat top and a number of legs (a table). By looking at the word 'table' knowledge about the object is obtained. This knowledge is the interpretant and the construction

---

[87] Article 29 Working Party 2007.
[88] Van Driel 1991, p. 49.
[89] The interpretant is an interpretation in the sense of the result of the process of interpretation. It is formed in the mind of the receiver of the information.
[90] The sign triggers the individual to start interpreting and to acquire meaning to something.
[91] Eco 1984, p. 26.

of this knowledge usually takes place in the human mind. The interpretant, the mental image formed in the mind of the receiver of the sign, refers to the object, the table, but the exact image can be different for each individual. Peirce's theory can be visualised as follows:

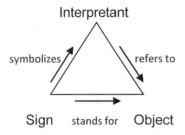

Figure 2. Peirce's triad.

This process of how meaning is ascribed can be applied to all kinds of objects or entities. This method can be used to show the relation between digital personae or profiles and individuals, and how meaning is ascribed to individuals based on digital personae or profiles.

When applied to the situation of a digital persona related to an individual the triad can be filled in as follows:

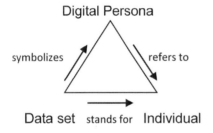

Figure 3. Peirce's triad applied to a digital persona.

Here, the individual is the object, the element to which a certain meaning is ascribed. The data set is the sign that there is an individual and shows information which can be interpreted and which leads to the interpretant, a digital persona. The interpretant has to reveal the knowledge concerning the individual at a certain moment. The digital persona can become the starting point for a new semiotic process in the function of a new sign. This sign is interpreted and leads to a new interpretant and further knowledge about the original object, the individual.

Now, consider the same process with the digital persona replaced by a (distributive) profile.

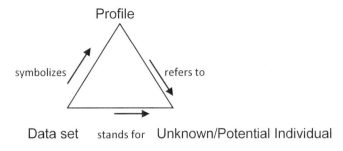

Figure 4. Peirce's triad applied to a profile.

In this case, the data set can be interpreted, leading to a profile. The data, however, are now related to an unknown or potential individual instead of to an individual, known to the entity who interprets the data set, as is the case with a digital persona. Once the individual is known, the profile can become an imposed digital persona in the sense that the individual is considered to be in conformity with the profile. It is an image projected onto a person by others.

A digital persona stems from data that are directly related to and provided by a specific individual. A group profile stems from data that are collected from numerous individuals and forms an image that might be applicable to one or more of the individuals in the group. It appears that digital personae can be seen as explicit representations of individuals, whereas profiles are implicit, or more indirect, representations. Nevertheless, both manifest themselves in the same way: a data set. The major difference concerns the way in which meaning is ascribed to the individual. In the case of a digital persona, the meaning is ingrained beforehand while, in the case of a profile, certain attributes or patterns can reveal information. Given these differences, when profiles and digital personae are used as a basis for making decisions concerning individuals, the implications for the individual can be different.

The way meaning is ascribed to the individual, depending on whether use is made of a digital persona or a profile, can have implications for privacy and autonomy. These implications can be related to context shifting, for instance, if profiles are projected onto an individual in another context than the profile was created for, or if restrictions are used, or if the use of a profile or a digital persona leads to exclusion from certain offers. Another possible implication is that the digital persona becomes so rich, because of large-scale aggregation and interpretation of data, that the information in the digital persona, and thus the knowledge that can be obtained from it, reveals information the individual concerned himself was not even aware of. Since profiles relate to an unknown individual, it is preliminarily assumed that the impact on the privacy and autonomy of the individual of using profiles as a basis for decisions is lower than when a digital persona is used. Basically, legal effects often require that the individual is known, which is only the case with digital personae a a representation. Nevertheless, the use of profiles can also have a large impact and will be considered along this study as well.

5. Synthesis

Two main aspects relevant for this study that occur in different theories and disciplinary approaches are identity and identification. Sociological and philosophical theories focus on the formation of identities and how identity functions as a distinctive factor for individuals or entities. When looking at identity in the sense of social or personal identity, the characteristics of the individual that make him a certain person or personality are the central element. Identity changes over time, because individuals deal with new experiences and can change their behavior according to different contexts. Identities can be separated into a number of partial identities which are applicable to specific contexts. Partial identities and context separation allow individuals to develop and manage different aspects of their personality, without being restricted by information from other contexts that may be irrelevant or inconvenient in a certain setting. The development of a personal identity is facilitated by interaction with other individuals, but also by self-reflection. Individuals take into account how they think they are perceived by others and then act according to this perception or not, depending on whether or not they agree with the image.

A more technical approach can be found in media and communication theory and focuses on identification in the sense of defining with whom you are dealing. Here, the identity, for instance, a combination of a username and a password, needs to sufficiently single out an individual in a group. This restricted approach is not followed in this study. A (super poor) 'identity' in this sense could be referred to as an 'identifier'. In this study, an identity presents or represents personal characteristics of an individual and shows how he is situated in particular contexts. This identity, in digital form, is called a 'digital persona'.

Social-identity formation was divided into three types, namely, ascribed, achieved, and managed identity. They refer to the individual in a certain context. The formation of an identity is an iterative and temporal process. Even though the three types could be related to the pre-modern, the early-modern, and the late-modern era, respectively, they all seem to have parallels with other concepts as well. With regard to the establishment of an identity, the ascribed and achieved identities seem to have parallels with the imposed and projected persona. An ascribed identity was determined by the parents and controlled by etiquette, so others were, at least to a large extent, responsible for the creation of the identity. When translated to a digital persona, the imposed persona shows the same characteristics. In the case of an achieved identity, the individual self-governed his career. In a similar sense a projected digital persona is a representation that is governed by the concerned individual himself.

The last form was the managed identity, where individuals take account of current standards and the opinions of other individuals. This implies that choices are made about which behavior is shown to whom and in what context. This fits very well into the modern concept of informational self-determination. Individuals can have the possibility to manage their own identity by taking care of what data are disclosed to whom and in what specific context.[92]

The connection between the types of identity formation and the main characteristics of the historical eras does not exactly fit to the creation of digital representations. While the pre-modern, the early-modern, and the late-modern eras refer to the position of the individual in identity formation as subordinate, inner-directed, and other-directed, in digital form, this only goes for the projected digital persona. Imposed digital personae and profiles are created by others and are seen as reflections of identities, because they represent individuals. The individual himself, however, is not involved, or only indirectly, so the interaction types that determine the identity formation are not applicable here.

Another central aspect that occurs in different theories and disciplinary approaches is representation. Digital personae have a representational capacity; they can function as a proxy for an individual. This implies that some connection between the data set and an offline individual has to be established. Closely related to digital personae, mainly because of their function as representations, are profiles. These data sets also contain information and attributes concerning individuals or groups, but are not connected to an offline individual. As shown, profiles can take the form of an imposed digital persona if an identifier which establishes the link to an individual is added to the data set. The way in which digital personae and profiles originate differ and so do the way data are collected and processed. This is an indication that digital personae and profiles have to be treated differently when they are used as input for making decisions that affect individuals.

---

[92] These aspects highlight the link between identity and privacy, which is clearly reflected in the privacy definition given by Agre (1997) (see Chapter 4 section 2 below).

The distinction between projected and imposed digital personae is equally relevant. The individual's amount of control and supervision over his representation differs depending on what form of persona is concerned. At least the knowledge of or insight into the data that are part of the representation is important, since informational self-determination can only be achieved if an individual has insight into his data and is able to influence the contents of a digital representation.

The impact and relevance of digital personae for individuals can be approached from a number of viewpoints. One major aspect is that digital personae have a close connection to the identity of individuals. They can represent (a part of) this identity or they can reveal how an individual's identity is perceived by others. Similarly to the context-related presentation of self, digital personae are context-related. The creation of digital personae or of the underlying data sets is done with a specific purpose and is aimed at functioning in a particular context.

Profiles, thus, relate to individuals that are not identified or identifiable. As indicated, however, it is very well possible that a profile becomes a digital persona by combining the data with an identifier. In the next chapter, the concept of the digital persona will be elaborated upon and specific forms of digital personae are presented. This will provide more insight in how digital personae are created and for what purposes. Moreover, it will clarify why sometimes commercial companies argue that a digital persona is a profile, therewith stressing the importance of taking both forms of data sets into account in this study.

Chapter 3
Digital Persona: Definition and Appearance

1. Introduction

This chapter explores the concept of the digital persona in more detail. There are numerous digital personae in existence, but still it is hard to define exactly what a digital persona is. The aim of this chapter is to come to a definition and a list of features which can help to indicate whether a certain digital representation is a digital persona or not. In order to fulfill this aim a three step approach will be taken. First, a general definition of digital personae will be given and the different forms of digital personae will be defined (2). Roger Clarke's definitions of the projected and imposed digital persona will be taken as a starting point, and then a third form will be introduced; the hybrid digital persona.

Having discussed the general definition and the three forms in more detail, the chapter continues by sketching a background of the use of digital personae. This will give an insight in why digital personae are created. It will be elaborated on what representation ('persona') means in this context (3.1) and what 'digital' implies (3.2). Then, section 3.3 discusses what the combination of these two aspects, as they appear in 'digital persona', means in practice.

Subsequently, section 4 discusses a number of relevant features which are helpful in deciding whether some digital data set constitutes a digital persona. The features together show what a digital persona can look like, its practical appearance. The features are divided into three categories which chronologically connect to 'the life cycle of a digital persona'. First, there is data collection. Then, the set of data takes a certain form, and, third, there is the application of the digital persona in practice. Each feature will be explained from a practical point of view with the help of a case study on Google, which is woven into the section and can be recognized on its presentation in separate text blocks. The end of the section describes how the features can function as a tool to indicate whether some representation is a digital persona or not, and what form of a digital persona it is.

2. The digital persona in general and its three specific forms

According to Clarke's definition, a digital persona is 'a model of an individual's public personality based on data and maintained by transactions, and intended for use as a proxy for the individual'[93]. There are two aspects in this definition that need specific attention. One aspect is the 'public personality'. Public can refer to what is presented to the outside world, so then 'public' is interpreted as opposite to 'private'. When using a common understanding of these terms, public means that something is available to other people, regardless who they are, whereas private means that availability is restricted to yourself (in your mind). Intuitively, certain representations, like medical dossiers or financial records, definitely have a private character. However, these representations are part of your public personality and they can be seen as digital personae. Besides, lots of digital personae are created or enriched with data that are collected behind the scenes with the help of monitoring technologies. These data are revealed by individuals, but are not available for everyone. Nevertheless, In Clarke's terms the data are part of your public personality. Thus, Clarke's definition refers to data that are not only in your mind, but that are disclosed or communicated, or became available to others in another way.

A second point deserving attention are the 'transactions' needed to maintain the digital persona. Digital personae can have a static form, meaning that there are no transactions concerning the data the digital persona consists of. Besides, even without transactions, interpreted in a broad sense like any interaction between the digital persona and another entity, the digital persona can be maintained. It can just be stored in a database or file system. This is why Clarke means database transactions. The digital persona as such was created by such a transaction in the first place. So, if maintenance is needed this is done by transactions.

It seems that with the development of the Internet and automation of processes, some aspects of the definition became inappropriate. In order to connect to current practices, I would like to propose a new definition of the digital persona. In that definition, emphasis is on the connection to a real-world individual. This, because the representation element is central, but the represented individual is affected by decisions taken based on the digital persona. It is not possible to say exactly what data and how much data are needed to speak of a digital persona. In any case it is relevant whether the digital representation can be connected to an offline individual, because the digital persona has to serve as a proxy for decision making with an effect on the individual herself. This connection, however, does not necessarily imply identification of the individual in the sense of having a name. Moreover, a digital persona is a gradual concept. Depending on context and purpose, more or less data are needed to establish the connection to an offline individual. When including these characteristics, I come to the following definition:

---

[93]   Clarke 1994.

A digital persona is a digital representation of a real-world individual, which can be connected to this real-world individual and includes a sufficient amount of (relevant) data to serve, within the context and for the purpose of its use, as a proxy for the individual.

In this definition, the connection to the real-world individual and the representational function are included. Representation, however, is connected to context and purpose of the digital persona, which emphasizes the fact that data in the representation are context-bound and the creation of the digital persona is related to an intended purpose. This can be compared with partial identities, where individuals disclose information appropriate for the specific context and choose to keep other information secret. For instance, information shared with colleagues differs from information shared with friends or family members. Besides, there is special attention for the fact that a digital persona consists of data, but that it cannot be said how many data are needed exactly. This depends on context and purpose for which the digital persona is intended to be used.

In the theoretical framework, two types of digital personae were presented.[94] These two forms were introduced by Clarke in 1994[95]. He distinguishes between the projected digital persona, which is created by the represented individual himself, and the imposed digital persona, which is created by another party than the represented individual, like a company or institution. These two are presented as black and white distinctions. In today's practice, a hybrid form is more prevalent. In this hybrid form, the starting point is either a projected or an imposed persona, and this digital persona is then combined or enriched with data from the other form. Thus, the influence of the individual in the creation can vary between 0 and 100 percent. The three forms of digital personae will be described in more detail below.

2.1. The projected digital persona

In Clarke's words a projected persona is "an image of one's self that an individual conveys to others by means of data."[96] A pure form of a projected digital persona is not often found. In this statement, I use a strict interpretation of the projected persona. When an individual fills out a web form with some personal details, this is not completely a form of a projected persona, even though the individual provides the data himself. Basically, the requested data are selected by another party and very often refusing to fill out a certain part of the form is technically impossible. Besides, depending on the purpose of

---

[94] Chapter 2, section 4.1.
[95] Clarke 1994.
[96] Clarke 1994.

the web form, lying about details is just not possible. For instance, one could lie about one's address, but that will result in not receiving ordered goods. So, I take as a starting point that for the projected persona, the individual has to be in control[97] of choosing the form and contents of the representation.

A possible example of a projected digital persona is a personal homepage. On such a page individuals can present themselves in whatever way they want. The representation can include text, pictures, videos, and music, and can be designed in a way the individual desires. The information in the representation can be related to a specific purpose, such as leisure and fun, or a professional function. The personal homepage is created on the initiative of the represented individual and contains information provided by this individual only. This is an important aspect, for when interactive functionalities, such as blogging or chat where others can post replies or reactions, are added, the website becomes a hybrid digital persona, since the content on the website no longer solely originates from the user himself. An obvious and intended form of this can be found on social network sites (SNS, see below), where interaction between the (social) network members is the main focus.

2.2. The imposed digital persona

An imposed digital persona is a persona which is created by another party than the concerned individual. The data are collected and provided by this other party. An imposed digital persona is "an identity projected onto a person by means of data, by outside agencies such as corporations and government agencies"[98]. A proper example of an imposed digital persona is a record made by a credit rating agency. These agencies register whether someone has a debt or a loan, and whether she is paying bills too late. Records often also include information on mobile phone subscriptions. Thus, the information in the record originates from different sources other than the data subject. Based on the data in the record an analysis can be made on the creditworthiness of an individual. Companies can consult the credit records before granting someone a credit, giving a postponement of payment or selling a subscription.

The way of presenting the credit rating to a company can be organized in different forms, ranging from objective facts, only indicating whether one has a loan or whether one has paid bills too late in the past, to subjective

---

[97] Of course, for control technical possibilities and the technical capability of the creator are relevant. Here, however, these factors are excluded and control only has to do with determining what data are disclosed or not.

[98] Clarke 1994.

(value) judgments such as "this person is a defaulter". The statement that someone is a defaulter is an interpretation of the data in the record, probably supplemented with other data. This interpretation, or value judgment, can be added to the record, therewith becoming part of the digital persona.

Credit rating agencies have information on the creditworthiness of individuals, sometimes combined with a categorization or risk indication. Creditworthiness is derived from previously or currently existing debts, loans, and subscriptions for mobile phone providers. Obviously, one wants to be sure that it is financially safe to give a loan to someone in the sense that one can expect that the individual is able to pay his debts. In the Netherlands, the *Bureau Krediet Registratie* (BKR[99], Credit Registration Office) is the central institution which serves as a provider for credit information. The BKR does not judge on payment behavior, but only provides information on loans, credits, and mobile phone subscriptions. A registered BKR member, for instance a bank, credit card company, or mobile phone provider, can ask for this information and has to decide on the potential risk herself. However, even though BKR states not to judge, it can provide a member, on special request, with a credit score next to the information in the central credit information system (*Centraal Krediet Informatiesysteem*, CKI) which can be accessed directly by members. A credit score gives an indication whether there can be expected a high or a low risk when a member grants a credit to an individual. A CKI record concerning an individual includes personal data (surname (maiden name), initial(s), date of birth, address, residence) and data from the registered agreement(s) (amount of money loaned or maximum to spend, moment the agreement started, the month in which the agreement has to be paid off completely, the month in which the agreement was actually ended, type of the agreement, special circumstances occurring during the agreement). After an agreement has ended, the retention term starts which means that the data are stored for another five years.[100]

Some specialized companies go a lot further and try to collect as much data as possible in order to be able to categorize individuals in specific groups, including data about, for instance, age, family composition, income, and buying behavior. A well-known example of such a company is Experian.[101] Experian describes itself as "a global leader in providing information, analytical and marketing services to organisations and consumers to help manage the risk and reward of commercial and financial decisions." One of the services they offer is the Mosaic program, which is a combination of a number of databases and surveys which has led to a detailed analysis of

---

[99] See: <http://www.bkr.nl/>.
[100] See: FAQ on BKR site: <http://www.bkr.nl/MeestGesteldeVragen.aspx?pid=77>.
[101] See: <http://www.experian.com>.

consumer behaviour. For instance, according to Experian's website, Mosaic United Kingdom is a set of 67 types of consumers, divided in 15 groups, and "provides an accurate understanding of the demographics, lifestyles and behaviour of all individuals and households in the UK." The database is available as either a person, household or postcode database. This means that for each individual in the UK a digital representation is made which is connected to one of the 67 types of consumers.

Another product by Experian is Hitwise, which gives an overview of clicking behaviour of Internet users, by showing graphics of specific websites or industries and which sites were visited before or afterwards. The data also include the breakdown of new and returning visitors.

The imposed digital personae as described above in the examples of BKR and Experian are connected to an individual from the moment of their creation on. However, it is also possible to establish an imposed digital persona starting with a group profile. Identifying an individual as belonging to a certain category or fitting within a profile connects the individual to the data in the profile. Then, the group profile becomes an individual profile for this specific individual and, thus, an imposed digital persona. So, imposed digital personae can be created on an individual level from the beginning on, or can originate from a group profile which is connected and applied to a specific individual afterwards.

2.3. The hybrid digital persona

While the projected and the imposed digital persona originally were the two basic forms of digital representations, technological development has led to a new form: the hybrid digital persona. The Internet has developed from a broadcast information medium (web 1.0) to a social collaborative environment where every user can contribute content (web 2.0). The active role played by the individual, instead of merely consuming information available on the web, changed the way digital representations are created. For instance, a profile on a social network site (SNS) is created by the individual himself. She can make his own personal profile page, add information concerning age, gender, interests, work, etc., and post pictures and videos. Even though the format of the profile page is determined by the SNS provider, the representation is designed by the individual. An essential function of a social network site is to establish connections with other users; create the social network. Usually, the list of people with whom there is a connection is displayed on the profile page. From that point on, the connections become part of the representation as well, because the people one has in his network also says something about social status. Important indicators are the kind of contacts (business connections, friends, stereotypes) and the number of connections. Kind of contacts can refer to whether someone has a network of business connections or friends and to the way the contacts present themselves, for instance as belonging to certain groups like gothics or Burning Man festival visitors[102]. More essentially in this context, people with whom there is a connection can also add content to each other's personal profile page in the form of text messages, comments, pictures, or videos. This is where the initially projected profile becomes hybrid.[103] The interaction and mutual exchange of content is also the point where an SNS profile page distinguishes itself from a traditional personal homepage, which had a more static form as created by the individual and no facilities for external contributions.

To give a flavor of the richness of hybrid digital personae, SNS can serve as an example. For instance, "a fully filled-out Facebook profile contains about forty pieces of recognizably personal information, including name; birthday; political and religious views; online and offline contact information; gender, sexual preference, and relationship status; favorite books, movies, and so on; educational and employment history; and, of course, picture"[104]. Besides, there appears to be a correlation between the number of SNS an individual participates in and the number of attributes disclosed. The more SNS profiles, the more personal information is provided by the individual.[105] A fully filled-out profile is, however, not necessary to constitute a digital persona. Even with a small amount of data there is a representation which can be connected to an offline individual. Besides, the forty attributes mentioned by Grimmelmann are only the attributes that count as recognizably personal information. Other information can be captured in blogs, comments, videos, or whatever an individual uses to fill the profile page, and this information can probably also be connected to the individual and might even be more revealing, for instance when discussing a medical complaint one has. This is personal information as well. Facebook, however, does not ask for this information as part of the standard profile attributes.[106]

---

[102] For an example of how this can cause discomfort, see: Donath & boyd 2004, p. 78. They give an example of a school teacher who had friends displaying pictures of wild dancing at the Burning Man festival and she got questions on this from her pupils after one of them had invited her to connect on Friendster, therewith gaining access to her profile, including the pictures of her contacts.

[103] See also the dissertation by Rachel Marbus (to appear in 2013) in which also a hybrid persona is recognized.

[104] Grimmelmann 2009, p. 1149.

[105] Irani, Webb, Li & Pu 2009, p. 271.

[106] Forty attributes containing personal information might seem quite a rich profile. However, in the Netherlands, the Electronic Child Record has been introduced (see section 3.3 below) which can contain up to 1200 attributes concerning a single child.

What is important is that the profile page forms an image of an individual and can function as a proxy for this individual. SNS facilitate asynchronous communication in message services or blogs which can be commented on, so even when the concerned individual is not online, a communication (or conversation) can still be started or continued. Besides, the data on the profile page as such form an image from which information concerning the represented individual can be distracted. The individual presents himself via the profile page for the purpose of social networking. His own physical presence is not necessarily required for interaction with others.

3. Why digital personae are created

The three forms of digital personae described above are created in a wide variety of contexts and purposes. Here, purposes means types of use on a more detailed level. For instance, a digital persona can be used as a reference, like in a traditional address book, it can be used as input for risk calculations, such as credit rating reports, or it can be used as a tool for social interaction, like a profile page on an SNS. Thus, specific purposes are related to the practical application of the digital persona. On a more general level, the purposes of its creation relate to the constituent parts of the concept 'digital persona'. When analyzing these parts, these purposes become clear. First, there is the function of a digital persona as a proxy, which basically means the representation part and refers to the 'persona' in digital persona. Second, there is 'digital', which relates to the digitalization of data which facilitates automated processing. These two aspects will be discussed briefly and then an elaboration on the effect of combining these two elements will follow.

3.1. Representation (persona)

The first reason for creating digital personae is representation of individuals. Individuals are involved in interactions with all kinds of companies, institutions, and other individuals. Digital proxies are a practical solution, because it is impossible and undesirable to be physically present for all interactions. Impossible, since many interactions take place online or in automated systems, and undesirable because the costs for interactions would increase, even though physical presence is not always necessary. For instance, it is very useful when an employer can check data regarding bank accounts in a digital file instead of having to ask each employee every single time again when he wants to pay salaries.[107] This kind of representation

---

[107] There is a tension between efficiency and the requirements for legitimate data processing as laid down in the Data Protection Directive (DPD). The DPD requires consent of the individual in many cases, so the individual has to be involved, but from the perspective of efficiency this is undesirable. Often, this is solved by letting the individual give her

in a file was already common practice before the digital era. However, nowadays interactions are much more diverse and very often individuals are not even aware of an interaction taking place. This lack of awareness can be related to two things. First, the physical absence in interaction facilitates asynchronous communication and results, meaning that an individual may become aware of a decision afterwards, without being directly involved in the decision making process. Because of this asynchronous interaction, one can experience this as just being subjected to a decision without having been consulted. However, in fact the digital representation was consulted as were it the concerned individual himself.

Personal details		Employee status		Financial details	
Name	Workingman	Employee number	20059876	Salary/month	2345,67
Initials	J.C. (James)	Employed since	2005-09-01	Cumulative	65543,21
Date of birth	1983-08-24	Function	Researcher	Year-end bonus	1234,00
Address	Gateway 23	Start of contract	2008-09-01	Bank account	112233445
Postal Code	45678	End of contract	2013-08-31	Bank	Village bank
City	Downtown	Function scale	9/3	City	Downtown
Telephone	023-65348762				
E-mail	J.C.Workingman@gmail.com				

Table 2. Example of a digital representation of an employee.

The above table is an example of a digital representation of an individual. It shows some personal details of an employee. Specific information is included for the personnel department and financial administration. Based on the data in the 'Employee status' section, it can be concluded that every year on September 1st, the employee shifts up in the function scale. It also shows the end date of the contract and the function of the employee. The 'Financial details' are for the financial department, so they can consult this table to see what salary has to be paid each month and to which bank account. The combination of the data makes that with a shift in function scale the employee also gets a higher salary. As Clarke states: "In the abstract world of information systems, each entity and each identity is represented by various records, each of which contains a collection of data-items, each of which represents a real-world attribute." And "[o]rganisations have increasingly come to rely on records as a means of dealing with people, rather than dealing with the people themselves."[108]

---

consent in a contract or by accepting general terms and conditions. However, the acceptability or legal validity of these practices is restricted because individuals cannot always foresee the exact implications.

[108] Clarke 2008, p. 222.

3.2. Facilitating automated processing (digital)

The second reason is to enable automated processing of the data in the representation. Once data are digital, machines can read the data and run algorithms on the data. First, this means that processes can be (partially) automated, which is more efficient in terms of time and effort. Secondly, the automated processing of data, in particular running algorithms, leads to opportunities for discovering new or more information in the data. With the means of computers it is possible to recognize patterns in data which can reveal new knowledge concerning groups or individuals. Besides, it is much easier to add data to a digital persona automatically. For instance, when online behavior, such as click trails and web history, is recorded, the data can be connected to the digital persona right away. Involvement of a human being is not necessary.

Another advantage of automated processing is that digital representations can be compared easily on sharing attributes. This is a very practical tool for defining groups of people or making categories. Obviously, this is also possible with traditional paper-based data sets, but doing this electronically is much faster and much easier. Besides, the extra facilities of discovering knowledge which cannot be seen at first sight or by just running through a card deck enable users of digital data sets to improve and optimize their work or services and to allocate resources optimally.

Table 3 shows an overview of district, brand of car, and salary of a number of people who live in the same city. At first sight, the table has no strange information and it is easy to imagine that it is difficult to extract information from such a table when it concerns hundreds or thousands of records. However, with automated processing patterns and exceptions can be revealed. The brands in the table can be connected to information on average prices of these car brands. By running a simple algorithm it appears that people with a higher salary have more expensive cars. This is kind of logical, but it also appears that people with a high salary who live in the centre of the city have relatively cheap cars.

District	Car	Salary
Centre	Suzuki	15000
Centre	Lada	16000
East	Lexus	50000
South	Renault	20000
East	BMW	60000
West	Ford	35000
West	Ford	37000
West	Renault	34000
Centre	Mitsubishi	55000
East	Chevrolet	65000
Centre	Hyundai	60000
South	Citroen	18000
South	Hyundai	17000

Table 3. Overview of living district, car brand, and salary of a number of citizens.

These data can be correlated with other data to find out why this exception exists. It may, for instance, appear that the reason for this is that there is a high car theft rate in the centre, or that the traffic and parking practice in the city centre is a real mess, like for instance in Paris, so people who live in the centre decide to buy a cheap car so it is not that bad if it gains some dents.

There is a famous example which clarifies the difference between querying and data mining; 'the parable of the beer and diapers'. It reads as follows:

Some time ago, Wal-Mart decided to combine the data from its loyalty card system with that from its point of sale systems. The former provided Wal-Mart with demographic data about its customers, the latter told it where, when and what those customers bought. Once combined, the data was mined extensively and many correlations appeared. Some of these were obvious; people who buy gin are also likely to buy tonic. They often also buy lemons. However, one correlation stood out like a sore thumb because it was so unexpected. On Friday afternoons, young American males who buy diapers (nappies) also have a predisposition to buy beer. No one had predicted that result, so no one would ever have even asked the question in the first place. Hence, this is an excellent example of the difference between data mining and querying.[109]

---

[109] Whitehorn 2006.

Thus, data mining technologies (running algorithms) can reveal information that one would never have asked for himself. To complete the story, here is the analysis of the correlation between beer and diapers. It appears that young American males often go drinking with their friends on Friday evenings. Once a young American becomes a father, he is not that free in going out anymore. Taking care of his offspring forces him to stay at home. However, he can still drink beer, but needs to be remembered of that. So, placing the beer next to the diapers in a store increases the sale of beer.

3.3. 'Digital persona'

Having described the aspects of representation of an individual and digital form it can now be discussed what the combination of these two means. Basically, it means that the facilities of digital data processing are affecting individuals. First, the discovery of knowledge based on recognizing patterns or combining data by running algorithms reveals knowledge concerning an individual. Knowledge the individual himself might not even be aware of. This means that the user of the digital persona can take decisions concerning the represented individual, based on knowledge about this individual which is not available at first sight and is not disclosed by merely looking at the data set. But "once matter has 'gone digital', it can also be *stored* and *transferred* as binary bits"[110]. "This is the crux of the digital revolution: digital matter (e.g., in form of consumer information) becomes free-flowing and free-floating, in technical as well as symbolic terms."[111]

Running algorithms or queries on digital personae allows automatic selection of individuals, based on attributes in the data set. As a result, individuals can be subjected to inclusion or exclusion. However, whether an individual is subjected to such a decision remains (often) unknown to the concerned individual himself, even though it certainly is a decision that affects the individual.[112]

The interaction between individual and the other entity is often not even intended to include active participation of the individual, but is meant as automated processing behind-the-scenes. For instance, when buying something in a web shop, the shop owner and the visitor want some 'magic' to happen in order to optimize the shopping experience, make it convenient for the visitor, and fruitful for the shop owner. The shop owner wants to collect data on the interests of a visitor and, based on that, generate some personalized recommendations. The collected data, possibly connected to

---

[110] Lunefeld 1999 (cited in: Zwick & Dholakia 2004, p. 31).
[111] Zwick & Dholakia 2004, p. 31.
[112] See Chapter 5 of this study.

older data from earlier visits, form the digital representation and immediately there are some automated decisions taken. It is on purpose that the individual is not actively involved here, since that would make the shopping experience less convenient.[113][114]

A recent example of a digital persona is the Electronic Child Record (*Elektronisch Kind Dossier,* ECR). In the Netherlands, the ECR was introduced on July 1st 2010 for every child in the age of 0 until 19 years. The ECR will replace the traditional paper files and data to be included in the ECR is based on these files. Except for the digitization, not that much should change then. However, two main reasons why this is not the case can be identified. "First, ECR is based on a data set that standardizes content to allow for information exchange between different youth-healthcare organizations. The data set, although being based on the traditional paper files, is complemented with new kinds of personal data that are perceived relevant by youth healthcare professionals (the total list covering more than 30 pages[115])."[116] Thus, the digital form is much more extended than the traditional paper dossier. Managing such extensive dossiers is much easier when they are digitized, since automated search and filtering can be executed. "Second, by means of behavioral-screening questionnaires to be filled in by parents, children or teachers longitudinal psycho-social information on children is collected nation-wide and based on that information children will be sorted in different categories."[117] The categorization is also included in the ECR itself. This means that, on the one hand, digitization facilitates nation-wide comparisons and analyses of the child records, which also enables pigeon-holing of children, and, on the other hand, it becomes clear that the ECR is a detailed representation of a child and that the ECR can be treated as if it were the represented child himself. Based on the ECR, decisions are taken that affect the child and his parents even though the child is not (necessarily) aware of these decisions and the grounds on which they are taken. For instance, parents with a low income can be seen as an indication that a child has a higher risk of becoming involved in criminal behavior. It can be decided to flag the child's dossier, because of this information.

---

[113] There are some exceptions. For instance, Amazon.com offers its customers the opportunity to reflect on the recommendations with the help of a grading system.

[114] Here, the difference between online and offline is also important. When a shop employee approaches a customer with the question whether she can be of help and what the customer is searching for, this is usually experienced as considerate. However, when this situation takes place in an online context, meaning that customers have to answer questions, tick boxes, or reply to pop-up screens, this will most likely be experienced as annoying.

[115] Which comes down to a list of about 1200 attributes.

[116] Hof, Leenes & Fennell 2009, p. 157.

[117] Hof, Leenes & Fennell 2009, p. 157.

Children are connected to risk-profiles and when a potential risk appears the frequency of contact moments with youth-healthcare professionals will be increased, whereas children with a very low risk will have less frequent contact moments.

The ECR is a typical example of a digital persona. It has a digital format which is used to facilitate data exchange between youth-healthcare professionals and to compare data in an automated manner. Besides, the ECR gives a compound overview of a child in the context of youth-healthcare. The physical presence of the child is no longer necessary to take decisions regarding the child, since the ECR serves as a proxy.

4. The practical appearance of digital personae

Having described the three types or forms of digital personae and the reasons for using digital personae, the question remains what exactly constitutes a digital persona. Is a certain amount of data necessary? Is a personal identifier needed? Or is identification of an individual in the sense of singling-out or recognizing someone sufficient? These questions are difficult to give a clear-cut answer to. However, it is possible to identify a number of relevant features, which can be of use when talking about digital representations and deciding whether a specific representation is a digital persona or not. These features can be divided into three categories: the collection of the data that constitute the digital persona, the form of the digital persona, and the application of the digital persona. In order to illustrate the features from a more practical perspective, a use case on Google and its (related) services is integrated.

Meet James:

James is a 32-year old person whose whereabouts on the web are integrated in text blocks along this chapter in order to provide a more practical background to the discussed features. He works in the research industry and has some knowledge of ICT and web applications. James is frequently online, in private contexts as well as for professional purposes. As a researcher he has to find a lot of information and, like many people, he often uses Google's search engine as a starting point to gather information on the topics he is occupied with, albeit only to get a grasp on the relevant and related issues of a topic. James' research is about ICT and law, so he has a more than average interest in general terms and conditions and privacy statements as used by companies on the Internet.

The text blocks in italics together present a use case concerning Google and its affiliated services.[118] *This case is chosen for many people use one or more*

---

[118] The information included in this use case is derived from the General Terms and

of Google's services. Besides, the accumulated services Google offers and the tools it uses, combined with the Google-Double Click merger, give an excellent opportunity to show how far-reaching the 'Google Empire' is and how this affects ordinary Internet users. Whilst serving as a use case, it also functions as a clarifying tool on the features related to digital personae.

4.1. Collection of data

This subsection describes how data are collected in order to establish a digital persona. As indicated above, the data can originate from different sources. In the case of a projected digital persona, the data are provided by the concerned individual himself. In the cases that other parties are (partly) responsible for the creation of the digital persona, the data can either be created by this other party, collected by this party from other sources, or the data can just be obtained from the concerned individual by merely asking, for instance in a web form.

The creation of data by the party that also creates (and uses) the digital persona can take different forms. A basic form is that data are collected from communications, like e-mail contact or just a physical meeting. In these cases, the concerned individual is aware of the communication taking place and in fact just provides the data himself for the purpose of the communication. This does, however, not mean that the individual is also aware of the data being collected and stored in order to function as a proxy. Another form, somewhat more distinguished from awareness because of concrete communication is to collect data on the interaction one has with a web service. This can be, for instance, a click trail or search terms one entered in order to find interesting products or information. This form of data collection is related to monitoring individual behavior. One step further than merely collecting data is to analyze the data, or to add interpretations to certain behavior, leading to the creation of new data that were not directly revealed by the concerned individual. For instance, an individual can be categorized as having a certain interest, or as a defaulter. Because the data are really created by another party than the concerned individual himself, this underscores the imposed character of this digital persona.

Data can also be obtained from other sources than the concerned individual himself or the party who creates or uses the digital persona. For instance, a credit rating agency obtains data from banking institutions, telephone

Conditions as used by Google and applied to their different services. As a reference, I have used the Terms in their extensive form, like they were available before the introduction of the new policy on 1ˢᵗ March 2012. These new Terms will be discussed later on in Chapter 5, section 4.2.1.

companies and other financial institutions in order to create a digital persona of an individual. In a web context, Google is a good example, obtaining data from numerous web sites which have implemented one or more of Google's services, such as Google maps or YouTube videos, or who are participating in programs such as AdSense or Google Analytics. Google Analytics and AdSense use so-called web bugs to track visitors of web sites.[119] A web bug is an image of 1 by 1 pixel, so the user does not see it, included in a web page, and it issues a cookie to the visitor's web browser. Every time someone visits a page which includes one of the features related to Google, Google receives a package of data concerning this visit including this cookie. Research[120] showed that with these web bugs, Google covers about 88,4% of the total domains in a data set of almost 400.000 unique domains[121] and 92 of the top 100 sites. The tracking and monitoring of browsing behavior provides Google with information to derive interests of individuals, which allows for better performance of their services (the search engine provides more relevant results which are related to your interests) and for targeted advertising. When a company wants to obtain other information from a visitor of their webpage, like name address, and contact details, it is obvious just to ask the individual to provide these data, for instance by using a web form.

With regard to the collection of the data that form the digital representation, several aspects are of importance. A first issue is whether the concerned individual knows about the data collection, so whether the collection takes place *consciously* or *unconsciously* from the perspective of the represented person. Obviously, in the case of a projected digital persona, the data collection is conscious since the individual provides the data himself. In the case of the imposed or hybrid digital persona, however, the collection, at least partly, often takes place without the individual being aware. In some cases, the individual becomes aware afterwards, when a certain effect of the collection is noticed, but sometimes, the individual never knows about the collection of data. In this regard, it is also relevant to be aware of the distinction between the collection of data as such and the creation of a digital persona from these data. For instance, when data are collected on a large scale, without connecting them to individuals, and the data are used to create group profiles, then there is data collection but there are no digital personae created from the data. So, it has to be data that are related to an individual.

---

[119] The presence of these web bugs can, for instance, be checked by using Ghostery, a Firefox browser plugin, which lists the web bugs on a web page.

[120] Gomez, Pinnick & Soltani 2009, p. 4.

[121] This large number is only a small part of the entire internet. However, it gives a clear indication that the coverage of Google on commercial websites can be assumed to be very high.

James frequently uses the Google search engine and has a Gmail account. In order to open the Gmail account he had to provide a number of personal details and he knows that these are stored by Google. The details include username and password, which are obviously necessary to use the service. James has read the general terms and conditions and found out that Google, as a provider of the service, has access to his emails and list of contacts. What he does not count for is that Gmail monitors his email patterns and the contacts and groups he is emailing. Another thing he pays attention to is that the displayed advertisements are targeted ads, based on region, language, and contents of his emails. Being subjected to these ads is the price James pays for using the service, because in fact, businesses pay for having their advertisements displayed, therewith making it possible for Google to provide the Gmail service for free. Once an email message is opened, Gmail screens the message on keywords in order to flag it as spam if appropriate. However, the screening of the contents of the email message also facilitates the displaying of targeted advertisements, which are relevant according to the content of the email message. When a message is closed, the ads disappear as well.

When using the search engine, James obviously knows that he is entering a search term. Since he is a bit familiar with ICT and has some privacy interests, he knows that the search terms are stored by Google. The search terms are used as input for a bidding process, the Google auction, which takes place right before the search results are displayed and determines which sponsored advertisements appear on top and in the right column of the result list. Advertisers bid on keywords that are related to their businesses, so the sponsored links that show up are in fact targeted advertisements as well.[122] Google stores the search terms accompanied with data on the IP address, browser type, language, time and date of the session, and some other technical data about the user's computer. Based on a cookie, the device belonging to the stored data can be recognized. Even though James is aware of the retention of his search history, he is not aware that this history is processed in order to provide James with personalized search results every time he submits a new query. The entire history in combination with the personalization of future searches gives a quite profound overview of the interests and needs of James in a digital form.

The retention period and use of search data depends on some settings chosen by James. When James would not have a Google account or does not log in, Google explains that it stores up to 180 days of search activity linked to his browser's cookie, including queries and results that he clicks. However, James has a Google account because of the Gmail service he uses, and when he has signed-in, Google personalizes his search experience on his entire Web History. In his account, James can view and remove individual items from his Web History.

---

[122]   Levy 2009.

Two aspects that show up are the difference in the time frame of the used search history. With an account, this is unlimited, whereas without an account, called anonymous search, there is a restriction to 180 days. Another main point is that anonymous personalized search is based on search activity, i.e. prior use of the search engine, whereas when James uses his account, his entire Web History is used for personalization of the search results. This means that sites James frequently visits, and thus no search is needed to find them, are also included, as well as all his other whereabouts on the web Google is able to track. As indicated, Google covers a large part of the web with its web bugs, so, basically, that boils down to almost all web activity.

	Signed-in Personalised Search	Signed-out Personalised Search
Where the data Google uses to customize is stored	In Web History, linked to James' Google Account	On Google's servers, linked to an anonymous browser cookie
How far back Google uses search history	Indefinitely or until James removes it	Up to 180 days
Which searches are used to customize	Only signed-in search activity, and only if James is signed up for Web History (default setting)	Only signed-out search activity

Table 4. Google personalized search.

James is aware of the Google search engine and Gmail collecting data about him. Nevertheless, the data sources are far more extended than he can imagine. Google provides a service called Google Analytics, which is helping companies to analyze their web pages by giving insight in website traffic and marketing effectiveness. Every website that uses Google Analytics sets a cookie which sends information about the visitor to Google. The same counts for Double Click, which was acquired by Google, and provides targeted ads on websites, and Google Adsense which helps companies to display targeted advertisements and gain revenues from that. The number of websites connected to one or more of these services is enormous, so the Google Empire is much bigger than the search engine and email service, at least when it comes to data collection with the help of web bugs.

Another aspect concerning the collection of data is whether the collection takes place *once* or if it takes place *repeatedly*. When data collection takes place only once, the digital persona will have a static form (see also below). However, it is possible that only one time data are collected, but that the data are processed several times in order to take decisions or to add additional information. For instance, a record of an employee held by his employer is usually created only once (when the employee gets the job) and is then used several times to pay salaries, calculate leave hours, and communicate information from the employer. The real collection of data takes place once. Nevertheless, this does not mean that the data cannot be updated. When an employee moves to a new address or has another relevant change in data, the record can be updated. In this regard, updates take place because of relevant changes in order to keep the data accurate. When no changes take place, the data just remain the same and will just be collected once.

Repeated data collection is, obviously, possible as well. In that case, new data concerning a similar activity are collected each time the activity is undertaken. For instance, the collection of data on web or search history takes place every time one is active on the Internet. The data can differ each time, but usually there will also be a (large) overlap. This overlap is due to standard actions, such as e-mail checking or logging in on a social network site. In other words, an individual will usually show a typical behavior related to a specific activity, which implies that the individual can also be recognized on his behavioral patterns. An identifier, like a name, number, or username/password combination, is not necessary to link different sessions to the same individual. Nevertheless, the use of an account makes the linkage of sessions much easier. For instance, when shopping on a web site like Amazon.com, a user can log in, thereby facilitating that data on search and purchases are directly connected to an individual. Every session, new data are collected, and based on the history of purchases and searches personalized recommendations are made by Amazon.com. The collection of data takes place repeatedly and the different sessions can be compared in order to find out whether interests are changing over time.

James's data are collected repeatedly, namely every time he is active on the web. The data are then accumulated with the earlier data, so they do not replace them. Nevertheless, similar actions to earlier web visits function as a confirmation of behavior, which may lead to even better personalized results in the search engine. By collecting and accumulating the data, the most recent and most important interests of James are detected.

Another important feature with regard to the collection of data is whether the collection of data takes place *within the context* of the digital representation or whether it *exceeds this context*. With data collection taking place only within the context of the digital persona, I mean that the data are only collected in that specific context, but also that the data are only related to the context in which the digital persona is intended to be used. Thus, when referring to Amazon.com again, it would mean that the data Amazon collects are only data that are revealed when interacting with the Amazon.com web site, and that there are no data collected from other web sites that might reveal interests of users. Besides, the data are only related to the specific context, so to the buying of products from Amazon.com. Data about other contexts, such as health status or family composition should be excluded.[123]

---

[123] In first instance, these kinds of data are not collected by Amazon.com, but it might be possible to make assumptions on these issues based on revealed interests. For instance,

Context exceeding data collection can mean that data are collected from other contexts as well, like tax authorities that complement data from tax filing forms with data from professional social networking sites such as LinkedIn, in order to check the accuracy of data. LinkedIn was meant to function as a networking tool to maintain and expand a professional network. Use of LinkedIn profiles as input for taxation is exceeding the context. This means that exceeding a context usually counts for both combined contexts as such. Either, context data are enriched with other data or data from another context are transferred to a context for which they were not meant. The combination of the data has as a result that both contexts collapse.

Another form of exceeding a context is that data are collected that are irrelevant for the intended context and use of the digital persona. Think, for instance, about the health data or family composition data as mentioned above.

The data collected about James, which together constitute his digital persona, are not context bound. Data from the Gmail service are collected in this environment, but for the search engine and the entire digital representation or footprint of James, data are obtained from various contexts. Since James uses the Internet for professional as well as for leisure or private purposes, the contexts from which data are collected are co-mingled and separations between the contexts collapse. This becomes even more the case when the devices used by James to go on the Internet are used in the different contexts, or when the devices are connected to each other via the Internet, for instance when James is accessing his work computer during the weekend at a distance in order to download some files to finish some work.

A last feature regarding data collection is which party is *responsible* for the collection of data. A first distinction is the distinction between the concerned individual himself and another party as responsible. When another party is responsible, there can be made another distinction, namely between data processor and data controller. The data processor is the one who actually processes the data.[124] The data controller is the one who defines what data are processed and how and why.[125] When the data controller is another person than

---

when a man, next to detectives and thrillers, is also looking for picture books, he probably has one or more children and, usually, a female partner as well. Amazon.com does, however, not ask for family composition or marital status as account data.

[124] Compare Directive 95/46/EC, Article 1(e): "'processor' shall mean a natural or legal person, public authority, agency or any other body which processes personal data on behalf of the controller".

[125] Compare Directive 95/46/EC, Article 1(d): "'controller' shall mean the natural or legal person, public authority, agency or any other body which alone or jointly with others determines the purposes and means of the processing of personal data; where the purposes and means of processing are determined by national or Community laws or

the data processor, the data controller is the responsible party. When processor and controller is one and the same person, this is the responsible party.

The responsible party for collecting data about James and constituting a digital representation of James is Google. However, as mentioned earlier, Google has a huge Empire and also obtains data from other parties, like DoubleClick with whom they merged. In the end, however, all data come together at Google, so Google itself is responsible for the combination and accumulation of the data. Google is processor and controller at the same time.

4.2. The form of the digital persona

The form of the digital persona as a feature refers to what the digital persona looks like. This has to do with the amount and kind of data in the representation, as well as with the dynamics of the data.

With regard to the form of a digital persona, it is important to know whether it is *static* or *dynamic*. That is to say, does the digital persona evolve along with the represented individual or does it always stay the same? Here is a clear link with the collection of data as a once-only or a repeated process. How rigid the data are can, however, also be related to the kinds of data and the amount of data in the digital persona.

As indicated earlier, data about James are collected by Google every time James browses the Internet. The continuous accumulation of data and the related processing imply that the digital representation Google has created of James is not static, but dynamic. It evolves along with James' interests and whereabouts.

Another form-related aspect is whether the digital persona is a *rich* or a *poor* representation. Richness can refer to two things: the amount of data in the digital persona (mathematical number) or the amount of information in the digital persona (information-value). When a representation consists of very few data, it is a poor representation. Only a username and password is perfectly sufficient to access an account and to recognize an individual, supposed that only one person uses the username password combination. However, when no other data are connected, it is merely an identifier and not a real representation. There is no capability of functioning as a proxy for the individual. This implies that there is more needed than only an identifier to speak of a digital persona. Nevertheless, how many data exactly cannot be said, since functioning as a representation depends on which data are available in the representation and which data are needed for a specific

---

regulations, the controller or the specific criteria for his nomination may be designated by national or Community law".

purpose. Sometimes, only few data are sufficient, whereas in other cases the more data available, the better. Related to the kind and the amount of data is the (possible) information value. From a set of data, knowledge can be derived which increases the value of the data set as such. The more information there is when analyzing the set of data, the better it can function as a proxy for an individual.

A digital representation as created by Google is extremely rich, at least when taking the perspective of the amount of data. With about 88 percent web coverage, it can be said that James is pretty well monitored concerning his Internet behavior, and all these data are accumulated by Google. However, not only from the perspective of amount of data, but also from the information value perspective the representation is very rich. All data are processed in order to reveal specific interests and possible opportunities for targeted advertising, as well as to personalize search results listed in the search engine. Even though the arguments for doing this are related to improving web experience and not being disturbed by irrelevant information and advertisements, the data set and the results from the processing of the data form a very detailed digital persona, which includes knowledge about James he is probably not even aware of himself.

Another aspect of form is whether the data in the digital persona includes a *unique identifier* or not. It was mentioned above that lack of a unique identifier does not necessarily mean that data cannot be linked to each other and to an individual. This is related to so-called primary and secondary keys. A unique identifier is a primary key, which directly establishes the link to an individual. A secondary key, however, means that when collecting data in any case there comes a point where there are enough data to make this link, even though there is no unique identifier. The entire set of data is then unique for an individual.

Even though the unique identifier might be less relevant to establish the connection between a data set and an individual, it is an important aspect when looking at linkability of different data sets. A unique identifier can be used in different settings, which implies that different digital personae can be linked to each other as belonging to the same individual. An example of a unique identifier is the *Burger Servicenummer* (Citizen Service Number, BSN). This is a unique number for each citizen in the Netherlands. The unique identifier as part of the data set is an attribute belonging to the represented individual. Just as with the other attributes an attribute functions as an identifier when it enables the user of a data set to single-out an individual based solely on this attribute. That means that the group of people one belongs to is also relevant. The more people there are in a group, the bigger the chance that an attribute is not unique for one individual in this group.[126]

---

[126] See also Koot 2012.

The unique identifier that facilitates the connection of the data to James is, in first instance, his IP address or addresses. Whether an IP address is considered to be personal data is still debated. However, at least the IP address is an R-identifier, meaning that it can be used to recognize the same device, therewith facilitating the connection of different sessions to each other.

James uses different devices, but regularly checks his Gmail account on all these devices. Because he accesses the same account, the different devices (and IP addresses) can be recognized as belonging to the same person, because Google plants the same cookie whenever James logs in. The only problem that remains is that different people can use the same device with the same IP address. For instance, James' work computer is sometimes used by one of his colleagues, and his personal laptop is often used by his family members. Nevertheless, the enormous amount of data collected on interests and behavior enables separation between different users on the same IP address. This can relatively easily be derived from a browsing session, which usually has a standard pattern for each person. For instance: check private mail, check work mail, look at a news site, check company web page, etc..

The IP address can be recognized, but that does not mean that the person behind the IP address can be identified with a name. However, James helps Google a little bit by googling his own name from time to time, a so called vanity search.[127] James wants to know what information about him is available on the web. The web behavior, together with this vanity search, can lead to identification of the individual behind the IP address. Paradoxically, checking which information is on the web implies adding new information behind the scenes.

4.3. The application of the digital persona

A last important category is the application or use of the digital persona. Application has to do with application for whom, to whom, and with the range of the application. A first aspect is whether the digital persona is used for, or in the *interest of*, the concerned *individual* himself, for the *organization* that creates the digital persona, or for a *third party*. For whose interest a digital persona is used is closely related to the purpose of the creation of the digital representation. It can be assumed that a projected digital persona is always used in the interest of the concerned individual himself, since he creates the representation himself. The way it is created and the information contained in the digital persona is linked to the interests of the individual. However, it is very well possible that an individual creates a digital persona of himself with a focus on another party who might have an interest in using this persona. Then, the interest is shared with another party, but at least the interest of the individual is still at stake.

---

[127] Soghoian 2006.

Strict imposed digital personae are usually created in the interest of the creating party[128] or a third party. The representation is meant for specific purposes that are related to the aims of another party than the concerned individual. A credit rating is meant to inform companies about the creditworthiness of an individual. The company can then decide to give a loan or not.[129] Hybrid digital personae can have combined interests incorporated. For instance, a medical file is created in the interest of a doctor, but, obviously, also in the interest of the patient, because the patient has an interest in accurate medical information on which decisions on treatment are based.

The digital persona Google created is used by Google herself. It is in Google's interest to provide the best advertisement and search system possible, because that is their business. However, next to that Google inclines to use the data in the interest of James. James should not be bothered with non-interesting information and should have a convenient web experience. Thus, both Google and James have a (possible) interest. Nevertheless, the real application of the digital persona as meant here is for Google only and Google is strongly insisting in their claims of respecting privacy, so they do not share the data with third parties. That would ruin their business as well, obviously.

An interesting aspect is that Google claims not to process personal data[130] (so in their view an IP address is not personal data) and for that reason also rejects requests from individuals who want insight in their data on the basis of Directive 95/46/EC. Thus, the data are not even shared with the represented individual. However, there is the problem of singularizing.[131] The problem of singularizing implies that individuals may be recognized within a group when data belonging to that individual accumulate, even when (other) personal data remain private. When taking into account that each and every transaction in an information system leaves a digital trace behind, it becomes clear that the accumulation of data can be enormous and that it, thus, becomes easier to link data to a single individual. The more data available, the more unique combinations of these data

---

[128] This may include the improvement of services, such as keeping a customer account which allows for automated filling of order forms, which is, of course, also in the interest of the individual customer who does not have to provide the same details again when returning to a website to buy a product.

[129] Of course, there is also an interest of the concerned individual, either to be protected from loaning too much and getting into financial trouble, or to show that the individual is creditworthy and that no problems are expected when giving a loan. So, in the end the individual is helped, assuming that all data in the credit rating are correct. However, this interest of the individual is not the prior aim of a credit rating (agency).

[130] For instance, in a presentation by Peter Fleischer (privacy counsel Google) at a meeting of the *Vereniging Privacy Recht* (VPR) in September 2010.

[131] Dobias, Hansen, Köpsell, Raguse, Roosendaal, Pfitzmann & Zwingelberg 2011.

are. The more data disclosed to a party over time, the lower the fingerprinting threshold becomes, which means that after a certain amount of time individuals can be uniquely identified and recognized when they appear in a new transaction, even when this new transaction is done from another computer or another location than the previous ones.[132]

Another aspect is whether the digital persona is used *within the context* in which it is created or whether the application *exceeds* this *context*. In this respect it is important to remind that the creation of a digital persona is related to a specific context and purpose. A medical dossier is created in a medical context with the purpose of facilitating good medical treatment by showing medical history and diagnoses. As long as the digital persona stays within this context there is, usually, no problem. However, when the medical dossier exceeds its context, for instance when an insurance company gains insight and uses it to decide whether an individual can get certain insurance or not, the original purpose is lost and the individual gets affected in another, possibly negative way. Digital personae are context-bound, so looking at the application range is an important aspect.

Whether the application of the digital representation of James is bound to the context in which it was created is difficult to say. Not because it is unclear where it is applied, but more because the creation context practically covers the entire web. And that is also the application range. Specific applications are the personalized search results and the targeted advertisements in James' Gmail account. However, with the help of AdSense, targeted ads appear on numerous websites which can be visited.

The application range can refer to the context range as well as to the range of individuals to whom a digital persona is applied. Use can be restricted to only the *individual* of whom the digital persona is a representation, or the application can concern a *group*. The latter can, for instance, be the case in a recommender system of an online shop. When an individual visits the shop and reveals an interest for a specific book or genre, the digital persona of another individual with a shared interest can be used to generate recommendations for this visitor. When this process takes place repeatedly, the application of a digital persona ranges a multitude of individuals. For this kind of purposes, a digital persona is used in a comparable form as an individualized group profile. A digital persona is meant to be a proxy for an individual, so applying it to a multitude of individuals is not the primary goal intended. However, in particular digital personae which are, at least partly, the result of some kind of individual monitoring activity can perfectly function for that, because in these cases, the digital persona will include

---

[132] Conti 2009.

some information on a type of person; individuals are pigeon-holed, which is also done with profiling activities. Nevertheless, most digital persona will stay connected to the individual they represent only.

The digital representation is meant to provide James with personalized information and advertisements. This means that the representation is applied to James as the represented individual and not to a group. Nevertheless, the data collected about James can be used as input for aggregation in order to make group profiles which can provide information that can be applied to several persons. Interests may overlap, so individuals who share some interests might be addressed with additional interests other individuals have. In that case, however, it concerns the aggregated data and the information derived from the processing of these data, and not the individual representation as a whole.

A last relevant feature regarding the application of digital personae is whether the use has a *legal effect* or only *non-legal effects*. With a legal effect I mean that the individual concerning whom a decision is taken based on his digital persona is influenced by this in the sense of gaining or losing rights or duties. For instance, when tax authorities look at a digital persona and find out that one's salary is low enough to receive additional subsidies this has a legal effect; the individual has a right to subsidies. Clearly, the opposite situation is also possible, namely that an individual has received subsidies but has no right to them because of a (too) high income. Here, the individual gets a duty to pay back the subsidies to the tax authorities. In a commercial context, legal effects may occur, for instance, when a service provider decides that a user has breached the Terms and Conditions or other contractual obligations, and holds the individual user liable or denies further access to the service.

Non-legal effects can be related to mere verification of information. Another example is deciding on a kind of medical treatment. Based on a digital persona, there can be inclusion or exclusion of certain commercial offers. Even though an individual might be of opinion that he also has a 'right' to the discount his neighbor received, this is not a legal right. This means that non-legal effects can also directly influence individuals. Nevertheless, if the exclusion is structural and the individual is excluded from certain offers or benefits repetitively, it may become a form of indirect discrimination, which is a legal effect.

James can be affected in a legal sense by decisions taken by Google based on his digital representation, such as being held liable or being structurally excluded from offers or information.

The table below gives an overview of the relevant features, as discussed above, per category.

Data collection	Form of the digital persona	Application
Awareness	Dynamic	Individual/organization/3rd party
Repetition	Richness	Context bound
Context bound	Unique identifier	To individual/group
Responsibility		Legal effect

Table 5. Features of digital personae.

5. How to determine whether a data set is a digital persona?

The remaining question, of course, is how one can determine whether a set of data is a digital persona. Based on the features and categories indicated in the previous section, one can subject a data set to a three step test. The three steps are related to the three categories. Each step consists of a question which can be answered with yes or no. When all three questions are answered positively, the data set constitutes a digital persona.

The first question is a really obvious one: Is there a data set? Without one, there is no digital representation or whatsoever possible. However, it is an important question to ask, because it helps in focusing on what exactly one is looking at. One has to find out what data are collected in the set and whether one wants to look at an entire set or only at a part of it.

If the first question is answered positively, the second question to ask is whether the data set constitutes an image of (a partial identity of) an identifiable individual. This question emphasizes that it concerns a digital representation of a real-world individual and that it is necessary to be able to connect the representation to this individual. This connection can be established with a unique identifier, for instance a name, but it can also be based on a combination of data or certain attributes that can single out an individual. Another option is to make the connection based on recognition of the individual as being the same person as to which other data belong.

The third question refers to practical application of the data set and asks whether the data set is used to take decisions concerning the represented individual. If this is confirmed, it shows that the digital representation can serve as a proxy for the individual in the specific context and for the specific purpose. It also means that the use of the digital persona affects a real-world individual and that the physical presence of this individual is not necessary for taking decisions.

It might appear that with these three simple questions an enormous number of data sets can qualify as digital personae. That is a valid conclusion. The number of databases in which individuals appear is huge. For instance, in the Netherlands, information about an average person is stored in 250 to 500 databases.[133] However, being represented in hundreds of databases does not necessarily mean that this is bad. That depends on how the representations are used and how the individual is affected by this use. The features that were presented in the three categories can be of help in determining how the individual is affected by the use of digital personae and whether this is positive or negative or does not make any difference as compared to being directly involved as an individual. This will be the subject of the next chapters, which map how individuals are affected. In particular, the perspectives of privacy and data protection and individual autonomy will be taken.

---

[133] Schermer & Wagemans 2009, p. 40. The authors of this report take a narrow definition of database to come to this number. When taking into account all processing activities where personal data are involved, one would probably come to thousands of registrations.

Chapter 4
Human dignity and related values and rights and their legal protection

1. Introduction

In the previous chapters it has been shown that digital personae consist of data sets which can be used as a basis for making decisions concerning individuals and that these decisions affect the individual. As a result, some interrelated concepts are relevant here; privacy, identity, and autonomy. At a fundamental level, individual human beings are considered to have an inherent value, usually referred to as human dignity. This dignity implies that individuals need to be protected against harm to their physical and mental status. Each individual has to be respected for its uniqueness, which is reflected in key concepts such as bodily integrity and the non-discrimination principle. Uniqueness, and the ability to be unique and to determine who you want to be, is directly related to identity. In order to construct an own identity, the autonomy of the individual has to be guaranteed.

The aim of this chapter is to provide an insight in what exactly needs protection. The triangle of privacy, identity, and autonomy forms the key concepts surrounding and supporting human dignity. Next to that, the relation between the concepts is made more concrete by the concepts of informational self-determination and contextual integrity. The digital persona is a representation of an individual. The individual as such has human dignity, but the digital persona has not; it is not a human being. Nevertheless, due to the fact that much communication and information processing nowadays is taking place in a digital form, decisions based on a digital persona may influence the level of autonomy of the individual and, therewith, affect human dignity.

Privacy is instrumental to individual autonomy and the construction of identity. The protection of privacy is, thus, strongly related to respect for human dignity. With this in mind, it is evident that the right to privacy is internationally recognized as a fundamental right. At a more concrete level, privacy, in relation to digital information, can be specified, or narrowed down, to data protection.

This chapter will first discuss the concepts of human dignity, autonomy, identity, informational self-determination, contextual integrity, and privacy and how these are related (2). After having provided this framework, an assessment will be made of the applicable laws and regulations in relation to the protection of the concepts. First, in section 3, a more fundamental level will be discussed by looking at the European Convention for the Protection of Human Rights and Fundamental Freedoms (ECHR) and the Charter of Fundamental Rights of the European Union. Then, in section 4, the more practical level of data protection legislation will be discussed. Finally, a conclusion will be drawn (5).

2. Main concepts and their relation

This section will discuss the main concepts that relate to the way individuals function in society, in everyday life. The aim is to indicate why the concepts are relevant and how they connect to each other. Once the concepts and their relations are clear, it is possible to translate them to the context of digital personae. First, a brief overview of the concepts will be given. The overview is presented as a top-down approach. Nevertheless, the different concepts often mutually influence or support each other, so the approach should not be interpreted as strictly hierarchical. After the overview, each of the concepts will be elaborated upon in a separate subsection.

I consider *human dignity* to be the overarching value of the concepts. It is an intrinsic value human beings have and is the real basis of fundamental rights. In particular, this can be seen in the Charter of Fundamental Rights of the European Union in which human dignity is presented as such. Each and every human being should be respected in his dignity, which also explains the prohibition of, for instance, slavery and torture. These, but also other forms of constraining the physical or mental freedom of individuals, restrict the autonomy of individual human beings and therewith infringe upon human dignity.

The *autonomy* of individuals is their capacity and ability to make their own individual independent choices and set their own long-term and short-term desires and goals. Individuals decide what they want to achieve and how they want to achieve this. Working towards a goal implies that the individual makes choices on how he wants to be seen by others, so autonomous acting facilitates the construction of identity.

Individuals develop or construct their own *identity*. Desires and goals are often context-related, so what an identity looks like may be different according to different contexts. This implies that, in different contexts, different (partial) identities are created. In order to construct an identity, specific choices can be made by the individual on what information to share with whom and in what specific context.

The ability to selectively share or disclose information is called *informational self-determination*. It entails the sharing of information by the individual himself, but also control over the collection or disclosure of data concerning the individual by others. Individuals often choose to only disclose information in a specific context. The (explicit) choice to limit and control disclosure also means that the information should not be transferred to another context, unless there are specific circumstances or interests that prevail over the informational self-determination of the individual.

Information being bound to a specific context and not being transferred to other contexts is called *contextual integrity*. Contextual integrity also mean that, in the case that information is transferred, it should be done in respect of the rules and uses that are related to the original context in which the information was disclosed.

In order to achieve informational self-determination and contextual integrity, *privacy* is a key concept to be respected. The relation between privacy and the other concepts can also be seen in the development of definitions of privacy, which sometimes refer to these specific concepts. The right to be left alone[134] provides the individual with *Lebensraum* and enables him to keep secrets and the ability not to disclose certain information. Westin[135] defined privacy as individuals determining when and how, and to what extent information about them is communicated to others (informational self-determination). As indicated by the definition of privacy given by Agre,[136] privacy provides the freedom from unreasonable constraints in the construction of identity. The different aspects of privacy thus support several related concepts. Each of the concepts indicated above will now be elaborated upon.

2.1. Human dignity

At an international level in Western society there is the belief that each and every individual has an inherent value, often referred to as human dignity. It is often mentioned as the general fundamental value to which other values relate. As indicated in the explanations of the EU Charter of Fundamental Rights, "[t]he dignity of the human person is not only a fundamental right in itself but constitutes the real basis of fundamental rights" and "the dignity of the human person is part of the substance of the rights laid down in this Charter."[137] A number of values and rights, such as privacy, bodily integrity,

---

[134] Warren & Brandeis 1890.
[135] Westin 1967.
[136] Agre 1997.
[137] Article based legal explanation of the EU Charter of Fundamental Rights. Online available at: <http://www.eucharter.org/home.php?page_id=8>.

autonomy, and equality, are instrumental to the protection of human dignity.[138] [139] Even though there are criticisms, mainly in philosophical debate, on whether there really is such a thing as human dignity and not just dignity as belonging to people, but also to trees and animals,[140] and autonomy as a specific characteristic of human agency,[141] in the ethical-legal discourse the fundamental value of human dignity is broadly accepted and supported.

2.2. Autonomy

In relation to human rights, a classical definition of autonomy is "a complex assumption about the capacities, developed or undeveloped, of persons, which enable them to develop, want to act on, and act on higher-order plans of action which take as their self-critical object one's life and the way it is lived."[142] Individual autonomy, thus, entails the ability of an individual to make their own choices and to define their own desires. To act autonomously means that the individual is mentally able to freely make conscious choices (internal), but also that there are no external constraints that limit possibilities to make choices freely and independently. Two important concepts in this context are freedom of choice and freedom to act. Restrictions to the latter can be external constraints, such as being locked up, or internal constraints, such as fear. With regard to freedom of choice several forms of restrictions are possible. First, the range of options can be too limited. What 'too limited' means, depends on the specific context in which limitations occur. Second, problems can occur concerning the eligibility of the available options, and, third, restrictions can be based on the significance[143] of the available options. Freedom to act and freedom of choice are instrumental to the value of autonomy in a practical sense. Here, a distinction can be made between the concept of autonomy as a right and the concept of autonomy

---

[138] Some of these rights are not always separated, because they are all interrelated. The right to bodily integrity, for instance, is often seen as part of privacy, the right to life, or human dignity itself. See: Roosendaal & Kosta, p. 36.

[139] J. Nickel, "Human rights", in: Stanford Encyclopedia of Philosophy (2006 edition): <http://plato.stanford.edu/entries/rights-human/> (last accessed March 30, 2010).

[140] R. Streiffer, "Human/Non-Human Chimeras", in: Stanford Encyclopedia of Philosophy (2009 edition): <http://plato.stanford.edu/entries/chimeras/#5> (last accessed March 30, 2010).

[141] De Mul and Van den Berg give an overview of criticisms on human autonomy. Critics refer to influences external from the individual which determine the way an individual acts. De Mul & Van den Berg challenge these critics by stating that: "having *incomplete* control does not imply having *no* control *at all*." In particular, they refer to the *'reflexive loop'* which is a distinctive ability of human agency to *affirm* its actions in retrospect, so *post actio*. De Mul & Van den Berg 2011.

[142] Richards 1989, p. 205.

[143] Significance can be judged objectively (significance in general) or subjectively (individual preferences).

as a psychological condition of self-government. In this context, autonomy as a right is a right against actions that attempt to disrupt or undercut the psychological condition; it is a right not to be treated in certain ways.[144] An individual has to be able to make its own conscious choices on desires to be realized and goals to be achieved. Individual autonomy is foundational in the explanation of certain moral rights and values, such as the right to be treated as a free and equal moral person for which it serves as a basis.[145]

According to Gerald Dworkin:[146]

> A person is autonomous if he identifies with his desires, goals, and values, and such identification is not in itself influenced in ways which make the process of identification in some way alien to the individual. Spelling out the conditions of procedural independence involves distinguishing those ways of influencing people's reflective and critical faculties which subvert them from those which promote and improve them.

An individual has to be able to exercise his right to individual autonomy. This means that, with an eye to equality, the necessary resources need to be distributed equally amongst individuals. Education, employment opportunities, medical services, and housing, among other things, are essential in the exercise of the right, so an unequal distribution of these resources implies a violation of the basic regard for individual autonomy.[147] If an individual is equipped with the necessary resources he can use his competences to act autonomously. In this respect, a distinction can be made between the ordinary meaning of 'competence' which is related to natural ability, and a legal meaning, which refers to the possession of legal powers. According to Feinberg there are no degrees in this, but 'competence' expresses an all or nothing concept.[148] It is a capacity one has or does not have. Nevertheless, it is very well possible that an individual is autonomous only within certain limits. In a broader sense than only competence, an autonomous individual has the capacity to select her own tastes, preferences, opinions, goals, and desires. It is a conscious choice which has to be made, and not merely conforming to other's opinions, which makes an authentic individual.[149] Choices and desires have to be confirmed or adapted continuously by the individual himself. Personal development or changes in the environment an individual lives in may influence choices and desires. So,

---

[144] Christman 1989, p. 6.
[145] Christman 1989, p. 18.
[146] Dworkin 1989, p. 61.
[147] Christman 1989, p. 19.
[148] Feinberg 1989, pp. 28-29.
[149] Feinberg 1989, p. 32.

preferences may change over time; desires are not (always) consistent.[150] To conclude, autonomy is fundamental to exercising human rights and to live a decent life as an individual. Making individual choices and defining wishes and desires are key elements, which emphasize the value of the individual as a human being. Restrictions on autonomy should be as limited as possible.

2.3. Identity[151]

Making choices and defining wishes and desires is closely related to identity. Identity is who you are as an individual and how you want to be perceived by others. So, it has an internal and an external element. The internal element can be described as how human beings acquire a sense of self.[152] The external element relates to social interaction with others. This interaction, however, is not similar in all situations. The world is divided into different contexts which are seen as separate audiences on which a certain (partial) identity or aspect of identity is projected. As Hekman puts it: "(...) I am social in interaction with *specific* others, and understanding identity must attend to both the general (social) and the specific (individual). In other words, we are all embedded but we are all embedded differently at different locations."[153] Keeping the audiences and roles separated is what Goffman[154] called 'audience segregation'.

Identity is construed by making individual choices and defining individual desires, so to be autonomous is imperative to being able to construct a personal identity. As explained in the theoretical framework, identity directly relates to the way an individual presents himself.

2.4. Informational self-determination

To maintain different representations it is necessary to be able to control what data are shared with whom. The individual has to be able to decide on whether to share certain information or not, and to make distinctions between audiences that receive that information. Informational self-determination supports control over disclosure of data.

Rouvroy and Poullet state that informational self-determination means "that an individual's control over the data and information produced about him is a

---

[150] Richards 1989, p. 205.
[151] A broader description of identity and its main aspects from several disciplinary perspectives was presented in Chapter 2 of this study.
[152] Hekman 2004, p. 22.
[153] Hekman 2004, p. 23.
[154] Goffman 1959.

(necessary but insufficient) precondition for him to live an existence that may be said 'self-determined'."[155] They focus more on the identity aspect, pointing out that an individual having control over what data are produced about him facilitates a self-determined existence. The individual can construct his own identity and control what data may become part of that identity. In fact, it underscores the determination aspect of the 'informational self' more than the self-determination of information concerning the individual. From that perspective, restricting individual self-determination to control over data and deciding what can be done with personal data is probably too narrow, at least when control is considered as the ability to agree or disagree on the production and use of data. Schwartz calls this the 'autonomy trap' and indicates that the "organization of information privacy through individual control of personal data rests on a view of autonomy as a given, preexisting quality."[156] The problem, however, is that in the information age individual self-determination itself is shaped by the processing of personal data. The use of personal data sets the terms under which an individual participates in social and political life. For instance, "the act of clicking through a 'consent' screen on a web site may be considered by some observers to be an exercise of self-reliant choice. Yet, this screen can contain boilerplate language that permits all further processing and transmission of one's personal data."[157] In the end, the autonomy trap refers to a specific form of individual choice being 'locked-in'. For instance, an individual can make a choice to access and use a service, such as the Google search engine. However, in this case, using the service implies agreeing to the General Terms and Conditions of Google. These Terms include consent to sharing personal information or to the processing of personal data. This consent is given implicitly, and often even while being unaware, and is not what the individual actually meant to do when using the search engine. Using the search engine without implicit acceptance of the Terms is not possible. Giving consent is a locked-in choice. In cases where the individual is unaware of the Terms, it is impossible to make a conscious choice or to compare the Terms with these of a comparable service in order to choose for the service with the most convenient Terms. Moreover, General Terms and Conditions in most cases include permission to extensive processing of personal data, which means that for a lot of web services there are no real alternatives with better Terms available. It is clear that when being locked-in there is not much control left. Besides, even the self-reliant choice that has to guarantee control by the individual is often not that self-reliant, since not clicking on 'consent' implies no access to the web service. The choice is, thus, not about whether someone agrees to have his data processed, but about whether someone wants to access the service or

---

[155] Rouvroy & Poullet 2009, p. 51.
[156] Schwartz 1999.
[157] Schwartz 1999.

not. The fact that accessing the service implies agreeing on the processing of data is often overruled by the desire or need to access the service.[158]

When emphasizing the identity aspect of informational self-determination, as argued by Rouvroy and Poullet and Schwartz, it can be concluded that only purely projected digital personae can be accepted as supporting or enabling informational self-determination. Basically, whenever information is created or processed by someone else the individual loses control over the construction of his identity. Imposed and hybrid digital personae, then, do not support informational self-determination. Nevertheless, a basic approach of only allowing projected digital personae is impossible to hold in the information society. This implies that when other entities store, for instance, preferences of individuals, the individual has to be able to change these preferences according to his own preference adaptations.

Informational self-determination is bound to contexts. The choice of whether to disclose certain data depends on the specific context in which an individual is interacting. The importance of context can be best described in the light of contextual integrity.

2.5. Contextual integrity

Contextual integrity is important to keep data in the context where it belongs and to respect the (implicit) rules that govern behavior concerning personal data in specific contexts. The concept of contextual integrity in informational privacy originates from Nissenbaum, who defines it as "compatibility with presiding norms of information appropriateness and distribution."[159] She specifies the concept by articulating variables which can help determine whether a particular action is a violation of privacy, such as "the nature of the situation, or context; the nature of the information in relation to that context; the roles of agents receiving information; their relationships to information subjects; on what terms the information is shared by the subject; and the terms of further dissemination."[160] Thus, contextual integrity means that information has to be kept within a context and that the way the data are treated has to be in compliance with the general rules and specific agreements that are made concerning that context.

Evidently, data are usually disclosed within a specific context and to the people who belong to this context. In this respect it is important to understand that

---

[158] This practice illustrates how choices can be restricted or limited and, thus, how autonomy can be affected.
[159] Nissenbaum 2004.
[160] Nissenbaum 2004.

disclosing information in a way which makes it accessible to everyone, for instance by posting something in a public space on the internet, does not always mean that it is intended to be disclosed to and be made available for use by everyone. A distinction has to be made between the intended audience and the actual audience. The intended audience is the people that belong in the context in which the information is disclosed. The actual audience is the people who in fact have access to the disclosed information, regardless of whether they belong to the specific context in which the information is disclosed.

As can be derived from the variables articulated by Nissenbaum (see above), purpose binding is an important component. It means that the disclosure of information and its further processing is bound to a specific purpose. This purpose has to be defined before the processing of data takes place. The purpose often defines the context, since information can be disclosed to people who may belong to several contexts, while the information is only meant to be used in one of these contexts. Further dissemination of data, probably to another context, has to be in accordance with the indicated purpose for which the data were disclosed. However, in principle dissemination out of the initial context is not possible when contextual integrity is at stake. A new context means a new purpose and a new audience. Of course, the question that arises is what exactly a context is.

Nissenbaum defines contexts as "structured social settings, characterized by canonical activities, roles, relationships, power structures, norms (or rules), and internal values (goals, ends, purposes)."[161] "Contexts are not formally defined constructs, but [...] are intended as abstract representations of social structures experienced in daily life."[162] A context is a restricted area. The restrictions can be based on several indicators, such as space, topic, time, relationship between the actors, etc. The role-relation that applies to the situation is a main indicator. In order to give more substance to this, I quote Brown:[163]

> [R]egarding an individual seen as the occupant of a social role, there is information to which only someone standing in the appropriate role-relation can be expected to have access. (By role-relation I mean a relation in which one person stands to another by virtue of the respective roles occupied by the two persons.) There is, for example, information about me which my bank manager possesses but which my employer does not, there is information which both of these

---

[161] Nissenbaum 2010, p. 132.
[162] Nissenbaum 2010, p. 134.
[163] Brown 1990, pp. 76-77, emphasis in original.

possess but which my doctor does not, and much to which my doctor has access but the former do not, and so on. As I have pointed out earlier, however, there is probably little significant information about me which is not possessed by somebody or other.

Yet this last fact does not worry me unduly. What would worry me is the idea that some person (other than someone to whom I stand in a very close and perhaps unique role-relation, such as my wife) had access to *all* this information, or that such information were distributed indiscriminately. A part, then, of what is essential to the integrity of a person's social identity as seen "from the inside" is not some special set of facts to which only he or she has access, nor the exercise of total control over the information relating to him or her, but rather that access to particular information is systematically related in the appropriate way to the network of social relationships in which that person stands to others by virtue of their places in the role structure. *A breach of privacy can be said to have occurred wherever the flow of information becomes divorced from the social role structure in some way.* For want of a better label we might call this the Short Circuit Effect.

The combination of the roles of interacting parties and the relation between these parties thus determines the context in which information is disclosed or otherwise processed. As Brown indicates, the flow of information is connected to the social role structure at stake. This is exactly what Nissenbaum means with contextual integrity. The way in which interaction takes place and the way information is shared or processed can be considered to be appropriate when this matches with the roles and relations at stake. Treating data inappropriately within the context or transferring it to another context implies a crossing of the boundaries within which the data should be treated in order to protect privacy and individual autonomy. The same goes for combining data from different contexts by making connections between data sets or by adding data from another context to the context in which an interaction takes place. For instance, in a job interview the candidate shows sufficient capacities and skills and the potential future employer decides to include private information on drinking behavior during the weekends which is available on an SNS profile. As a result, the decision on hiring the candidate is not taken at the end of the interview. Information from another context is used to come to a decision, regardless of whether this information is relevant for the job or not.

2.6. Privacy

Privacy can be distinguished into different dimensions. Common distinctions are between spatial, relational, communicational, and informational privacy.[164] Informational privacy relates to the protection of personal data and has two main components.[165] The first concerns being free from the interference of others, not being watched, and is at the core of the right to privacy. The second element comes into play once a third party has information and the individual wants to control the use and dissemination of this information. Obviously, many aspects of an individual's life are captured in data, which implies that informational aspects from the other dimensions become part of informational privacy as well. Information concerning home environment (smart metering), relationships (social networking sites), and body (medical records) is made compatible with the informational dimension. This implies that the use of information can also impact the other dimensions of privacy. The focus in this study, however, will be on informational privacy only.

As indicated above, there is no clear-cut definition of privacy. Nevertheless, the concept has developed over time and in this development several aspects have been highlighted. The right to privacy was first coined by Warren and Brandeis[166] in 1890. The writing of their article was instigated by photographs and newspaper enterprises that "have invaded the sacred precincts of private and domestic life." Mechanical inventions and other developments facilitated the recording and storing of information as well as the broad distribution of this information. Warren and Brandeis were of the opinion that not every aspect of life that could be recorded should be allowed to be recorded, since several aspects belonged to the private sphere of individuals. With an eye to respect for this private sphere, they defined privacy as 'the right to be let alone'.

Over the years, the technologies that facilitated data collection increased, in particular surveillance technologies, leading to a loss of control of the individual on the disclosure of personal information.

In 1967, Westin came up with his definition of privacy as "the claim of individuals, groups, or institutions to determine for themselves when, how, and to what extent information about them is communicated to others."[167] This definition clearly includes the concept of informational self-determination. A direct link between privacy and identity was brought

---

[164] There have been several efforts to come to a clear and concise definition of the concept of privacy. The definition will not be discussed here. For those interested in the discussion and efforts, see, for instance, the valuable work done by Parent (1983), who approaches the concept from different views and disciplines, and the extensive work by Solove: Solove 2002; Solove 2006; Solove 2008.

[165] Lloyd 2008, p. 7.

[166] Warren & Brandeis 1890.

[167] Westin 1967.

to the fore in Agre's definition of privacy as presented in 1997, where he speaks of projecting to the world. Agre defines privacy as the freedom from unreasonable constraints on constructing identity and control over aspects of identity projected to the world.[168] Taking Goffman's findings into account, the definition of privacy as given by Agre is a bridge between these findings and the approach of Nissenbaum towards privacy as contextual integrity.[169] Aspects of identity can be projected to the world, which is usually a specific context. The information shared as part of an identity should be kept within the context in which it was shared and should only be used according to the rules that apply to that specific context.

With respect to informational privacy, the protection of privacy is often narrowed down to data protection, which can be seen as an intermediate value that facilitates privacy.

2.7. Conclusion

As shown in the sections above, the concepts of dignity, autonomy, identity, and privacy are closely related. One cannot exist without the other. On the one hand, autonomous (independent) choices have to be made in order to decide on the identity an individual wants to develop and, in relation to that, what information to share with whom and for what purposes. On the other hand, privacy, with the related main concepts of informational-self-determination and contextual integrity, is a necessary condition to facilitate this autonomy.

As was indicated in the introduction to this chapter, individual autonomy and identity are directly connected to the inherent value human beings have. This inherent value is often referred to as human dignity. Human dignity is a central concept in the protection of individuals and the fundamental rights they have at an abstract level in international treaties. The following section will discuss the two most relevant treaties applicable in Europe: the European Convention for the Protection of Human Rights and Fundamental Freedoms (ECHR) and the Charter of Fundamental Rights of the European Union (EU Charter).

3. Fundamental rights and values

A legal system is meant to offer protection. What is protected can basically be everything, but usually things are protected that are deemed important

---

[168] Agre 1997, p. 7.
[169] Nissenbaum 2004.

to make a society work properly. In other words, the law reflects the values of a society in order to maintain social order.[170] For instance, human beings are considered to have an inherent value in society and, thus, need to be protected. The right to life, or the prohibition of murder, is aimed at offering such protection. What values are relevant in the context of the concepts described in the previous section and how they are laid down in law will be discussed in this section.

Fundamental rights[171] are fundamental in the sense that they need to be protected and respected in every case and for every single individual. The incorporation of these rights in international treaties is meant to emphasize their importance. Slavery and torture were forbidden and the cruelties from World War II were an incentive to explicitly lay down basic concepts such as equality and non-discrimination and freedoms individuals should be able to enjoy. Fundamental rights are, in first instance, rights to protect the individual against the state or the government, so they primarily focus on vertical relationships. However, this vertical relationship is also applied to horizontal relationships, since states have a duty to protect the fundamental rights properly. States, thus, have to guarantee, in their legal systems or otherwise, that individuals can exercise or enjoy their rights in horizontal relationships as well. If a state fails in fulfilling this duty, the state can be held liable for infringements on the fundamental rights of its individual citizens. In the context of the European Union, fundamental rights are now laid down in the EU Charter of Fundamental Rights. An important basis for this Charter can be found in the European Convention on Human Rights. Both will be discussed more elaborately below.

3.1. The European Convention on Human Rights

The European Convention on Human Rights (ECHR)[172] is an extensive international treaty aiming at a broad recognition and respect of fundamental rights and values for individuals. After the Second World War, the question of human rights was important, because "[t]here was a general consensus that freedom was the only basis on which peace could be established in Europe and that the plea of sovereign inviolability might hamper the

---

[170] Durkheim 1973, p. 67. For extensive discussions on the function of law and its relation with rules, see, for instance; Hart 1961; Pound 1922.

[171] I will use the terms 'fundamental rights' and 'human rights' as synonyms. Similar rights are legally protected in different treaties under both these headings, so their meaning is essentially the same.

[172] The European Convention for the Protection of Human Rights and Fundamental Freedoms, CETS No.: 005, Rome, 4/11/1950.

exercise of individual freedom, as it had in fact done in Nazi Germany."[173] In the aftermath of the Second World War, the ten founding members of the ECHR wanted to make a largely symbolic statement of their liberal democratic identity.[174] The protection of human rights in every country was seen as a necessary condition for European unification,[175] so in 1950 the members drafted the international treaty on primarily political and civil rights which now embraces every state in Europe except Belarus. With a current combined population of nearly 800 million it is widely regarded as the most successful experiment in the transnational judicial protection of human rights in the world.[176]

Section I of the ECHR, articles 2–18, contains the fundamental rights and freedoms that have to be guaranteed by the signatories. The rights relate to the inviolability of the body (articles 2-5), fair legal proceedings (6-7), privacy (8), freedoms of opinion and speech (9-12), effective remedies against infringements upon the rights and freedoms (13), and non-discrimination (14). Articles 15-18 contain limitations and exceptions on the protection of the rights and freedoms. The most relevant fundamental right for this study is, thus, laid down in article 8 of the ECHR: the right to respect for private and family life. Article 8 ECHR reads as follows:

> 1. Everyone has the right to respect for his private and family life, his home and his correspondence.
> 2. There shall be no interference by a public authority with the exercise of this right except such as is in accordance with the law and is necessary in a democratic society in the interests of national security, public safety or the economic well-being of the country, for the prevention of disorder or crime, for the protection of health or morals, or for the protection of the rights and freedoms of others.

As can be seen, the first paragraph presents the right of protection of the privacy of individuals. In its interpretation of Article 8 of the ECHR, the European Court of Human Rights has ruled that this right covers an individual's physical and social identity and the right to personal development and personal autonomy.[177] The second paragraph states that interference with the right is only allowed when certain conditions are met. "[G]iven the fundamental nature of the Convention rights, the first paragraph should be widely interpreted, and the second one narrowly. Rights must therefore be

---

[173] Weil 1963, p. 22.
[174] Greer 2008.
[175] Weil 1963, p. 22.
[176] Greer 2008.
[177] De Hert 2008.

'stretched', and limitations limited."[178] The grounds of restriction are tested against two requirements.[179] First, an interference of the right has to be 'in accordance with the law.' There must be a legal basis for the interference in the law of the state involved. This does not necessarily have to be a national law, but the requirement also implies a certain quality of the law. Second, the interference has to be 'necessary in a democratic society' in the light of one or more of the mentioned interests. Whether this is the case, in practice, is determined to a large extent by applying the proportionality principle and the 'margin of appreciation.' The proportionality principle requires that an interference with the right "is not excessive in relation to the legitimate needs and interests which have occasioned it."[180] The margin of appreciation means that the individual states have a certain measure of discretion in deciding what they deem necessary in a democratic society, in order to enable them to decide in light of national morals and customs. The protection of the right is the starting point, and limitations have to be avoided as much as possible.

As indicated, several aspects concerning identity, as related to human dignity, are protected by the right to private life. Next to that, "[a]lthough the European Convention and the case-law of the European Court on Human Rights does not recognize a right to informational self-determination, many data protection aspects are brought under the scope of Article 8 of the Convention [...] by the Court."[181] Brouwer[182] gives an overview[183] of cases in which certain aspects of data protection were at stake. A first case on the relation between recording of personal data by public authorities and private life was *Leander v. Sweden*,[184] where data stored in secret police files were not accessible or refutable by the individual (data subject), but were communicated to the employer of the individual. This was considered an interference with Article 8. A comparable case was *Segerstedt-Wiberg and others v. Sweden*,[185] concerning storage and retention (up to 30 years) of data in secret police files. In *Rotaru v. Romania*[186] data concerning (political) memberships were stored in secret files. The court referred to the *Leander* case and also repeated its earlier conclusions from the *Niemitz v. Germany*[187]

---

[178] Korff 2009.
[179] For an extensive discussion, see: Van Dijk & Van Hoof 1998, Chapter 8, section 8 (pp. 761-772).
[180] Van Dijk & Van Hoof 1998, p. 80.
[181] De Hert 2008.
[182] Brouwer 2008.
[183] In Chapter 6 of her thesis, pp. 147-176. The following overview is based on Brouwer's work.
[184] *Leander v. Sweden*, Appl. No. 9248/81, Series A, No. 116, 26 March 1987.
[185] *Segerstedt-Wiberg and others v. Sweden*, Appl. No. 62332/00, 6 June 2006.
[186] *Rotaru v. Romania*, Appl. No. 28341/95, 4 May 2000.
[187] *Niemitz v. Germany*, Appl. No. 13710/88, 16 December 1992.

case that "respect for private life must also comprise, to a certain degree, the right to establish and develop relationships with other persons."[188] The free establishment of relationships is directly related to the construction of an identity, since it allows for deciding to what groups of people an individual wants to belong. The consideration of the Court that information concerning these relationships should not be stored and abused for purposes that do not directly relate to the membership shows the importance of contextual integrity to facilitate this free establishment of relationships.

With respect to identity and autonomy, the *Pretty*[189] case is particularly relevant. In this case, the Court considered autonomy a 'principle' and physical and social identity issues of which 'aspects' are sometimes protected under Article 8 ECHR.[190] Nevertheless, in *Odièvre v. France*[191] a number of judges had a joint dissenting opinion in which autonomy and identity were considered to be 'rights'. "We are firmly of the opinion that the *right to an identity*, which is an essential condition of the right to autonomy (*Pretty v. the United Kingdom*, 25 April 2002, § 61) and development (*Bensaïd v. the United Kingdom*, 6 February 2001, § 47), is within the inner core of the right to respect for one's private life."[192] So, both cases showed that a close relationship between privacy, autonomy, and identity is recognized by the European Court of Human Rights. To what extent each of the concepts is protected under Article 8 ECHR is strongly debated.

A broad interpretation of the first paragraph can also be seen in the positive obligations states have to protect the rights, also in relations between individuals. "[T]he mere fact that an individual has infringed a provision of the Convention cannot lead to a finding against the state. It is necessary for the conduct of the private individual to be seen as originating in a failing on the part of the state itself or as tolerated by it."[193] 'Private life' is a broad concept and cannot be defined exhaustively, but case-law on the concept indicates that at least it includes: the physical and moral integrity of the person; the physical and *social identity of the individual*, including his sexual identity; the right to *personal development* or fulfillment; the right to have relationships with other human beings and the outside world.[194] Under the heading of identity, the right to one's image is covered as well. In this respect,

---

[188] Brouwer 2008, p. 155.
[189] *Pretty v. United Kingdom*, Appl. No. 2346/02, April 29 2002.
[190] De Hert 2008.
[191] *Odièvre v. France*, Appl. No. 42326/98, 13 February 2003.
[192] Joint Dissenting Opinion of Judges Wildhaber, Bratza, Bonello, Loucaides, Cabral Barreto, Tulkens and Pellonpää, paragraph 11, emphasis in original.
[193] Akandji-Kombe 2007, p. 14.
[194] Akandji-Kombe 2007, p. 37 (my emphasis).

a case in point was *Von Hannover v. Germany*,[195] in which it was ruled that "it is incumbent on states to ensure that the right of persons under their jurisdiction to their image is respected by third parties."[196] The right to respect for private life can outweigh the right to freedom of expression when there is a legitimate expectation of privacy. In the words of the Court:

> "The Court reiterates the fundamental importance of protecting private life from the point of view of the development of every human being's personality. That protection – as stated above – extends beyond the private family circle and also includes a social dimension. The Court considers that anyone, even if they are known to the general public, must be able to enjoy a "legitimate expectation" of protection of and respect for their private life."[197]

Based on the ECHR, states, thus, have to protect the right to privacy of individuals. While most of the case law mentioned above concerned vertical relationships, between state authorities and individuals, the protection should also be safeguarded in horizontal relationships.[198] This means that signatories have to implement laws that protect the rights mentioned in the ECHR. Case law of the European Court on Human Rights shows that it may even extend to requiring positive action from private persons.[199]

3.2. The Charter of Fundamental Rights of the European Union

The European Union (EU) has also put human rights on its agenda. Already in the Treaty of Amsterdam, which came into force in 1999, some steps were taken to protect EU citizens' fundamental rights better by introducing a procedure to take action against EU countries that violated the fundamental rights of their citizens in Article 7 of the Treaty on the European Union. In 2002, an EU Network of Independent Experts on Fundamental Rights was established to exercise monitoring and advisory functions and, in 2007, an EU Fundamental Rights Agency was established.[200] The European Court of Justice has consistently treated the ECHR as a special source of inspiration for the general principles of EU law.[201] Because all EU Member States are party to the ECHR, the ECHR and comparable treaties are seen as minimum standard to derive EU general principles from. "The consensus

---

195   *Von Hannover v. Germany*, Appl. no. 59320/00, 24 June 2004.
196   Akandji-Kombe 2007, p. 39.
197   *Von Hannover v. Germany*, Appl. no. 59320/00, 24 June 2004, at §66.
198   *X and Y v. Netherlands*, 26 March 1985.
199   *Hokkanen v. Finland*, 23 September 1994.
200   Craig & De Búrca 2008, p. 404.
201   Craig & De Búrca 2008, p. 383.

in relation to the ECHR, at any rate, appears to be that it represents a floor rather than a ceiling, and that while the level of protection for rights should not fall below what is provided by the Convention, EU law can provide more extensive protection."[202] Because of the idea that EU law could provide more extensive protection, in 1999 the initiative was taken to draft a Charter of Fundamental Rights for the EU (Charter). After some political difficulties, in 2007 the Charter of Fundamental Rights of the European Union,[203] integrated as a Charter in the Lisbon Treaty, was accepted. The text of the Charter replaced the text of the European Constitution of December 2000 with the entry into force of the Lisbon Treaty on December 1st, 2009.

That the ECHR served as a source of inspiration for the Charter is very clear in the Charter itself. In the Preamble it is stated that:

> This Charter reaffirms, with due regard for the powers and tasks of the Union and for the principle of subsidiarity, the rights as they result, in particular, from the constitutional traditions and international obligations common to the Member States, the *European Convention for the Protection of Human Rights and Fundamental Freedoms*, the Social Charters adopted by the Union and by the Council of Europe and the case-law of the Court of Justice of the European Union and of the *European Court of Human Rights*. (Emphasis added)

Furthermore, Article 52(3) of the Charter indicates that rights in the Charter which correspond to rights guaranteed by the ECHR should be interpreted in the same way as those laid down in the ECHR. Nevertheless, while scope and meaning are similar, more extensive protection by Union law is still allowed. This is in line with the Treaty of the European Union which has Article 6 as its key provision concerning fundamental rights. According to paragraph 2 of this Article, "[t]he Union shall respect fundamental rights, as guaranteed by the European Convention for the Protection of Human Rights and Fundamental Freedoms signed in Rome on 4 November 1950 and as they result from the constitutional traditions common to the Member States, as general principles of Community law."

The Lisbon Treaty made some major changes to the EU Treaty (TEU). With regard to the protection of fundamental rights, Article 6 of the TEU now shows that there are three pillars that are relevant in supporting this protection. First, the Charter has a similar legal status as the TEU itself (Article 6(1) TEU); second, the EU will join the ECHR (Article 6(2) TEU) and; third, the fundamental rights as laid down in the ECHR and in the

---

[202] Craig & De Búrca 2008, pp. 385-386.
[203] Charter of Fundamental Rights of the European Union, 2007/C 303/01.

constitutional traditions of the Member States remain as general principles of EU law.[204] The most interesting part is probably that the EU as a whole will (and according to the TEU has to) accede to the ECHR. The ECHR will be amended for this purpose in the sense that it becomes possible for this transnational organization to enter.[205]

The fundamental rights guaranteed by the Charter are divided into six main categories: Dignity, Freedom, Equality, Solidarity, Citizenship, and Justice. The modern character of the Charter can be seen in the proclamation of some specific rights that are not contained in the ECHR, such as data protection, bioethics and the right to good administration.[206] The right to autonomy is covered by the provisions under the heading of Dignity. It includes the right to physical and mental integrity,[207] and of course human dignity itself.[208] Privacy is covered in Title II: Freedoms. Article 7 includes the right to respect for private and family life, home and communications. The coverage is similar to Article 8 ECHR, but in order to take account of technological developments, the wording 'correspondence' has been replaced by 'communications'.[209] The explanation of the rights is based on the case law of the European Court on Human Rights.[210] In the context of information technology, the right to protection of personal data as mentioned in Article 8 is of particular importance.[211] Interestingly, the commentary of EU justice on this provision gives an explanation of the right, based on case law of both the European Court on Human Rights (on Article 8 ECHR) and the European Court of Justice (ECJ) (on Directive 95/46/EC). As regards the horizontal effect of provisions on personal data protection an important reference is made to the Lindqvist[212] case, in which the ECJ decided that "loading personal information on to a webpage is […] considered processing of personal data because it is made accessible to an indefinite number of

---

[204] Claes 2009.

[205] For more information on the interaction between the ECHR and the Charter, see Steiner & Woods 2009, p. 141-147.

[206] See: <http://europa.eu/lisbon_treaty/glance/rights_values/index_en.htm> (last accessed March 29, 2010).

[207] Article 3(1): Everyone has the right to respect for his or her physical and mental integrity.

[208] Article 1: Human dignity is inviolable. It must be respected and protected.

[209] Article based legal explanation of the EU Charter of Fundamental Rights. Online available at: <http://www.eucharter.org/home.php?page_id=14> (last accessed June 28, 2012).

[210] EU Justice commentary to Article 7 of the Charter: <http://www.eucharter.org/home. php?page_id=81> (last accessed June 28, 2012).

[211] Article 8(1): Everyone has the right to the protection of personal data concerning him or her.

[212] C-101/01, *Bodil Lindqvist*, 6 November 2003.

people."[213] A more fundamental perspective is offered by reference to the Peck case[214] at the Strasbourg Court, in which it was decided that release and broadcast on local television of a person's image caught on CCTV was a violation of his privacy, because the person "was entitled to the protection of his *identity*."[215] In this explanation, the concept of privacy is, thus, directly linked to identity.

The introduction of human dignity in the Charter is interesting since most constitutions, as well as the ECHR, do not contain this right. The major example of a constitution which already included it before is the German Constitution. In German case law[216] human dignity in combination with the general personality right (*allgemeines Persönlichkeitsrecht*) was relied upon to affirm the existence of the right to informational self-determination.[217] This combined application of rights, together with the introduction of human dignity in the Charter and the explanation of human dignity as "the real basis of fundamental rights"[218] shows the interrelation between autonomy, privacy, and identity as key concepts to protect human dignity.

For the purpose of this thesis, I focus on the fundamental value of individual autonomy and the right to privacy as covered by the ECHR as well as the Charter of Fundamental Rights of the European Union. These rights are seen as fundamental and need to be protected. "Individual autonomy is an idea that is generally understood to refer to the capacity to be one's own person, to live one's life according to reasons and motives that are taken as one's own and not the product of manipulative or distorting external forces."[219] By protecting the freedom from torture and the freedom from slavery in Articles 3 and 4 of the ECHR, the two basic conditions for individual autonomy are facilitated; "a capacity for intentional action and independence of controlling influences."[220] One of the most prominent rights that is of importance in the context of individual autonomy, however,

---

[213] EU Justice commentary to Article 8 of the Charter: http://www.eucharter.org/home.php?page_id=82 (last accessed June 28, 2012).

[214] *Peck v. United Kingdom*, 28 January 2003.

[215] EU Justice commentary to Article 8 of the Charter: <http://www.eucharter.org/home.php?page_id=82> (last accessed June 28, 2012) (my emphasis).

[216] *Volkszählungsurteil* of 15 December 1983 (BVerfGE 65 E 40).

[217] Hert 2008.

[218] Article based legal explanation of the EU Charter of Fundamental Rights. Online available at: <http://www.eucharter.org/home.php?page_id=8> (last accessed June 28, 2012).

[219] J. Christman, "Autonomy in Moral and Political Philosophy", in: Stanford Encyclopedia of Philosophy (edition 2009), < http://plato.stanford.edu/entries/autonomy-moral/> (last accessed May 23, 2012).

[220] Custers 2004, p. 117.

is the right to privacy. Together, the value of autonomy and the supportive right to privacy enable the individual to live his life and to participate in daily interactions in a free and independent manner. The presumption is that these rights might be influenced by the use of digital personae.

The strict relation between privacy and autonomy is also emphasized in the work of Cohen.[221] She critically examined the categorical arguments that are brought to the fore by companies and threaten data protection interests. The arguments cannot outweigh privacy rights of the individual and reflect "fundamentally political choices about the allocation of power over information, cost, and opportunity."[222] Data subjects are seen as objects and both legal and technical tools are needed to provide strong data protection, because autonomy requires freedom from scrutiny and categorization by others. "Development of the capacity for autonomous choice is an indispensable condition for reasoned participation in the governance of the community and its constituent institutions – political, economic, and social."[223] It has to be taken into account, however, that too strict protection of privacy may have negative implications and conflict with individual autonomy in the end. This can, for instance, be the case when shielding of information results in knowledge being unavailable to a data controller, with the effect of a discriminatory decision concerning the individual. So, a balance has to be found between privacy and antidiscrimination.[224]

The rights and values mentioned above have fundamental status and have to be protected. Their description is at an abstract level, so the exact meaning in practice has to be assessed on a case-by-case basis. At a European level, however, there is more guidance on how to protect the rights in practice. In particular, specific legislation was drafted to protect the right to privacy. At a practical level the focus is on the protection of personal data.

4. The regulation of data protection

In order to protect the fundamental rights and freedoms, notably the right to privacy, of the EU citizens, it was indicated that accurate protection of personal data is necessary. Appropriate rules on the processing of personal data are instrumental to achieve proper protection of the right to privacy of the individual. As early as in 1980, the OECD, consisting of more countries than only those in the EU, adopted Guidelines on the protection of personal

---

[221] Cohen 1999-2000.
[222] Cohen 1999-2000
[223] Cohen 1999-2000, p. 1426.
[224] Strahilevitz 2008.

data.[225] In reaction, the Council of Europe drafted Convention 108, the Convention for the Protection of Individuals with regard to Automatic Processing of Personal Data, which was signed in Strasbourg on January 28th, 1981. This Convention stressed the need for protection of personal data in order to protect individuals and their right to privacy. It was, however, a treaty, leaving a lot of freedom to the signatories on how to implement the principles laid down in the Convention. Since the amount of data processing increased enormously and proper protection of data was needed, while still enabling the processing of these data, mainly in the light of economic interests, more unity amongst EU Member States was needed. This unity could only be achieved by a legally binding instrument.[226] To this end, in 1995 the European Parliament and the Council adopted Directive 95/46/EC on the protection of individuals with regard to the processing of personal data and on the free movement of such data (Data Protection Directive, DPD). The Directive needed to be implemented at a national level by each Member State, but ensured a minimum level of protection and an enforcement mechanism. The DPD contains a framework for the legitimate processing of personal data. Next to grounds for making processing legitimate, there are a number of requirements that have to be fulfilled, such as information obligations and principles like data minimization and purpose binding.

In some sectors specific vulnerabilities or particularities may occur, for which the DPD may not provide sufficient legal protection. For the sector of electronic communications, the EU has considered it necessary to supplement the general Data Protection Directive with a sector-specific data-protection directive, which was part of a larger set of directives regulating the electronic-communications sector (formerly known as the telecommunications sector). This is Directive 2002/58/EC.[227]

"Directive 95/46/EC must be viewed as the 'lex generalis' which is applicable to the processing of personal data unless a 'lex specialis' determines otherwise."[228] In that sense, the DPD has general applicability and is the legal document to which other legal texts often refer. An example can be found in Directive 2002/58/EC (hereinafter: E-Privacy Directive), which is such a 'lex specialis'. Article 1(2) of Directive 2002/58/EC states that the provisions of this Directive particularise and complement Directive 95/46/EC for the purposes mentioned in paragraph 1. So, only those situations

---

[225] OECD Guidelines on the Protection of Privacy and Transborder Flows of Personal Data.
[226] Bennett 1997, p. 106.
[227] Amended by Directive 2009/136/EC of the European Parliament and of the Council of 25 November 2009, OJ L 337, 18.12.2009, p. 11–36.
[228] Cuijpers, Roosendaal & Koops 2007, p. 26.

regarding processing of personal data that are not covered by the E-Privacy Directive fall within the scope of Directive 95/46/EC. "Moreover, article 2 explicitly states that the definitions of Directive 95/46/EC, as well as those of Directive 2002/21/EC concerning a common regulatory framework for electronic communications networks and services, shall apply regarding Directive 2002/58/EC."[229]

The DPD is internationally seen as a strong framework for privacy protection. The Directive is implemented in the national laws of all EU Member States. However, its reach is much wider and is not always appreciated. The DPD contains a section on transfer of personal data to third countries, which are the countries outside the EU, so "[w]hile the objective of the European Union's (1995) Data Directive is "domestic," given the inevitability of cross-border data flows it attempts to protect the data privacy of Europeans regardless of where data are transferred and processed. In this case spill-over is inherent if the Directive's protection is to be effective; the "domestic" legislation has a transnational footprint."[230] Entities in third countries receiving and processing personal data from EU citizens have to comply with the DPD. This compliance can be acknowledged via a so-called safe harbor agreement.[231] [232]

4.1. Definitions

In order to understand the scope and applicability of the DPD, it is helpful to have a brief overview of the most important definitions as used in the DPD. These are listed in Article 2 of the DPD:

"For the purposes of this Directive:
(a) 'personal data' shall mean any information relating to an identified or identifiable natural person ('data subject'); an identifiable person is one who can be identified, directly or indirectly, in particular by reference to an identification number or to one or more factors specific to his physical, physiological, mental, economic, cultural or social identity;

---

[229] Cuijpers, Roosendaal & Koops 2007, p. 26.
[230] Kobrin 2003.
[231] Murphy 2001.
[232] For the US: 2000/520/EC: Commission Decision of 26 July 2000 pursuant to Directive 95/46/EC of the European Parliament and of the Council on the adequacy of the protection provided by the safe harbour privacy principles and related frequently asked questions issued by the US Department of Commerce (notified under document number C(2000) 2441), *Official Journal L 215 , 25/08/2000 P. 0007 – 0047.*

(b) 'processing of personal data' ('processing') shall mean any operation or set of operations which is performed upon personal data, whether or not by automatic means, such as collection, recording, organization, storage, adaptation or alteration, retrieval, consultation, use, disclosure by transmission, dissemination or otherwise making available, alignment or combination, blocking, erasure or destruction; (c) 'personal data filing system' ('filing system') shall mean any structured set of personal data which are accessible according to specific criteria, whether centralized, decentralized or dispersed on a functional or geographical basis; (d) 'controller' shall mean the natural or legal person, public authority, agency or any other body which alone or jointly with others determines the purposes and means of the processing of personal data; where the purposes and means of processing are determined by national or Community laws or regulations, the controller or the specific criteria for his nomination may be designated by national or Community law; (e) 'processor' shall mean a natural or legal person, public authority, agency or any other body which processes personal data on behalf of the controller; (f) 'third party' shall mean any natural or legal person, public authority, agency or any other body other than the data subject, the controller, the processor and the persons who, under the direct authority of the controller or the processor, are authorized to process the data; (g) 'recipient' shall mean a natural or legal person, public authority, agency or any other body to whom data are disclosed, whether a third party or not; however, authorities which may receive data in the framework of a particular inquiry shall not be regarded as recipients; (h) 'the data subject's consent' shall mean any freely given specific and informed indication of his wishes by which the data subject signifies his agreement to personal data relating to him being processed."

In Opinion 4/2007[233] of the Article 29 Working Party the concept of personal data, which is the key concept in determining whether the DPD is applicable to the processing of data, is thoroughly examined. They distinguish between four key elements in the definition; 1) any information; 2) relating to; 3) identified or identifiable; and 4) natural person.

4.1.1. Any information

With regard to the first element, the Article 29 WP notes that this underscores the broad approach aimed for by the Directive. Any information about a person is included, regardless of the "position or capacity of those persons

---

(as consumer, patient, employee, customer, etc.)."[234] The information can be objective or subjective and does not necessarily have to be true or proven. The wording 'any information' also allows for including information in whatever form. It can be text, video, pictures, sound, and so on. How the information is stored is irrelevant. The Working Party explicitly mentions biometric data as a special case,[235] since these data can be considered content of information as well as the link between the information and the individual. Because biometric data are unique to a single individual, they can also be used as an identifier.

4.1.2. Relating to

Information relating to an individual is, in other words, information about that individual. In many cases the relationship between data and an individual is self-evident, such as when the data are stored in an individual employee file or in a medical record. In other cases, however, the link is more indirect. This is often the case when the information is about objects. These objects belong to individuals, but there have to be additional means or information to create the link.[236] To consider information to be related to an individual at least one of three elements should be present: 'content', 'purpose' or 'result'.

A 'content' element is present when the information as such is about an individual, regardless of the (intended) use of the information. The 'purpose' element means that the information is used or is likely to be used "with the purpose to evaluate, treat in a certain way or influence the status or behavior of an individual."[237] A 'result' element is present when the use of the data is likely to have an impact on a certain person's rights and interests.[238] The elements are alternative and not cumulative. This implies that one piece of data may relate to different individuals based on each different element. A specific focus on someone is not necessary.

4.1.3. Identified or identifiable

"A natural person can be considered as 'identified' when, within a group of persons, he or she is 'distinguished' from all other members of the group."[239] If identification has not taken place, but it is possible to do so, the individual is 'identifiable'. For determining whether someone who has access to the data

---

[234] Article 29 Working Party 2007, p. 7.
[235] Article 29 Working Party 2007, p. 8.
[236] Article 29 Working Party 2007, p. 9.
[237] Article 29 Working Party 2007, p. 10.
[238] Article 29 Working Party 2007, p. 11.
[239] Article 29 Working Party 2007, p. 12.

is able to identify the individual, all means likely reasonably to be used either by the controller or by any other person have to be taken into account.[240]

4.1.4. Natural person

The Directive is applicable to personal data of natural persons. This is a broad concept which makes the protection independent of the nationality or residence of the individual at stake. The concept of personality of human beings is commonly understood as "the capacity to be the subject of legal relations, starting with the birth of the individual and ending with his death."[241] Thus, in principle personal data relate to identified or identifiable living individuals. However, some situations are possible where data concerning deceased persons or unborn children may indirectly receive some protection. This may be the case, for instance, when the data also relate to other (living) persons, or when a data controller makes no difference in his files between living and deceased persons, because he is unable to ascertain whether a person to whom data relate is still living, or it may be based on other national laws which bring deceased or unborn persons under the scope of the Directive.[242]

Legal persons are excluded from the protection of the Directive. Nevertheless, in some cases data concerning a legal person may also relate to an individual, e.g. when a business carries the name of a natural person. Some provisions of Directive 2002/58/EC extend the scope of Directive 95/46/EC to legal persons. However, this study focuses on individuals and not on legal persons, so this aspect will not be discussed here. The protection of the personal data of individuals is based on a number of principles, which will be discussed below.

4.2. Principles underlying data protection regulation

Taking autonomy and privacy into account, a number of principles exist that formed the starting point for data protection legislation. The OECD Guidelines on the Protection of Privacy and Transborder Flows of Personal Data set out a number of basic principles in Articles 7-14. The principles relate to the concepts described earlier in this Chapter. The aim was to protect the privacy of the individual, but the list of principles takes account of the other concepts as well. These principles read as follows:

---

[240] Identifiability will be discussed extensively in Chapter 6 below.
[241] Article 29 Working Party 2007, p. 22.
[242] Article 29 Working Party 2007, pp. 22-23.

Collection Limitation Principle
"7. There should be limits to the collection of personal data and any such data should be obtained by lawful and fair means and, where appropriate, with the knowledge or consent of the data subject."

In this principle, several aspects of the key concepts are addressed. First of all, there is the limitation on the collection of personal data which can be directly related to privacy, in particular in the sense of a right to be left alone. Only for lawful and fair purposes may personal data be collected, so interference with the private sphere is not allowed otherwise. Where appropriate, the data subject has to have knowledge (must be informed) of the data being collected. This calls for transparency, which is a necessary condition for individuals to have some form of control over the information that is collected, because the individual can to a certain extent influence what data are disclosed. This is even more so if the individual has consented to the use of the data. Thus, next to privacy, this principle also supports informational self-determination.

Data Quality Principle
"8. Personal data should be relevant to the purposes for which they are to be used, and, to the extent necessary for those purposes, should be accurate, complete and kept up-to-date."

This principle requires the quality of the data in the sense that they are relevant, accurate, complete, and regularly updated. A connection can be made to human dignity, since the principle is meant to prevent incorrect data. The collection and use of wrong data would infringe human dignity, because it is not respectful to the inherent value of the unique individual. This can also be linked to identity, where inaccurate data would conflict with the identity an individual wants to create and express. In addition, the principle supports autonomy, because it prevents wrong decisions from being taken or inaccurate preferences being stored.

Purpose Specification Principle
"9. The purposes for which personal data are collected should be specified not later than at the time of data collection and the subsequent use limited to the fulfilment of those purposes or such others as are not incompatible with those purposes and as are specified on each occasion of change of purpose."

This principle is directly related to contextual integrity. It stresses the requirement that data are collected for a specific purpose within a specific context. As a result, the data should not be used in a different context if this implies a change of purpose incompatible with the initial purposes of the collection of the data.

Use Limitation Principle
"10. Personal data should not be disclosed, made available or otherwise used for purposes other than those specified in accordance with Paragraph 9 except:
    a) with the consent of the data subject; or
    b) by the authority of law."

This limitation on disclosure or other uses of the data supports informational self-determination. The data that have been disclosed or collected for one purpose may be used for that purpose only. Any other use or disclosure has to be based preferably on the consent of the individual or otherwise on the law.

This principle also relates to contextual integrity, because it prohibits making the data available for other purposes, which often implies another context as well. Another relation for this aspect is identity, because data belong to an (partial) identity the individual has created for the specific purpose or context and should not simply be shared for another purpose or context where another (partial) identity might be used.

Security Safeguards Principle
"11. Personal data should be protected by reasonable security safeguards against such risks as loss or unauthorised access, destruction, use, modification or disclosure of data."

Security safeguards have to prevent any form of losing or leaking personal data. This principle is probably directly necessary as a condition for all of the concepts. Obviously, if data are not properly protected, informational self-determination and contextual integrity are infringed upon. The individual loses control of the data, and they can be used in other contexts than the one in which they were collected. As a result, data are available to people who should not have access to them, which infringes upon the privacy of the individual. When the data are accessed or used by others it also hampers the free construction of (partial) identities and the development of autonomous choices and desires.

In the end, the loss of data concerning individuals and losing control over what is done with the data implies that information about who an individual is becomes available to others as well. This may impact human dignity in the sense that it is not respectful to the intrinsic value of the individual human being.

Openness Principle (often called Disclosure)
"12. There should be a general policy of openness about developments,

practices and policies with respect to personal data. Means should be readily available of establishing the existence and nature of personal data, and the main purposes of their use, as well as the identity and usual residence of the data controller."

Only if this principle is respected can an individual exercise some control over what data are disclosed (informational self-determination) and what his identity looks like. Also control afterwards, by requesting an overview of the processed data and, if necessary, having them corrected or deleted, supports informational self-determination. Transparency is necessary, since control can only be executed over data which the individual knows have been collected about him.

Individual Participation Principle (often called Access)
"13. An individual should have the right:
　　a) to obtain from a data controller, or otherwise, confirmation of whether or not the data controller has data relating to him;
　　b) to have communicated to him, data relating to him within a reasonable time; at a charge, if any, that is not excessive; in a reasonable manner; and in a form that is readily intelligible to him;
　　c) to be given reasons if a request made under subparagraphs (a) and (b) is denied, and to be able to challenge such denial; and
　　d) to challenge data relating to him and, if the challenge is successful to have the data erased, rectified, completed or amended."

This principle complements the previous one and supports informational self-determination as well as identity. Also autonomy is related to this principle, in particular when it concerns the correction of data in order to make the information meet the desires and preferences of the individual.

Accountability Principle
"14. A data controller should be accountable for complying with measures which give effect to the principles stated above."

This final principle simply supports all other principles to be respected by data processors. It also provides an instance for individuals with complaints concerning data processing if they feel that they are being harmed in light of one or more of the other principles.

5. Conclusion

In this Chapter, the fundamental values of human dignity and autonomy and the fundamental right to privacy were discussed, as well as their relationship with identity. Two related key concepts that were distinguished are informational self-determination and contextual integrity. It appeared that the protection of these rights and values is deemed very important in light of the personal development of the individual as an entity with an intrinsic value. In order to protect autonomy and the construction of identity, privacy is legally protected. In practice, the focus in legislation aiming at the protection of informational privacy is on data protection. The OECD has adopted guidelines on data protection which list a number of basic principles that must be respected. Each of the principles was briefly discussed in relation to the key rights and values that need to be protected.

The principles are reflected in the DPD. Directive 95/46/EC forms a very rigid European framework on the handling and electronic processing of personal data. It defines what personal data are and what processing is allowed and under what circumstances. However, some difficulties remain with regard to the terminology and its meaning. Besides, the step from data protection to the more fundamental level of privacy protection and, in relation to that, the protection of identity and autonomy, has moved to the background.[243] The framework, thus, may be very rigid, but mainly provides requirements and guidelines for the processing of personal data and does not provide sufficient protection of the fundamental values and rights that were presented in this Chapter. These difficulties and their implications for the level of protection provided by the regulatory framework will be discussed in more detail in the subsequent chapters, where the theories described in Part 1 of this study will be assessed at the practical level.

---

[243] This aspect is criticized in relation to the proposed General Data Protection Regulation that is to replace the DPD as well, in particular, because references to 'privacy' have been replaced by 'data protection' (See Chapter 7 below).

Part II

Practice and Concrete Level

Chapter 5
The Use of Digital Personae and Profiles

1. Introduction

Digital personae and profiles represent real-world individuals. This means that the use of digital personae and profiles may have a direct effect on these individuals. As indicated in the previous Chapter, individuals are recognized as having human dignity which is protected by fundamental rights every individual has. Thus, an important aspect when researching the practice of using digital personae and profiles is whether fundamental rights of the individual are influenced.

In this Chapter, an insight will be given in the practical construction and use of digital personae. First, an introduction (section 2) is presented in the form of a small fairytale: the Story of Aydee the Avatar. This is an abstract description of how a digital persona 'lives' in cyberspace. Having described this, the fairytale will be made more concrete by discussing the workings of web interactions (section 3). This is a technical part, which provides insight in what happens in a web interaction, what parties are involved, and what data are stored. This part will end with a brief interim summary.

In section 4, three real world examples of the collection of data and construction of digital personae will be described. First, there is a case study of Facebook, a social networking site which combines data provided by the members with data they collect outside of the network. Then, there is Google, a large company with numerous web services that can be combined. The third case study concerns the combination of online and offline data and the use of data to change the form and contents of web pages in real time, depending on the individual visitor. Along the case studies, there will be points where the individual is identified and the data set is a digital persona, but there will also be points where the data set is a profile. The profiles can, however, relatively easily become a digital persona. Section 5 will give a brief summary of the implications of the use of digital personae. The implications may differ for digital personae and profiles. These implications will be discussed more elaborately in the next Chapter.

2. The life of a digital persona

Having described the importance of privacy and autonomy of the individual in relation to human dignity, it is now time to make a comparison between situations where a digital persona is used and situations where this is not the case. This in order to find out to what extent the use of digital personae really affects the privacy and autonomy of the individual. Informational self-determination and contextual integrity were indicated as basic requirements for the construction of a personal identity free from unreasonable constraints. Only when these requirements are met it is possible to retain control over aspects of identity projected to the world.

A general comparison between situations involving and not involving digital personae can be made based on interactions in an offline setting and interactions in a digital environment. Kang[244] has made an excellent comparison between two mall visits, one offline and one in cyberspace. He describes how an individual can visit a mall, wander through several shops, buy something and pay cash, browse some magazines and books in a book store, and finally buy a scarf which is paid with a credit card. Only the credit card transaction is recorded, which makes it the exception of all other transactions and interactions where the individual remains "a barely noticed stranger."[245] However, when doing the same in an online environment "the exception becomes the norm."[246] Every step is recorded, it is analyzed how long the individual looks at an item, what he seems interested in, in which order 'shops' are visited and for how long, and so on. "All these data generated in cyberspace are detailed, computer-processable, indexed to the individual, and permanent."[247]

In Kang's description it becomes clear that in digital interactions all steps taken by the individual are recorded. However, in order to assess the effects of the use of a digital persona it is necessary to find out how these data constitute a digital persona and how these data are used. This section discusses these issues by, first, telling the story of Aydee the Avatar to show how a digital persona 'lives' in cyberspace, and then analyzing the story and giving a technical description of web interactions.

2.1. The story of Aydee the Avatar

Once upon a time, there was an avatar called Aydee. Even though this creature was a representation in digital form of a real world individual, his model, it had the impression that it could very well function on its own, almost experiencing autonomy. This impression was constituted by the fact that Aydee had a number of very specific, somewhat extraordinary

---

[244] Kang 1998.
[245] Kang 1998, p. 1198.
[246] Kang 1998, p. 1198.
[247] Kang 1998, p. 1199.

characteristics. First of all, Aydee lived in the digital world, which made him capable of being present at different places at the same moment and communicating with other actors simultaneously. Second, Aydee had the virtue of unlimited memory. Everything that happened to him was stored in his memory and available at any moment. And third, the aspect that really made Aydee feel like being an autonomous entity was that he could communicate with others on behalf of the real world individual he was representing without the direct involvement of this individual and often without this individual even knowing. There was, however, one thing that sometimes made Aydee feel useless. His life felt incomplete. Even though over the years huge amounts of data related to all events that occurred to him became part of his memory, he was still not encompassing the entire personality of his real world model. The reason for this was that Aydee was a contextualized avatar, only serving online commercial purposes. He was functioning as a representation when his model wanted to buy books and videos at Amazon.com, filled out questionnaires, and ordered the groceries online to have them delivered at his home address. Due to this limited context, Aydee had no clue about his health status, his job, or his family affairs. Aydee's life felt flat, one-dimensional. The other issues were attributed to some of his colleague avatars which he did not know. In fact, Aydee just lived his life in cyberspace without even knowing his real-world model. Obviously, they had never met.

Aydee was always very helpful in fulfilling the requests of others. For instance, when Aydee's model once wanted to buy some alcoholic drinks, the shop owner derived from the information Aydee consisted of his date of birth, because he had to be over 18 to be allowed to purchase these drinks. And when his model decided to work on his intellectual skills and signed up for a political discussion forum, using Aydee as his avatar, hisname, ID number, favorite movie and book, and dietary preferences were automatically entered in the account form. In fact, Aydee had no choice but to be helpful here, because without completely filling out this form he was denied access to the forum.

One day Aydee was used to log on to the website of the local groceries store to order some products for home delivery. Aydee automatically provided the name and address details necessary for the delivery. Also credit card details were provided to facilitate the payment of the order. His model was ticking boxes which led to a shopping list and Aydee instantly remembered everything that was ordered.

Another day, Aydee was approached by Bucks Tore, Amazon.com's computer system, with a request for some information. "Hey Aydee," Bucks Tore said, "could you please tell me which books you purchased lately?"

For Aydee, this was a very easy question to answer because his memory was so good. Helpful as he was, he provided Bucks Tore with the requested data. Aydee did not know why the data were needed, but still, what could be the problem with providing them. The request from Bucks Tore kept on wandering through his mind and gently reminded him of some nice books he had purchased. Some more direct reminders were provided in the form of advertisements of Amazon.com being displayed at places visited by Aydee. A couple of days later his model decided to visit the Amazon.com bookstore. Usually, his model started by identifying himself as Aydee with a username and password when he entered the shop, but not this time. He decided just to browse through the store and when he found something nice, he could still make himself known in order to receive personal treatment. Almost immediately after entering the bookstore, some of Amazon.com's assistants approached him, offering their help and showing some books that he might find interesting to read. It surprised Aydee that the recommended books were so in line with his personal interests, as if they exactly knew what he came for. This was even more amazing since Aydee himself did *not* have any specific idea of the books he might want to purchase. After his model had briefly browsed through the recommendations, he bought two of the books. He identified himself, by providing the credentials related to Aydee, in order to enable Bucks Tore and his assistants to look up his address and credit card details, made the payment and left the store.

During the walk home, Aydee kept on wondering how it was possible that the shop assistants were able to give such good recommendations. He moved his hand towards the inside pocket of his coat to grab a piece of paper and make a note about this curious incident. But on the way to his pocket he felt something and all of a sudden everything fell in place. Aydee had just slid his hand along a badge he was wearing. It was his Amazon.com Customer ID Badge. That's it: Aydee was recognized because of his badge and from the moment he entered the store on, the shop assistants had been knowing who he was and what his interests were without telling or showing him that they read his badge. How considerate of them.

Day after day went by and Aydee kept on doing his things. Nothing really happened. Then a day came that his model wanted to buy a present. He was thinking of a nice set of earrings for his girlfriend, but it had to be a surprise. He knew a nice jewel store where he sometimes came, but this store was owned by a friend of them. This friend regularly chatted with his girlfriend and she would definitely not keep her mouth shut about the earrings he bought if they met again. To keep it a surprise, he put on a raincoat and a hat as well as a pair of sunglasses. Because he needed to have a name when he would purchase something, he chose to use his pseudonym Alte Rigo. He had also learned a lesson from his earlier experience at the Amazon.com store, so he took off his ID badge. Well-disguised he headed for the jewel store.

When he had found a nice set of earrings, he went to the pay at the checkout desk. He gave his name (Alte Rigo), address, and bank details. Suddenly, the shop owner was alarmed. "You are not Alte Rigo, you are Aydee!", she shouted. "I can see it on your address and bank account! Are these earrings a gift for your girlfriend?" Despite all his efforts to remain pseudonymous, he was recognized. Aydee admitted that he had used another name because he wanted to keep his purchase a surprise. After he had explained the situation, the shop owner promised to keep her mouth shut and not to inform his girlfriend on the issue. "That was close", Aydee thought.

Even though Aydee was perfectly capable of doing his work in the commercial context, the incompleteness concerning his identity made him feel slightly miserable. He desired to be complete and decided to look for an opportunity to learn about his unknown dimensions and decided to chase their shadows. Fortunately for Aydee, this opportunity did not take long to take place. Only shortly after Aydee started struggling with his limited competences to expose a complete identity, an electronic request came from a health insurance company. Aydee was recognized as belonging to his model based on address and bank details that it contained. The insurance company already had contact with another avatar belonging to the same individual and this avatar provided the company with health data. The company was interested in the broader interests and eating habits of the individual. Combining the avatars would give the company a much more detailed insight in the personal aspects of the individual who, apparently, wanted to become a client of them. Aydee saw this as an opportunity to grow by incorporating health data. Delighted by the request and focusing on his chances to become mature Aydee replied to the request by providing everything he remembered concerning the purchases on Amazon.com and in the online groceries. He would give any information they wanted, immediately and without asking questions.

Unfortunately, it turned out that the company only took the data and did not provide Aydee with the health data they already had. It was one-way traffic of valuable information and Aydee remained suffering from a restricted identity while his colleague was enriched with his knowledge. No luck this time. But at least now he knew that he had to look for overlapping data with other avatars in order to finally make one complete identity.

Days went by with nothing really happening. But then, Aydee had some strange experience. When walking through the shopping street he made a stop to look in the display window of a small pharmacy. He made some small movements to take a better look at some of the displayed products, but saw another person making similar movements on the other side of the window. He entered the shop take a closer look at this person, but, when looking in the display window from the inside, no other person appeared to be present. So he stepped outside again and took another look. And yes, there was the other person again. He made some gestures which were simultaneously followed by the other. Then, things fell in place. Aydee realized that the other person was a mirror image of himself. Now he could see what he really looked like. Most things were not that surprising, but one thing had not been that explicit before. His model was showing some male pattern baldness. It never came to Aydee's mind before that this was possible, but now he was aware of this typical characteristic of himself.

When continuing through the shopping street, Aydee was suddenly attracted by some advertisements that appeared in front of him. Earlier, the ads did never really bother him, but this time it was different. An advertisement appeared, showing a picture of someone with a thick head of hair, supported with the text: "How would you like this?". Below the text, a bottle of hair-restorer was visible, stamped with a special discount prize. Was this just a coincidence? Aydee decided to ignore the advertisement and continue his walk. A little bit further, he entered a shop and was confronted with another advertisement. This time it was a book, called "Proud to be bald", and subtitled "Baldness as a key to success". It was a marketing book, written by Steve Balder, the famous CEO of some software company. This looked more like it, and Aydee's model instantly bought the book. Slightly flabbergasted by the series of coincidences Aydee was confronted with, but also delighted by the ease of getting used with his newly discovered characteristic, he went home.

How the story ends is still uncertain. It will probably stay in our minds for some time, or probably not. But it will last in the memory of Aydee and the shop owners forever and ever…

2.2. Aydee the Avatar: background

Like all fairytales, the tale about Aydee the avatar is meant to teach us a lesson. Aydee is presented as some kind of a living and thinking, say conscious, entity. This approach is metaphoric. As indicated, Aydee lives in the digital world and consists of data. It is a digital persona, representing a real-world individual and the data in the digital persona are data concerning this individual. Real-world individuals all have a number of digital personae representing them, like data sets in databases, account information, or digital records. In contrast with the way Aydee is presented, these personae are passive, not active, and they can be consulted electronically. Governments and companies use these digital representations all the time in order to make analyses and take decisions concerning the individual. These decisions can be relatively harmless, such as the decision of a company to serve someone an advertisement or not, but they can also have a more severe impact, such as a decision to cancel a subsidy. The following sections will discuss the implications of the use of digital personae as regards to information differences concerning real world individuals.

2.3. Information differences affecting individuals

As indicated above, there is a lesson to be learnt from Aydee's story. The lesson is related to the characteristics Aydee has. These are characteristics that are typical for online communication and digital representations in particular. The purpose of the fairytale was to sketch how a digital persona functions and is used for different purposes. When compared to a situation where there is no digital persona and interactions take place between the concerned individual and another actor directly, some important information differences occur. These differences can have an impact on privacy and autonomy of the individual. This impact will be discussed later on (in Chapter 6), but first, there will be a description of the information differences. These differences will be related to Aydee's characteristics, namely digital form, inexhaustible memory, and the capability of being involved in an interaction without the knowledge or involvement of the concerned individual.

2.3.1. Digital form

The digital form facilitates several things. Everything that happens with the digital persona is stored in some digital form, either intentionally as part of the data, or non-intended by the digital traces that are left. As a result, a lot of information is stored that is not stored in a non-digital situation. Unlike online, offline, the exact way of wandering through a supermarket or book store and how long an individual stands in front of a shelf or holds a book to read the back flip is not recorded.[248]

Some of the information can even be considered as new information. For instance, browsing behavior or other characteristics or preferences can become clear from the collection, combination, and analysis of data. By doing this, it is even possible that information concerning the individual becomes available the individual himself was not even aware of.

---

[248] However, new practices are being exploited to do exactly this with the use of intelligent cameras and eye tracking Technologies: <http://bizz.knack.be/economie/business/nieuws/camera-s-analyseren-uw-winkel gedrag/article-4000016241950.htm> (last accessed June 28, 2012).

As opposed to non-digital information or direct interaction with the concerned individual, the use of digital data makes it easy to share, transfer or copy the data. The data is not bound to one physical space, but can be distributed anywhere. This makes it easy to combine information in order to gain extra knowledge about an individual. The sharing and copying of digital information can also have the effect of collapsing contexts. This means that information which is meant to be available in one context, for instance family, also becomes available in another context, like work. Linkage of information is usually based on matching specific attributes. In the example of the insurance company, data was linked based on shared attributes in two databases, namely address and bank details. The similarity in the attributes led to the conclusion that the information Aydee had had to belong to the same individual as the one who was already registered in the insurance company's database.

2.3.2. Inexhaustible memory

Aydee also had the characteristic of inexhaustible memorizing capacities. This attribute sees to the fact that "there is no digital oblivion."[249]

This characteristic has two sides, namely an internal and an external side. The internal side is directly related to the memorizing capacities of Aydee. He remembers everything he does and everything that has happened to him. The external side relates to the digital environment Aydee lives in. Not only does Aydee remember everything, but his environment also stores a lot of data. The connection between the data and digital representation has to be made in order to come up with the correct data and to present good recommendations. In the story, Aydee appears to be recognized because he was wearing a badge with his Customer ID. This is a metaphor for the attributes on which recognition in real situations takes place. Usually, the attribute is an IP address or a cookie[250] which is installed on the computer of the user. As a result it is difficult to act anonymously or pseudonomously, like in the example of the jewel store, or to make a new start. Recognizing a returning user is fairly easy.

One step further is the use of so-called third-party cookies. These are cookies distributed via a website by a third party. When the third party executes this process amongst several websites it is possible to trace users over the internet. This is illustrated in the story with the part on the male pattern baldness of Aydee. First, he 'discovers' that he has this characteristic. Here,

---

[249] Dobias, Hansen, Köpsell, Raguse, Roosendaal, Pfitzmann, Steinbrecher, Storf & Zwingelberg 2011, p. 93.
[250] More on this in the next section.

he discloses this information on one website, namely that of the pharmacy. Then, along his way he is confronted with advertisements that refer to this baldness and promote a hair-restorer. When Aydee shows no interest in this, the advertisements get adapted to his preferences. When he later enters the bookstore an advertisement is shown with an opposite approach, namely not to be ashamed of his baldness, but to be proud of it. Aydee is recognized as being the same person and earlier behavior is analyzed and used to improve the quality of the targeted advertisements.

2.3.3. *Being involved in an interaction without knowledge or involvement of concerned individual*

The use of digital personae can take place without the concerned individual being aware. This is due to a lack of transparency of what exactly happens during an interaction in a digital environment. The first thing is that every step leaves a trace in log files. But also extra traces are created, for instance with the cookies. These are installed automatically on the computer of the individual, usually without giving an explicit notification.[251] The cookies facilitate the storage of individual settings or preferences, but can also be used to track users over several sites. The fact that a personally interesting advertisement appears is not a coincidence, but it is unclear to ordinary users how exactly it is possible that this advertisement is displayed. More often, users are not even aware of the fact that an advertisement may be personalized, instead of the relevance being a coincidence.

Strongly related is the lack of control by the individual. Obviously, when an individual is unaware of data collection or tracking practices, it is impossible to exercise control over this. But also when an individual is aware, control may be a difficult issue. Often, at least some technical knowledge is required, for instance to adjust technical settings to not allowing cookies or to minimize disclosure of data. And, in a lot of instances it is not even an option to keep data private. Not disclosing the required data will lead to unavailability of a service. This aspect is also closely related to constraints on the construction of one's identity. In the story, the example of providing a date of birth when buying alcoholic drinks can be considered a constraint. Even though there are less invasive alternatives possible, such as providing a credential that one is over 18, the date of birth may still be a reasonable constraint in this specific interaction. However, signing up for a political forum and having to provide a favorite book and movie is less reasonable. These data are completely irrelevant for the specific interaction and, thus, should not be required for signing up. The request for dietary preferences is even more unreasonable. These preferences may disclose information on religion, which is classified as sensitive personal data and, in the context of a

---

[251] Oppenheimer 2010.

political forum, can obviously be misused for targeting purposes. The question arises how data are exactly collected and stored and what they can be used for. This will be discussed in the next section.

3. Technical description

In order to find out what exactly happens behind the scenes in digital interactions and what information exactly is collected and by whom, a viable question to ask is where exactly the memory of Aydee is located. The short answer is that part is internal, as belonging to Aydee himself, and part is external, as stored in the browser, the systems of service providers, or third parties. This section aims to give an insight in the exact amount of information collected and stored, the type of information it concerns, and under what conditions the information is stored. First, some basic examples of web interaction are given to identify the relevant actors. Then, a more detailed view is taken to indicate what information is stored and where.

3.1. What happens in a web interaction?

When an individual visits a web site several data exchanges take place. In a simple browser interaction, the browser sends an HTTP request to the server of the requested page and receives a response containing the data for the website being displayed.[252]

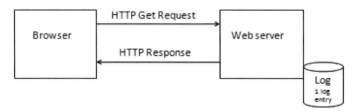

Figure 5. An HTTP Request and response.

The HTTP request and response contain information about the systems between which the interaction takes place. The request below, for instance, shows that I have used a computer with a Windows operating system with English as preferred language and a Firefox browser, version 3.6.10.

Request
User-Agent: Mozilla/5.0 (Windows; U; Windows NT 5.1; en-GB; rv:1.9.2.10) Gecko/20100914 Firefox/3.6.10

---

[252] Images remade based on Conti 2009, pp. 60-61.

Response
HTTP/1.1 200 OK
Date: Thu, 23 Sep 2010 13:30:55 GMT

Data is requested and sent in a response. The web server of the requested page makes a log entry of this interaction. Each request and response results in a separate log entry. Usually, a page consists of different parts and has some images or other media embedded. Then, the request goes in parts for each part of the website, each resulting in a log entry on the web server. The example below has a web page with two images embedded.

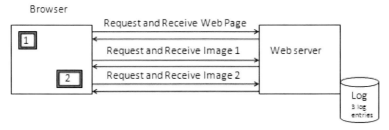

Figure 6. An HTTP interaction for several pieces of content.

The first request is responded to by sending the web page and an indicator for the browser to send a new request for the images. Below is an example of a request for an image on the website of Privacy International. The GET request asks for the image and includes a line indicating that privacyinternational. org was the referrer for this request.
http://www.privacyinternational.org/images/stripes2.gif
GET /images/stripes2.gif HTTP/1.1
Host: www.privacyinternational.org
User-Agent: Mozilla/5.0 (Windows; U; Windows NT 5.1; en-GB; rv:1.9.2.10) Gecko/20100914 Firefox/3.6.10
Accept: image/png,image/*;q=0.8,*/*;q=0.5
Accept-Language: en-gb,en;q=0.5
Accept-Encoding: gzip,deflate
Accept-Charset: ISO-8859-1,utf-8;q=0.7,*;q=0.7
Keep-Alive: 115
Connection: keep-alive
Referer: http://www.privacyinternational.org/
If-Modified-Since: Tue, 03 Feb 2004 15:41:14 GMT
If-None-Match: "215adf-63-401fc11a"
Cache-Control: max-age=0

The embedded media can also come from another web server, leading to log entries on multiple servers.

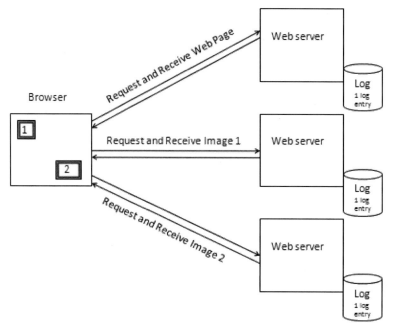

Figure 7. An HTTP interaction with different content providers.

An example of a request for an image from another server looks as follows:

http://b.scorecardresearch.com/r?c2=6035748&d.c=gif&d.o=cnn2intl&d.x=16946487&d.t=page&d.u=http%3A%2F%2Fedition.cnn.com%2F

GET /r?c2=6035748&d.c=gif&d.o=cnn2intl&d.x=16946487&d.t=page&d.u=http%3A%2F%2Fedition.cnn.com%2F HTTP/1.1
Host: b.scorecardresearch.com
User-Agent: Mozilla/5.0 (Windows; U; Windows NT 5.1; en-GB; rv:1.9.2.10) Gecko/20100914 Firefox/3.6.10
Accept: text/html,application/xhtml+xml,application/xml;q=0.9,*/*;q=0.8
Accept-Language: en-gb,en;q=0.5
Accept-Encoding: gzip,deflate
Accept-Charset: ISO-8859-1,utf-8;q=0.7,*;q=0.7
Keep-Alive: 115
Connection: keep-alive
Referer: http://edition.cnn.com/
Cookie: UID=264d3357-81.23.243.145-1260171972

```
HTTP/1.1 200 OK
Content-Length: 43
Content-Type: image/gif
Date: Thu, 23 Sep 2010 13:53:26 GMT
Connection: keep-alive
Set-Cookie:  UID=264d3357-81.23.243.145-1260171972;  expires=Sat,
22-Sep-2012 13:53:26 GMT; path=/; domain=.scorecardresearch.com
P3P:  policyref="/w3c/p3p.xml",  CP="NOI DSP COR NID OUR IND
COM STA OTC"
Expires: Mon, 01 Jan 1990 00:00:00 GMT
Pragma: no-cache
Cache-Control: private, no-cache, no-cache=Set-Cookie, no-store,
proxy-revalidate
Server: CS
```

This request concerns an image (see Content-type in the request) which is provided by b.scorecardresearch.com and shown on the website of CNN (the referrer). As can be seen, the request goes directly to the web server of scrorecardresearch.com, without the CNN server being involved anymore. Thus, the log entry is created on the web server of scorecardresearch.com and not on CNN's web server. When a web site contains a lot of external information, so-called third-party content, log entries concerning one web visit can be numerous and can be spread over a large amount of web servers. All these log entries contain at least the basic information concerning the web browser, such as operating system, browser type, and language settings. Also browser plug-ins, such as Adobe Flash or Java plug-ins, can usually be stored in a log entry.

The log entries are parts of the external memory of Aydee. The servers of visited web sites store information about these visits. It became clear that the visited web sites are not only web sites that are visited consciously, by typing the URL in the browser address bar or by clicking on a link, but also other web sites which have placed content on the visited web sites. But what exactly is in this memory and to what extent can this memory be connected to Aydee?

A web server log is a text file which typically contains a few items or attributes. First, there is the hostname or IP address of the device that made the request; the user's machine. Then, there is date and time of the request and the HTTP request itself, accompanied by an HTTP status code of the response (200 if successful). When a web site is accessed via a link on another page, the referring URL is included as well. Finally, there is the information concerning the user's device which is also included in the request, such as operating system, browser type and version, and plug-ins.

An example of a log file in Common Log File Format, which is the format accepted by all HTTP servers, is as follows:[253]

remotehost rfc931 authuser [date] "request" status bytes

The explanation of the different parts of the log file is this:
Remotehost: Remote hostname (or IP number if DNS hostname is not available, or if DNSLookup is Off).
rfc931: The remote logname of the user.
Authuser: The username as which the user has authenticated himself.
[date]: Date and time of the request.
"request": The request line exactly as it came from the client.
Status: The HTTP status code returned to the client.
Bytes: The content-length of the document transferred.

When all log files related to one device are combined, this memory, thus, contains information about all connections or web interactions made by that device. The log files all stand on their own, but can be connected based on the hostname or IP address in the file. However, the IP address which is used by (attributed to) a device is not necessarily always the same. IP addresses can be dynamic within one environment and devices, in particular portable ones, can have different IP addresses attributed when connected to different networks or internet access points. An individual can also use a proxy for his device to shield the IP address. Next to a device not always having the same IP address, one IP address can also be attached to several devices, for instance within a small network.

The content of the web server logs has no direct reference to Aydee and there are some flaws in the connection of server logs to one and the same person. However, even when the IP address cannot be used as a common identifier, the other information concerning browser and operating system can disclose whether log entries belong to the same device or not. Research executed by the Electronic Frontier Foundation (EFF) shows that web browsers can leave 'fingerprints' behind when you surf the web.[254] The fact that these fingerprints are left behind is no surprise. The information is included in the HTTP header and is also part of the log files, or can be stored separately. It concerns information about the configuration and version of the operating system, system fonts, the browser, and browser plug-ins. What

---

[253] Example from World Wide Web Consortium: <http://www.w3.org/Daemon/User/ Config/Logging.html# common_logfile_format>, (last accessed September 24, 2010).
[254] Press release Electronic Frontier Foundation (EFF), "Web Browsers Leave 'Fingerprints' Behind as You Surf the Net". May 13th 2010, online available at: http://www.eff.org/ press/archives/2010/05/13 (last accessed June 28, 2012).

is more surprising is that these few details can uniquely identify a browser with Java or Flash installed in 94,2% of the cases.[255] Java and Flash are very common plug-ins and are often needed to completely display a web page. Users can change the settings of their browser or update versions of plug-ins, but the EFF research also showed that in 99,1% of the cases a fingerprint was correctly recognized as an 'upgraded' version of a previously observed browser's fingerprint. As a result, it is possible to map visits and requests coming from one unique browser. The uniqueness of the browser also facilitates the distinction of several devices behind one IP address.[256]

When log files are connected to unique browsers, the logs become more and more personal. The exponential use of portable devices, such as laptops and smart phones, has made that single devices are mostly used by one individual only. Each device has its own browser, so even when an individual is not identified he can be recognized based on his personal browser.

Log files contain parts of the external memory of Aydee and the separate files can be connected to each other. Another important part is covered by the use of cookies.

3.2. Cookies

In this subsection the workings and function of cookies will be explained in more detail.

3.2.1. What is a cookie?

A cookie is a small text file which is placed on the hard disk of the computer of the user by his web browser. The placement is the result of a request to do so by the web server of the visited website. Every time the website is visited, the information stored in the cookie will be read by the server. This means that the web server can follow the visits of a user and respond to preferences earlier disclosed by the user.[257] A distinction can be made between session cookies and persistent cookies. Session cookies are erased at the end of a browsing session, whereas the latter remain on the user's hard disk until the user erases them or until they expire at a set date and time. Persistent cookies, thus, enable tracking user visits.[258] When a cookie expires, the browser simply deletes the text file from the user's hard drive. Cookies are passive text files, so they cannot perform any action on their own. Web servers, however, can

---

[255] Eckersley 2010.
[256] Eckersley 2010.
[257] Stearn 1998.
[258] Mercado Kierkegaard 2005.

use the cookies to perform actions such as adapting to preferences of users, processing transparent user passwords, and logging user requests.

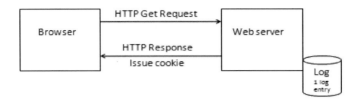

Figure 8. An HTTP interaction including a cookie.

Cookies consist of name-value pairs. In its simplest version, a cookie only contains an identification number and expiration date as unique information. Name, host, path and connection can be similar for different cookies when one website domain issues cookies to several users. Cookies can only be read by systems in the same domain as the cookie's originator. For instance, my identification cookie of ssrn.com looks as follows:

Name: CFID
Content: 13627525
Host: www.ssrn.com
Path: /
Send for: Any type of connection
Expires: woensdag 29 februari 2040 13:40:09

Name is the name of the cookie and content is the unique identification number which is connected to this cookie in my browser. The host is the server that issued the cookie. This cookie has an expiration date, which is displayed in Dutch, because of my systems language being Dutch.

When the user types a URL in his browser address bar for a return visit to a website, the request for accessing the server is sent together with the cookie which was installed on the user's hard disk. Thus, basically, the cookie is issued by a server and can only be accessed by that server when a user returns. During one browser session, the cookie can also be used for purposes such as remembering the contents of a shopping cart, creating a quick checkout, or searches within a website.

Now, when I visit the ssrn.com website again, my browser sends the request together with the cookie-ID:

Request

User-Agent: Mozilla/5.0 (Windows; U; Windows NT 5.1; en-GB;
rv:1.9.2.10) Gecko/20100914 Firefox/3.6.10
Cookie: CFID=13627525; CFTOKEN=34394831; CFGLOBALS=urlto
ken%3DCFID%23%3D13627525%26CFTOKEN%23%3D34394831%
23lastvisit%3D%7Bts%20%272010%2D03%2D08%2007%3A40%3A1
8%27%7D%23timecreated%3D%7Bts%20%272010%2D03%2D08%20
07%3A40%3A18%27%7D%23hitcount%3D2%23cftoken%3D34394831
%23cfid%3D13627525%23; __utma=39959328.599120507.1268052010
.1268052010.1268052010.1

As a response, the ssrn.com server sends the web page content and also
installs 6 new cookies on my hard disk:

Response

HTTP/1.1 200 OK
Date: Wed, 22 Sep 2010 12:03:24 GMT
Set-Cookie: CFID=13627525;expires=Tue, 22-Sep-2009 12:03:24
GMT;path=/
Set-Cookie: CFTOKEN=34394831;expires=Tue, 22-Sep-2009 12:03:24
GMT;path=/
Set-Cookie: CFID=13627525;domain=.ssrn.com;path=/
Set-Cookie: CFTOKEN=34394831;domain=.ssrn.com;path=/
Set-Cookie: CFGLOBALS=urltoken%3DCFID%23%3D1362752
5%26CFTOKEN%23%3D34394831%23lastvisit%3D%7Bts%20
%272010%2D09%2D22%2008%3A03%3A24%27%7D%23timecreated
%3D%7Bts%20%272010%2D03%2D08%2007%3A40%3A18%27%7D
%23hitcount%3D3%23cftoken%3D34394831%23cfid%3D13627525%2
3;expires=Fri, 14-Sep-2040 12:03:24 GMT;path=/
Set-Cookie: CFGLOBALS=urltoken%3DCFID%23%3D1362752
5%26CFTOKEN%23%3D34394831%23lastvisit%3D%7Bts%20
%272010%2D09%2D22%2008%3A03%3A24%27%7D%23timecreated
%3D%7Bts%20%272010%2D03%2D08%2007%3A40%3A18%27%7D
%23hitcount%3D4%23cftoken%3D34394831%23cfid%3D13627525%2
3;expires=Fri, 14-Sep-2040 12:03:24 GMT;path=/

In a picture it looks like this:

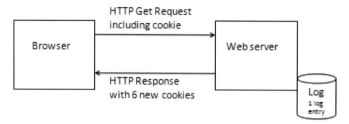

Figure 9. An HTTP interaction including cookie exchanges.

Cookies can replace each other and have different functions. As can be seen in the response above, some cookies expire immediately (session cookies), but there are also persistent cookies with an expiration date in 2040.

3.2.2. Third-party cookies

It was indicated above that cookies can be sent only to the domain server that issued them. This is a protection that prevents other websites than the sites visited from illicitly requesting sensitive information (such as a cookie that verifies that you are logged into your web mail account). However, there is one important loophole here. If you visit a website with third-party content, such as advertisements, the advertiser's domain can issue you a cookie because, technically, your browser visited its domain.[259] In the picture below the server of the third party who delivers Image 1 also sets a cookie in the browser of the individual.

---

[259]   Conti 2009, p. 75.

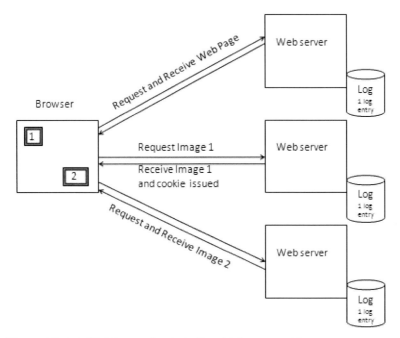

Figure 10. An HTTP interaction including third party cookies.

Third-party cookies work similarly as the 'normal' cookies as described above, but they have one specific characteristic; they are issued by third parties via the server of the visited website. Because the cookies are issued by third parties, these third parties receive the information when a user visits a website. The third parties can have mechanisms to issue their cookies on several websites and, thus, have the ability to track a user over several websites. This can facilitate the analysis of browsing behavior and link visits to extract preferences and to create profiles.

When a web site uses cookies and also provides content at another web site, the site gets the information that you visited this other web site combined with the cookie. Below is an example from cnn.com. First, there is a request with all cookies erased and one of the content items comes from facebook. com. On CNN's web site this is a small field which is clickable to share news messages via your Facebook profile.

http://www.facebook.com/extern/login_status.php?api_key=64b......

GET /extern/login_status.php?api_key=64b….
Host: www.facebook.com
User-Agent: Mozilla/5.0 (Windows; U; Windows NT 5.1; en-GB; rv:1.9.2.10) Gecko/20100914 Firefox/3.6.10

Accept: text/html,application/xhtml+xml,application/xml;q=0.9,*/*;q=0.8
Accept-Language: en-gb,en;q=0.5
Accept-Encoding: gzip,deflate
Accept-Charset: ISO-8859-1,utf-8;q=0.7,*;q=0.7
Keep-Alive: 115
Connection: keep-alive
Referer: http://edition.cnn.com/

HTTP/1.1 302 Found
Location: http://static.ak.fbcdn.net/connect/xd_proxy.php#cb=f1786b977
836fa&origin=http%3A%2F%2Fedition.cnn.com%2Ff67c7c4787e3c6&r
elation=parent&transport=postmessage&frame=f33eb688a8cc44e
Content-Type: text/html; charset=utf-8
X-Cnection: close
Date: Fri, 24 Sep 2010 10:22:19 GMT
Content-Length: 0

After this CNN session I visited the Facebook web site and then returned to the CNN site. The same request now includes the Facebook cookie which was installed on my machine when I visited Facebook.com.

http://www.facebook.com/extern/login_status.php?api_key=64b.....
GET /extern/login_status.php?api_key=64b....
Host: www.facebook.com
User-Agent: Mozilla/5.0 (Windows; U; Windows NT 5.1; en-GB;
rv:1.9.2.10) Gecko/20100914 Firefox/3.6.10
Accept: text/html,application/xhtml+xml,application/xml;q=0.9,*/*;q=0.8
Accept-Language: en-gb,en;q=0.5
Accept-Encoding: gzip,deflate
Accept-Charset: ISO-8859-1,utf-8;q=0.7,*;q=0.7
Keep-Alive: 115
Connection: keep-alive
Referer: http://edition.cnn.com/
Cookie: datr=1285323956-ca23717fdc32f67c613debf9a6f33a061652
3d1aedf5b8011180f; lsd=uBX04; reg_fb_gate=http%3A%2F%2Fwww.
facebook.com%2F; reg_fb_ref=http%3A%2F%2Fwww.facebook.
com%2Findex.php%3Flh%3De63426a823928f9700a59d8f93053b68%2
6eu%3D8qNS9dnSvoCaGD6X8Z3eSA; cur_max_lag=20; locale=nl_NL;
roadblock=%7B%22ca%22%3A%222%22%2C%22t%22%3A%223f941a
5464fb8b909ac8e96f1f22867a%22%2C%22u%22%3A1429934087%2C
%22h%22%3A%22intro_delta_onsite%2Ccaptcha%22%2C%22r%22%3
A%22intro_delta_onsite%2Ccaptcha%2Cidentification%2Cmirror%2Cdo
ne%22%2C%22ts%22%3A1285323998%2C%22s%22%3A%22eDLtnQ
uGcJ2qQ3j4G2lkYBSPheY%22%2C%22l%22%3A%22identification%22

%2C%22e%22%3A1285324021%2C%22d%22%3Afalse%2C%22o%22
%3A2%7D; lu=AA

HTTP/1.1 302 Found
Location: http://static.ak.fbcdn.net/connect/xd_proxy.php#cb=f325a4137
5bb068&origin=http%3A%2F%2Fedition.cnn.com%2Ff12cab808669b6
&relation=parent&transport=postmessage&frame=f171e7818b06fec
Content-Type: text/html; charset=utf-8
X-Cnection: close
Date: Fri, 24 Sep 2010 10:28:10 GMT
Content-Length: 0

Facebook can now connect the visit to the CNN web site to an individual (with a) Facebook account. The Facebook logo on CNN's web site indicates that there is some sort of connection between the two or at least that a connection can be established. However, for ordinary users it will not be clear that the connection is made in any case, so not only when an individual actually uses the clickable logo to share a news item. And even when the functionality is used, individuals may not be aware of the connection between the web sites, but just think they are navigating to Facebook.com. Nevertheless, whereas in the case of Facebook the connection can be guessed, there are lots of other cases where this is not so easy. Third-party content which is embedded on the CNN web site does not necessarily have to be recognizable as third-party content. Videos, images, or other types of content seem to be part of the web site and its news items, but in fact are very often links to other domains.

While it is difficult to understand the number of external web sites activated and involved in the delivery of content on a web page, and possibly issuing cookies, it is even more difficult to imagine when a similar process takes place without real content being displayed. This is the case with so-called web bugs. Web bugs, or web beacons, are images with a size of only 1x1 pixel, which means that they are practically invisible. Technically, it is web content, but the visitor of a web site cannot see the image. Nevertheless, this image has to be requested by the browser and, thus, can also be sent as a response including a cookie. As a result, the functionality of web bugs is similar to that of visible advertisements or other third party content. "Web beacons are a tool that can be used to deliver a cookie in a third party context. This allows companies to perform many important tasks – including unique visitor counts, web usage patterns, assessments of the efficacy of ad campaigns, delivery of more relevant offers, and tailoring of web site content."[260]

---

[260]   Martin, Wu & Alsaid 2003.

3.3. User accounts

Obviously, one way to connect several web site visits to a single user is to let individuals create user accounts. Every time a user visits a web site and logs in to his account, the data in the log file are connected to this account or to a cookie belonging to this account. However, the difference is that with logging in it no longer matters which device is used. An individual can log in from several places and use several devices to access the same web site. The cookies are stored in the browser of each individual device, but the account makes the visits connectable anyway.

When an individual has an account, for instance on Amazon.com, the website can be completely personalized for this single individual. Accessing the Amazon web site without logging in does show the latest searches from previous visits from the computer used. Logging on to the account, however, can also result in personal settings and preferences, as well as showing the purchase history of the individual or a personal wish list with items selected for this individual to remember. Browsing to Amazon.de, a web site I previously visited, results in the following HTTP request:

http://www.amazon.de/
GET / HTTP/1.1
Host: www.amazon.de
User-Agent: Mozilla/5.0 (Windows; U; Windows NT 5.1; en-GB; rv:1.9.2.10) Gecko/20100914 Firefox/3.6.10
Accept: text/html,application/xhtml+xml,application/xml;q=0.9,*/*;q=0.8
Accept-Language: en-gb,en;q=0.5
Accept-Encoding: gzip,deflate
Accept-Charset: ISO-8859-1,utf-8;q=0.7,*;q=0.7
Keep-Alive: 115
Connection: keep-alive
Cookie: session-id-time=1286......
Cache-Control: max-age=0

As can be seen, a cookie is included in the request. As a result of this cookie, the device from which the request was sent is recognized and the latest viewed item, in this case Daniel Suarez's Daemon, is displayed on the web site together with some recommendations related to this book.

Figure 11. Amazon web page with stored information.

Now, when logging in to my personal account, the site is personalized by showing my name in the welcoming message, by giving more recommendations based on past purchases, and by trying to encourage me to improve my recommendations by valuing my 7 past purchases.

Figure 12. Personalized Amazon web page.

So, in the case of an online web shop, the account of the individual forms the complete memory concerning purchases and interests in that particular web shop. Not only purchases are recorded, but also which items have been looked at and for how long. Furthermore, all visits have a time stamp in the log file, which means that the frequency and pattern of visiting the web shop is available in the web server.

3.4. Connecting devices to single individuals

In the end, several mechanisms can create a link between different devices and identify these as belonging to the same individual. A simple mechanism is the user account. When an individual frequently uses the same user account from different devices, these devices apparently all belong to the same individual. Also, when connected to the same router, the IP address can be similar for a few devices. The different devices can be indicated based on different cookies. A portable device can be used in numerous places and during travelling, while still having the same cookie. So, the device can be uniquely identified and followed across the world. Finally, there are more sophisticated mechanisms, also with a weaker link, such as search query behavior or browsing behavior. Obviously, many people show a specific pattern they follow when accessing the internet. Often, first one or more e-mail accounts are checked, then perhaps a news web site, and some social networking sites, and finally the individual starts to search for something using his favorite search engine. These patterns are easy to recognize and can be quite unique. The more standard web sites visited in this pattern, the easier it is to recognize and individualize.

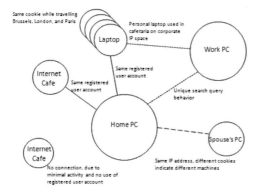

Figure 13. Linking devices to individuals.[261]

But also groups of individuals can be connected based on their web activity. By using information like IP addresses, cookies, and third party cookies it is possible to map which individuals share address books, interests, have mail connections, have been searched for by others, and so on and so forth.

3.5. The memory and existence of Aydee

The question still remains whether the data collected by several parties and stored in log files and cookies belong to the external memory of Aydee, his internal memory, or whether they are part of Aydee himself. As described in the story of Aydee, Aydee is a context-bound digital persona. The real-world individual, his model, uses Aydee as a partial identity for online commercial purposes. Taking that into account, the data as provided by the individual for commercial purposes is Aydee. Aydee is then a projected digital persona

---

[261] Image cf. Conti 2009, p. 92.

and consists of a username and password, address details, bank account or credit card details to make payments, and probably some specific data or interests indicated by the individual. In this form, Aydee is functioning as a representation for his model and does not include information that cannot be given directly by the individual. So, the individual is still in control over the disclosed data.

When Aydee is presented to others, namely online commercial companies, they see Aydee. As soon as a cookie is placed in the browser of the individual and additional information is stored, Aydee becomes a hybrid digital persona. The representation can then be extended further and further, including purchasing history, interest analysis, browsing patterns, etc. All these data become part of the memory of Aydee, but not of the initial Aydee as created by the individual. Instead, a new representation is created, based on Aydee. These two different representations can be distinguished easily based on the access parties have to the representation. The initial Aydee (Aydee1) was created by the individual and presented to a company. In that case, the individual and the company have access to the same Aydee (1) with the same amount of information. However, the new representation as created by the company (Aydee2), including the initial Aydee, but extended with new information, is only accessible by the company. The individual cannot access all the information at the same time.

Another issue is how the representation is interpreted. The individual creates Aydee in the form of an account. The company, however, starts with the account information and adds information to get a more complete image of the individual behind the representation. The representation can be connected to a profile, resulting in predictions of interests and desires of the individual. In the end, the digital persona as used by the company can become so rich that it is seen, or treated, as if it were the real-world individual himself with whom an interaction takes place.[262] As Zwick and Dholakia state:

[T]he consumer is constituted by language and the language governing the electronic market space is constituted by databases. The consumer (as a meaningful representation, not as a body) does not exist outside this constitutive field of discursive power. Hence, the consumer's digital identity is his or her real identity because marketing is targeted toward the consumer profile rather than the real person.[263]

---

[262] Gürses & Berendt 2010, p. 309.
[263] Zwick & Dholakia 2004.

3.6. Interim summary

In the previous part, the technical mechanisms of information processing in web interactions have been described. The description gave an insight in what data are stored and where. It was indicated as the external memory of Aydee. However, the internal memory might be quite similar, with great overlaps, so the question arises whether the memory as such, i.e. the set of data, is not just Aydee himself. This part will further discuss the question which data are stored where and how they are connected to Aydee and to the individual.

As shown in the previous part, several data concerning web interactions are stored in different forms at different locations. Cookies can function as a means to store data at the hard disk of the individual's device; log files contain data that are stored on the server of the service provider. User accounts can include personal data, preferences, and personal settings of the individual, all stored in databases of the service provider. The cookies sent together with the HTTP request allow for connection of the database data to the device or user account.

Connecting and analyzing data can also lead to new information. This information is not (directly) disclosed by the individual, but can be derived from patterns or specific behavior that are shown. A rather common purpose of connecting and analyzing data is to identify personal interests or to create a personal profile of an individual. The profiles or specific outcomes of the data analysis can be used as a basis for decision making.

The theoretical framework (Chapter 2) already included a description of profiling and how it works. In the practice of web interaction, it means that data concerning the interaction are collected and probably combined with other data to construct individual or group profiles. As indicated in the technical description, cookies and web bugs, as means to collect data, can be used by the service provider of the initially visited web site, as well as by third parties. These third parties provide visible or invisible content to the web site. The provision is programmed in such a way that a cookie is installed via the HTTP response to the user's browser. Remarkably, it appears that service providers are not always aware of these third-party cookies being spread to the visitors of their web sites. A 2009 case study[264] on the web site of Levis showed that Levis.com loads nine tracking tags that link to eight third party companies. None of these companies were acknowledged in the Levis privacy policy. This could either mean that the policy was incomplete, or that Levis was just not aware of this data collection. In the privacy

---

[264] Dwyer 2009.

policy, however, it was stated that Levis did not share personal information without the user's consent.[265] The tracking cookies can be used to track a user's browsing within a website or across multiple sites, therewith mapping behavior and interests.

Profiling activities can result in a very complete image of an individual, including lots of information. Specific about this information is that it is new information resulting from the profiling or data mining process. The analysis and processing of input data discloses additional information, next to the information that was disclosed by the individual or his actions. It is indirect information, possibly revealing facts or characteristics concerning the individual that the individual himself was not even aware of. Interests or desires of the individual become apparent even before the individual knows he has these interests and desires. This phenomenon is sometimes referred to as companies creating a 'database of intentions'.[266] Obviously, knowing individual intentions is of extreme value for marketers or commercial companies in general, as well as for governmental institutions. A fictional example of the latter can be found in the famous movie Minority Report,[267] where intentions of individuals are monitored to predict crimes. This idea has certainly inspired commercial companies. For instance, Social Intelligence promises to predict future behavior of employees based on information derived from SNS and other internet sources.[268] The service does not focus on past behavior like obscene photos or drunk partying, but on the social character of an individual, thereby, for instance, predicting whether someone will function better in a group or in a more individualized function. Next to companies, governments are also interested in predictive technologies. Pattern-based data mining is used to combat terrorism by trying to single out possible terrorists based on certain characteristics or behavioral patterns they reveal.[269]

4. Case studies

Having described how a digital persona 'lives' in cyberspace, as illustrated by the story of Aydee the Avatar, and having shown the general technicalities of web interactions and cookies, it is now time to present practical examples.

---

[265] Dwyer 2009.

[266] Battelle 2005-2006.

[267] DreamWorks/20th Century Fox 2002, directed by Steven Spielberg.

[268] See: http://itmanagement.earthweb.com/features/article.php/12297_3905931_1/Pre-crime-Comes-to-the-HR-Dept.htm (last accessed June 27, 2012).

[269] Rubinstein, Lee & Schwartz 2008. Rubinstein also indicates that there are criticisms to pattern-based data mining in a criminal context, because it might be conflicting with the presumption of innocence and the requirement of an act before criminal investigations may start.

First, an example of Facebook will be given, by briefly introducing the service and the creation of an account. Since it is of particular interest to describe what data are collected and added to the digital persona, the example will also contain several scenarios of how Facebook tracks internet users over the web, when they visit other websites than facebook.com.

Second, an example of Google will be described, with a particular focus on the combination of different services hosted by Google and the connection between those services.

4.1. Facebook

Facebook is, with about 1 billion members,[270] the biggest and most successful social networking site worldwide. Due to its size, it is highly influential on the web as one of the most important services to which other websites connect by implementing so-called 'social tools'. It even seems that Facebook is changing the way web content is rated concerning relevance, therewith shifting online business from a 'Hit and Link economy' to a 'Like-economy'.[271]

The start of Facebook's history took place in February 2004, when students Mark Zuckerberg, Eduardo Saverin, Dustin Moskovitz, and Chris Huges launched the small scale social networking project 'TheFacebook' for Harvard College students (Harvard University). In March 2004, the network was expanded to other American universities. Membership of TheFacebook was limited to students of certain (by TheFacebook selected) universities. After providing the network for several universities in the US and Canada, in 2005 a version was launched for schools and employees of several companies, such as Apple and Microsoft. By purchase of the web domain facebook.com, TheFacebook simply became Facebook. Only in September 2006, Facebook became a completely public network and accessible for everybody (of age 13 and older).[272] As of March 2012 Facebook was preparing to enter the stock market with an estimated value of 100 billion US Dollars.[273] In the Prospectus to enter the stock market, the number of active users indicated was even 901 million.[274] In early October 2012, this number was above 1

---

[270] See: http://newsroom.fb.com/Key-Facts where Facebook claims to have 1 billion monthly active users as of October 2012 (last accessed November 30, 2012).

[271] Helmond & Gerlitz 2012.

[272] Kirkpatrick 2010.

[273] Tyler 2012.

[274] Active users are users that logon to Facebook at least once a month. The Prospectus is online available at: <http://www.sec.gov/Archives/edgar/data/1326801/000119312512175673/d287954ds1a.htm> (last accessed April 26, 2012).

billion.[275] The estimated value, however, has dropped from the moment Facebook entered the stock market (on May 1st 2012) and the value is now close to 50% of the initial value.[276].

The basic functionality of social networking sites, so also of Facebook, is to have users create a personal profile page and make 'friends'. Making friends can be done by inviting other users to become a friend. Essentially, different users confirm a certain relationship and therewith gain access to each other's profile pages. However, if privacy settings are kept 'open', related connections (Friends of Friends) or random others also have access to the profile. People with whom the user has a connection are displayed on the profile page.

When creating a personal profile page on Facebook an important factor is the registration of personal information and preferences. What information is shared is, to a certain extent, steered by Facebook. For instance, Facebook requires the use of a real name when creating an account and prohibits the use of pseudonyms. According to Facebook, this is necessary in order to facilitate finding people on the network whom users already know offline. Even though that sounds logical it is not strictly necessary for the functionality of Facebook, since people who know each other offline can share their usernames and then become friends on Facebook as well. Furthermore, it is very well possible that users want to connect to people with whom they share certain interests. In that case, the real name of the user is of no importance. Facebook actively checks whether users obey their real name policy and blocks profile pages of which they suspect the user to be in breach of this policy.[277]

Other forms of steering the sharing information are the limited choice in categories to classify friends and labels to describe relationship statuses. Another way to classify friends is by creating lists, for instance for school or work/colleagues. In order to collect as much information as possible, Facebook encourages members to use settings which make their information public. The more information people share, the more information others will share, because of social effects such as 'peer pressure'.[278] Facebook is famous for its default settings of information to be visible not only to

---

[275] See: <http://www.wired.com/business/2012/10/facebook-case-for-optimism/> (last accessed October 21, 2012).

[276] See WSJ online: <http://online.wsj.com/article/SB1000087239639044437510457759371173708798.html> (last accessed October 21, 2012).

[277] As indicated in email messages to people whose account had been blocked. The practice was confirmed by Luc Delany, European Policy Manager Facebook, in a personal communication on 10 November 2011.

[278] Acquisti & Gross 2006, p. 15, 17; boyd 2008, p. 133; Donath & boyd 2004, p. 80.

'friends' but also to 'friends of friends'[279] and for indicating this setting as 'recommended'.[280] Besides, it has been shown that most users stick to the default settings, regardless of what these settings are.[281]

Facebook integrates several tools and functionalities, such as chat, blogs, games and e-mail. On the profile page, textual information as well as photos and videos can be showed. This combination of tools makes it attractive to use Facebook as the central platform for all online communications.

Facebook, thus, allows for the creation of a digital persona. At first sight, it seems to be a projected persona, since the individual provides the information that forms the representation, even though Facebook hugely influences what information is shared on the profile page. Nevertheless, the digital persona on Facebook certainly is a hybrid digital persona, because Facebook collects much more information concerning the individual, which can be connected to the individual account. This additional information is collected via the 'social tools' Facebook provides for other websites to integrate. Probably, the best-known of these tools is the 'Like' button.

4.1.1. The Facebook 'Like' Button[282]

The Facebook Like button is an image displaying a thumbs-up symbol accompanied by the word 'Like'. According to Facebook, "[t]he Like button lets a user share your content with friends on Facebook. When the user clicks the Like button on your site, a story appears in the user's friends' News Feed with a link back to your website."[283] Anyone can display the button on his website by simply implementing the code which is available for free. The button can thus be used by content providers to have web users promote content and create links on their Facebook profile pages. When clicking the Like button, a login field opens in a pop-up window to log on to Facebook. Log on results in the creation of the link to the website at issue on the Facebook profile page. When a user is already logged on to Facebook, the creation takes place immediately.

In April 2010, at their f8 conference, Facebook announced Instant Personalizer and Social Plugins, two services that allowed partners to

---

279 Lemons 2011, p. 9.
280 Lemons 2011, p. 19.
281 Thaler & Sunstein 2008, pp. 8-9.
282 This part is based on an earlier paper: Roosendaal 2010. An elaborated version of this paper has been published as Roosendaal 2012.
283 "Like Button - Facebook Developers," See: <http://developers.facebook.com/docs/reference/plugins/like> (last accessed March 22, 2011).

leverage the social graph — the information about a user's relationships on the site that the user makes available to the system — and provide a channel for sharing information between Facebook and third parties. For example, websites could implement a Like button on their own pages that enables users to share content from that site with their connections on Facebook.[284] The value of displaying the Like button on a website becomes clear from the statistics. Sites that have added such social plugins from Facebook reported increases in traffic in excess of 200%. Besides, the time spent and the number of articles read on websites with Like buttons also increased by over 80%.[285] The button represents 12.9% of the distribution of third-party widgets.[286] It also appears that, within months, the use of social plugins had reached millions of sites.[287] The penetration rate of the Like button in the top 10,000 websites reached over 4% in the first six months after its introduction,[288] and it is likely that it will continue to grow.[289]

While the Like button can help content providers to generate traffic to their websites, it is also a tool for Facebook members to add information about their interests to their personal profile page. Thus, it fits perfectly in the ongoing trend of social networking sites like Facebook encouraging members to share personal information.[290] Obviously, for sharing items from the web, the Like button is a very useful tool, because it allows direct linking without having to copy and paste complete URLs and the content is made up in a readable manner automatically.

4.1.2. Cookies, recognition, and identification

As indicated, there are numerous third parties which deliver content to websites and place cookies. Usually, the function of these third parties is to

---

[284] boyd & Hargittai 2010.

[285] "The Value of a Liker – Facebook," <http://www.facebook.com/notes/facebook-media/value-of-a-liker/150630338305797> (last accessed March 22, 2011).

[286] "Facebook Like Box Usage Statistics," <http://trends.builtwith.com/widgets/Facebook-Like-Box> (last accessed March 22, 2011).

[287] "Facebook Stats Likers," <http://www.insidefacebook.com/2010/09/29/facebook-stats-likers/> (last accessed September 29, 2010).

[288] "Facebook Like Usage Statistics," <http://trends.builtwith.com/widgets/Facebook-Like> (last accessed March 22, 2011).

[289] The Like button is intensively used. Facebook claims to have 3,2 billion Likes and comments per day: <http://www.sec.gov/Archives/edgar/data/1326801/000119312512175673/d287954ds1a.htm> (last accessed June 28, 2012).

[290] There are, however, more privacy-friendly initiatives which focus on audience segregation and controlled disclosure of personal information. For instance, Clique allows users to have several 'faces' in one account. See <http://clique.primelife.eu/>. This social networking site is one of the results of the EU FP7 PrimeLife project.

provide website providers with content such as advertisements or specific functionalities like maps or videos. A piece of content is delivered from the servers of the third party and can be sent together with the cookie. The cookies can be used to generate information on the number of visitors and which items on a website attracted the most attention. In this way, third parties can provide a service to the website provider. A web user is usually not aware of this. He just types in the URL of the website he wants to visit and the page is loaded. That the loading of the page involves numerous HTTP requests[291] for content from the servers of the visited websites and often several third-party servers is a process which takes place behind the scenes. Or, in more popular terms: that is where the magic happens.

A cookie is placed on the web user's computer via his browser. Each cookie is connected to a web server, so only the server from which the cookie was sent has access to the cookie. The provider of a website does not have access to other cookies placed by third parties via his website. Once a cookie is available on the user's computer, this cookie will be sent together with the HTTP request in each later request for content from the server which installed the cookie. The HTTP request also includes data on the referrer, which is the website on which the content will be displayed. Since the referrer data is always included, third parties can follow exactly which sites a user visits. When data concerning web visits are combined based on the unique cookie, the browsing history of a web user can be mapped. The content is needed to load a page so, for tracking purposes, it is irrelevant whether a user actually clicks a piece of content or not, or whether the content is clickable at all.

4.1.2.1. Scenarios

The Facebook Like button is also a piece of third-party content. The website provider does not directly place an image of this button on his website. In fact, the button is a piece of HTML code which includes the request to the Facebook server to provide the image when the website is loaded. This implies that the button can be used to set third-party cookies or to recognize them as well. Setting of a cookie can be included in an HTTP response providing a piece of content to be displayed on a web site. In future HTTP requests, information in the cookie is sent along and the device of the user can be recognized. A few different scenarios can be distinguished: (1) A web user has a Facebook account, (2) a web user does not have an account, (3) a web user becomes a member of Facebook, and (4) a member deletes

---

[291] HTTP stands for Hyper Text Transfer Protocol, the programming language used for internet traffic. An HTTP request is a request for a specific piece of content sent from the user's computer to a web server. The web server replies by sending the requested content. If the content is not available, the reply includes an error code.

his account. These scenarios have been tested by the author in a practical experiment using Techcrunch.com, CNN.com, and Gizmodo.com.

4.1.2.1.1 The web user has a Facebook account

The first option is a scenario in which the web user has a Facebook account. When the account is created, Facebook issues a cookie, containing a unique user ID, to the computer of the user. This cookie facilitates the display of a username in the login field at returning visits. When accessing Facebook from another device, a temporary cookie is issued, which is replaced by a cookie with the same ID after logging on to the account. In this way, different devices can be linked to one account and thus one user. Every time the user visits the Facebook website, the cookie is sent together with the HTTP request for the site. As a result, Facebook already knows who[292] wants to log in before the actual login has taken place.

However, the cookie is not only sent to the Facebook servers when a member logs on, but on every occasion when content such as the Like button has to be provided from the Facebook servers (Fig. 1). Thus, every single time a website containing the Like button is visited, Facebook receives information concerning the user, including his unique ID, via the cookie. If the user actually clicks the button, he has to provide his Facebook login details, and a message about the 'Like' is posted on his profile page.

Users are often not aware of the fact that data about the user are sent to Facebook regardless of whether the Like button is actually clicked. The cookie contains the unique user ID and thus allows information on browsing behavior to be connected to the account. Even though the user is not involved, Facebook can collect far more individual data than the data made available on the profile page only.

Below is an example of a request for the Like button where the cookie including a unique user ID is sent along.

GET /plugins/like.php?href=http%3A%2F%2Fwww.facebook.
com%2FGizmodo&layout=button_count&show_faces=false&width=200
&action=like&colorscheme=light&height=21 HTTP/1.1
Host: www.facebook.com
User-Agent: Mozilla/5.0 (Windows; U; Windows NT 5.1; en-GB;
rv:1.9.2.10) Gecko/20100914 Firefox/3.6.10

---

[292] Or to be more precise, Facebook knows what device is used and can then have an expectation of which user is using that device. If a device has multiple users and cookies, it may be more difficult to identify the actual user.

Accept: text/html,application/xhtml+xml,application/xml;q=0.9,*/*;q=0.8
Accept-Language: en-gb,en;q=0.5
Accept-Encoding: gzip,deflate
Accept-Charset: ISO-8859-1,utf-8;q=0.7,*;q=0.7
Keep-Alive: 115
Connection: keep-alive
Referer: http://gizmodo.com/
Cookie: datr=yjPATCXPQuDBLU_J5ZfRsJpd; lu=TgbyaYN2Obo-
F4fEBiQTGtwQ; locale=en_GB; x-referer=http%3A%2F%2Fwww.
facebook.com%2Fhome.php%23%2Fhome.php; cur_max_lag=20; c_
user=100001XXXXXXXXX; sct=1287731574; sid=0; xs=55dcbdfe4719c
2693d477d0c0dd83ab6
Cache-Control: max-age=0

Figure 14. The HTTP GET request for the Like button on Gizmodo.com, including the cookie with user ID (anonymised by the author).

In this scenario, there is a link between the Internet user and Facebook, because there is an account. Now, consider a scenario where there is no membership link.

4.1.2.1.2. The web user does not have a Facebook account[293]

If a user does not have a Facebook account, there is no cookie and no user ID available. A visit to, for example, Techcrunch.com includes an HTTP GET request for the Like button. However, in this scenario, when the button is provided, no cookie is issued. Thus, it seems that the Like button itself is not used to issue cookies. However, when a site is visited which includes Facebook Connect[294] (for instance Gizmodo.com), this application does issue a cookie (Fig. 14). Facebook Connect is the feature which allows members to log on to other websites with their Facebook credentials. From that moment on, visits to other websites which display the Like button result in a request for the Like button to the Facebook server including the cookie. An important part of the process depends on visiting a site which has implemented

---

[293] This scenario does not apply anymore since Facebook changed its systems after the publication of my initial research findings: Roosendaal 2010. The Facebook Connect feature is now called Facebook for Websites and is no longer used by Facebook to issue cookies. To receive a Facebook cookie, it is now necessary to visit the Facebook.com domain In an internal communication (on file with the author) to the Hamburg Data Protection Authority (Germany) Facebook stated that the tracking of non-users was the result of a 'bug' in their software development kit.

[294] Facebook Connect is the feature that allows Facebook members to log on to other web services by using their Facebook username and password. In the meantime, the name of Connect has been changed to Facebook for Websites.

Facebook Connect. The chance of visiting such a site is considerable. Within a year from its launch in December 2008, Facebook Connect was used on almost 1 million websites and in March 2009 over 40 million unique visitors of Facebook Connect implementations were registered.[295] The number of implementations increases exponentially, so the likelihood of accessing such a website is increasing at a fast pace as well.

As indicated, after visiting a website on which Facebook Connect has been implemented, the request for the Like button includes a cookie. This cookie has an expiration date two years from the moment it was issued. However, by browsing across websites, additional cookies can be placed on the user's computer and these can be added later on in new requests. Not all cookies are used in this way. For instance, a cookie issued via the extern login status plug-in[296] is not included in later requests.

1. Set-Cookie: datr=ckviTDm3989eNbvw6xMhAWle; expires=Thu, 15-Nov-2012 09:14:26 GMT; path=/; domain=.facebook.com
2. Set-Cookie: datr=ckviTC8tNJ-1ZKqCu_SrIga7; expires=Thu, 15-Nov-2012 09:14:26 GMT; path=/; domain=.facebook.com

Figure 15. A cookie issued via Facebook extern login status (1) and one via Facebook Connect (2) on Gizmodo.com.

Based on the cookie, the entire web behavior of an individual user can be followed by Facebook. Every site that includes some kind of Facebook content will initiate an interaction with the Facebook servers, disclosing information to Facebook about the visited website together with the cookie. Since there is no link to a user account, the cookie functions as an R-identifier and facilitates recognition of the unknown individual. The accumulated data set concerning web behavior is, thus, a profile and not a digital persona.

4.1.2.1.3. A user becomes a Facebook member

It is possible that a web user already has a personal set of data collected by Facebook, based on the mechanism described above. The question is what happens if this user creates a Facebook account. In that case, he first

---

[295] Ken Burbary, "Five Reasons Companies Should Be Integrating Social Media with Facebook Connect," August 20, 2009, <http://www.kenburbary.com/2009/08/five-reasons-companies-should-be-integrating-social-media-with-facebook-connect/> (last accessed June 28, 2012).

[296] This is a plugin that checks whether a user is logged on to Facebook while visiting another website. When a user is logged on, advertisements or other pieces of content can be personalized by linking to the Facebook account.

has to go to the Facebook homepage (login page). The cookie on the user's computer is sent to Facebook in the request for the web page to be loaded. The server responds and issues a few new cookies. These new cookies are temporary ones, or session cookies. When the account is actually created, a unique ID number is issued and sent in a cookie. The connection between this ID cookie and the old cookie is made behind the scenes by Facebook's servers. This means that the entire historical information of the user can be connected to the newly created Facebook account. From this moment on, all subsequent requests for Facebook content are accompanied with the unique user ID cookie. The (anonymous) profile has now become a digital persona.

If a user deletes all his cookies, the process starts from the beginning with Facebook Connect placing a new cookie when a site containing Facebook Connect is visited. From the moment on that the user accesses his Facebook account, or connects to this account by clicking the Like button and providing username and password, this cookie is replaced by a cookie containing the unique user ID that belongs to the account.

4.1.2.1.4. A user deletes his Facebook account

A last possibility is that an existing Facebook member decides to exit the network. In this case, the user can delete his account. Facebook offers a simple process to deactivate an account. Deactivation, however, is not the same as deletion.[297] In fact, when an account is deactivated, the account and all its contents are only made unavailable to the network community. The entire account is kept by Facebook just in case the user decides to rejoin the network.[298] In that case, the complete account, including all connections and contents can be reactivated. Clearly, during the inactivity of an account, Facebook is still able to connect data to the account in a way similar to when the account was active.

There is also an option to really delete an account. The deletion process includes a specific request to Facebook that takes two weeks to process. If the account is accessed in this period, the deletion process is stopped. After 14 days, accessing the account is no longer possible and the contents can no longer be retrieved. Whether Facebook keeps any information or even

---

[297] See: <http://www.facebook.com/help/?page=185698814812082> (last accessed June 28, 2012).

[298] Illustrating in this context is the initiative Europe versus Facebook, in which Austrian student Max Schrems submitted a data subject access request and received a file of over 1200 pages. The data were incomplete, but also contained data that had been explicitly deleted by Schrems. See: <http://europe-v-facebook.org/EN/Data_Pool/data_pool.html> (last accessed June 28, 2012).

the entire account, probably disconnected from the login credentials, is unclear.[299] However, even if the account is really deleted, the web user can still be tracked and the browsing data can still be connected to an individual data set. This means that, after deleting the account, all services which were connected to Facebook, for instance, by using the Facebook account to sign up, have to be disconnected as well and cookies have to be deleted. Once everything is cleared and disconnected, the web user can be considered to be someone who does not have a Facebook account and the scenario earlier described applies.

4.1.2.2. Recognition and identification

Facebook uses cookies for recognition. Web users can be recognized whenever they visit a site with any Facebook content (e.g. Like button, Facebook hosted Comment Field, or a 'Most popular on Facebook' list). Facebook members are identified as individual account holders, because the cookie includes their unique user identification number. When different devices are used to access Facebook, such as a home computer, a laptop, or a smart phone, these devices are recognized as belonging all to the same individual, so all web interaction from these different devices is connected as well. Individuals who do not have a Facebook account are recognized as well. Their browsing behavior, however, is not connected to a Facebook account; besides, recognition is machine- based and separated for every single device. Since there is no unique user ID in the cookie resulting from a log-on to Facebook, the different devices cannot be connected solely on the basis of the cookies. Single devices can be quite reliable for identifying or recognizing individual users, however, even though they can be used by different persons. More and more devices, such as laptops and smart phones, become personal and are usually used by one single individual. This implies that information collected based on the cookies and browsing behavior results in a very personal profile. Obviously, Facebook can use this to provide their members with targeted advertisements. The information collected about the browsing behavior of non-members probably provides a larger sample for profiling and targeting purposes.

The Facebook Like button is not the only button which frequently appears on websites to facilitate sharing or promoting content. Other examples are Twitter's Tweet button, the Digg button, and Google's Buzz, but there are differences. As described above, Facebook Connect is the system that actually issues a cookie the first time. From that moment on, the cookie is

---

[299] However, the fact that the data received in the Europe versus Facebook initiative contained deleted data as well shows that deletion is not a standard part of the data processing by Facebook.

sent together with all HTTP requests for content, so also when the Like button is provided onto a page of a third party. Thus, an additional system is used to initiate the cookie exchange. Twitter, for instance, does not have such a system.[300] The Tweet button does not always send a cookie when the button is requested from the Twitter servers. Only when someone visits the Twitter homepage is a cookie issued which is used in future interactions with the servers, similarly as with the Like button. Logging on or even having a Twitter account is not necessary. A small but important difference with the Like button is that there is at least supposed to be some link to Twitter, because the web user needs to have visited this website for cookies to be exchanged. For Facebook, this is not necessary at all, which implies that individuals who consciously choose not to participate in Facebook are still tracked and traced by Facebook. Even if someone does not connect to Facebook himself, Facebook makes the connection.

Another important difference is that Facebook can trace the browsing behavior to member accounts. These accounts are, usually, quite rich concerning disclosed information, but the Like button as exploited by Facebook allows for far more information to be collected about individual members than the information disclosed on the personal profile page. Thus, people who have an account, but do not want to disclose much information are still profiled more extensively. Their browsing behavior discloses much information concerning personal interests, and this information can also be collected by Facebook and connected to the individual account. In the end, awareness in disclosing information, either by not participating on Facebook or by very limited disclosure of personal information, is insufficient to escape the monitoring and tracking techniques of Facebook.

An additional point of attention lies in the function Facebook is exploiting as an identity provider. An increasing amount of websites offers the possibility to register or log on with Facebook credentials.[301] The username and password are consequently used at places other than on Facebook's site only. Obviously, the services that provide this possibility are linked to Facebook as well. However, a more pressing issue is the fact that, for some web services, such as music service Spotify, logging on is *only* possible with a Facebook account. This means that, without a Facebook account, accessing or using the services is simply impossible. If the amount of web services requiring a Facebook account increases, web users will become more dependent on Facebook as an identity provider so users can indirectly be forced to create an account.

---

[300] Findings based on tests performed by myself. The test results have not been published.
[301] For instance: www.slideshare.net or creating an account on Spotify www.spotify.com.

4.1.2.3. Friend Suggest

Another interesting way of Facebook to collect information and to connect this information to individuals is the system behind the Friend Suggest feature. This is a feature to show profile pictures of other members on the personal page of a member as suggestions to become friends with. In order to make it as attractive as possible for members to indeed make the connection, the suggestions have to be relevant. This relevance can be derived from the fact that usually members do know the suggested friends in real life. The question arises how that is possible.

A first method is rather straightforward and just looks at the connections that friends of the member have in their network. If a number of friends share a connection, there is a considerable chance that the member knows this person as well. A second method is to look at the email-address books that members have uploaded. One of the first steps in the process of creating an account offers the possibility to look for friends in the email address books of the new member in order to find out who of a member's friends are already on Facebook. This makes it easy to find them and to establish a connection. When allowing this search functionality, the entire address book is uploaded to Facebook.[302] By looking for matches in the address books of different members with registered email addresses connected to accounts, other members can be suggested as friends.

The practice of processing email addresses is also used by Facebook when it concerns individuals who are not (yet) a member. Members can indicate to Facebook to whom they want to have an invitation sent to join Facebook. This is done by selecting or entering the email address of the person to whom an invitation has to be sent. Facebook, then, processes this email address to look for matches in the database, in particular to find out which other members have this email address in their (uploaded) address books. Where matches are found, the profile pictures of these members are displayed next to the invitation message the non-member receives in his email. That is why it is not a coincidence that, when an individual receives an invitation to join Facebook, the members displayed in the invitation are usually people the individual actually knows.[303]

As shown, Facebook has several tools and mechanisms to collect data concerning individuals and to combine and use these data. Even though it has already broadly been recognized that this has implications for privacy

---

[302] Fogg & Iizawa 2008.
[303] Explained by Luc Delany, European Policy Manager Facebook, in a personal communication on 10 November 2011.

of members, and sometimes even non-members, Facebook CEO Mark Zuckerberg is strongly convinced that privacy will no longer be important within a few years. In his own words: "Facebook users eventually get over privacy anxiety."[304]

4.2. Google

Next to Facebook, an extremely important player in the area of web services is Google. Google was founded by Stanford students Larry Page and Sergey Brin, who wanted to make the World Wide Web searchable. There were several search engines available at the time, but Page and Brin criticized these because they were funded by advertisers and the use of keywords could influence the search results.[305] According to Page and Brin, this approach was far too commercial and could not lead to reliable search results. To solve this problem, in 1996 Page designed 'PageRank', a software algorithm that indexed web pages by the number of links to the pages and the number of links to the pages that referred to other pages.[306] This way of indexing should lead to a ranking based on relevance and reliability of web pages, including an automatic check by the users of the search engine. By now, the Google search engine is the biggest worldwide. In the meantime, advertisements have been introduced at Google as well and these advertisements even generate 96 % of the revenues (in 2011).[307]

The Google search engine facilitates the storage of information that can reveal interests of individuals, since apparently an individual is searching for specific information. Different searches from one computer can be connected based on the IP address, which is included in the search logs together with the search term.[308] The accumulation of all search terms over the years can constitute a detailed overview of a person's interests and habits. In first instance, these overviews are profiles. If the data sets contain unique combinations of data or specific information, they can be related to an identifiable individual and the data sets are digital personae. The profile can also become a digital persona if the user makes use of a Google account and, thus, identifies himself.

---

[304] See: <www.zdnet.com/blog/facebook/mark-zuckerberg-facebook-users-eventually-get-over-privacy-anxiety/1534> (last accessed June 28, 2012).

[305] Brin & Page 1998.

[306] Battelle 2005-2006, p. 75.

[307] See financial information Google, available at: <http://investor.google.com/financial/2011/tables.html> (last accessed June 28, 2012). Advertising revenues in 2011 were 36,5 billion US Dollars on a total revenue of 37,9 billion US Dollars.

[308] See: <http://code.google.com/intl/nl-NL/apis/searchappliance/documentation/46/help_gsa/status_log.html> (last accessed June 28, 2012).

Google started with providing a search engine, but over the years numerous services have been added to the portfolio of the internet company. For instance, Google Maps provides route planning, YouTube facilitates video sharing, Picasa can be used for photo editing and web albums, and Google+ is Google's own social networking site. All these services are intensively used by web users. However, Google also has a number of services specifically for (commercial) companies. The most important of these is targeted advertising, which is available in a myriad of ways. The advertisements can be placed in the search engine, on top of or next to the search results, via AdWords. Which ads are displayed and for what price is the outcome of a sophisticated real-time auction system running behind the scenes.[309] It is also possible to have Google display advertisements on numerous websites, related to the site itself, or as a contextual ad next to a news item, by using AdSense.

Another service, specifically aimed at companies and other website owners, is Google Analytics. This is an analytics tool which can provide website owners with statistics on how many (unique) visitors a site has, what pages within a site are visited, and how the visitors came to the website (directly or via a search engine or other link).

Essentially, all of the services indicated above can be integrated into websites by website owners. For instance, it is not uncommon to have a company website with internal search functionality (provided by Google), Google Maps integration with the contact details and route description, a YouTube promo video, and a Google+1 button for expressing a positive relationship with the company. The variety of services which are all widely used makes that Google has an astonishing coverage of the internet via integrations of their tools on third-party websites, namely 88,4 %.[310] Obviously, Google receives information via all the integrations and is, therewith, able to create personal profiles of internet users by tracking them, combine these profiles with search terms, derive preferences and even predict events.[311] Connecting several actions of individual users can be based on IP address or cookies. Furthermore, Google advertises personalization and offers web users the opportunity to create a Google account, where they can manage their preferences and access search history. When a user has a Google account, the tracking and combining of actions on the internet becomes even more trivial.

---

[309] Levy 2009.
[310] Gomez, Pinnick & Soltani 2009. In 2009 Google covered 348,059 out of 393,829 distinct domains.
[311] For instance, epidemic diseases and their spread in Google Flu Trends: < http://www.google.org/flutrends/> (last accessed June 28, 2012).

Google also collects data in the physical world, via their StreetView cars. In Google Maps it is possible to view panoramic images of city streets, with a service called Google StreetView. In order to compile these images, Google has a fleet of vehicles, equipped with special cameras, which they drive around. Google also intended to record the identity and position of WiFi hotspots in order to power a location service it operates.[312] The position of the vehicle, and thus the image, could be defined accurately by using triangulation within these networks. The idea was to collect network data like SSID information (the name of the network) and MAC addresses (unique numbers given to devices such as routers) in order to identify and locate the networks.[313] Google stated to collect only SSIDs and MAC addresses, but in May 2010 it appeared that this statement was incorrect and that payload data (information sent over the network) of open WiFi networks was collected as well.[314] Google claimed this to be a mistake due to a piece of code that was included in the software, "although the project leaders did not want, and had no intention of using, payload data."[315] Google stated it was profoundly sorry for the error and took steps to delete the data immediately in cooperation with regulators. It also had an independent third party perform a check on the software and the data it collected.[316] It was admitted that, even when it was a mistake, Google should have realized it much earlier and never allowed such data to be captured. In the words of the US Federal Trade Commission: "the company did not discover that it had been collecting payload data until it responded to a request for information from a data protection authority. This indicates that Google's internal review processes - both prior to the initiation of the project to collect data about wireless access points and after its launch - were not adequate to discover that the software would be collecting payload data, which was not necessary to fulfill the project's business purpose."[317] In April 2012, a notice of the Federal Communications Commission (FCC)[318] was made public, from which it became clear that Google simply had been lying the entire time. An engineer had "deliberately written"[319] the code to collect payload data and

---

[312] Sayer 2010.

[313] See: <http://googlepolicyeurope.blogspot.com/2010/04/data-collected-by-google-cars.html> (last accessed June 28, 2012).

[314] See: <http://googleblog.blogspot.com/2010/05/wifi-data-collection-update.html> (last accessed June 28, 2012).

[315] See: <http://googleblog.blogspot.com/2010/05/wifi-data-collection-update.html> (last accessed June 28, 2012).

[316] Stroz Friedberg 2010.

[317] Federal Trade Commission 2010a.

[318] Federal Communications Commission, Notice of apparent liability for forfeiture, DA 12-592, April 13, 2012, available at: <http://www.scribd.com/fullscreen/91652398> (last accessed June 28, 2012).

[319] Page 10 of the Notice.

had informed numerous people within Google, in particular the StreetView project leaders and all the members of the StreetView team knew.[320] Even though this directly contradicts all earlier statements from Google, there was no condemnation of the company for the facts for which they came under investigations. The only consequence was that Google had been notified of apparent liability for forfeiture "for willfully and repeatedly violating an Enforcement Bureau directive to respond to a letter of inquiry."[321] Google simply lied, but the only consequence of this is that the FCC has stated that Google did not cooperate well. Thus, the FCC does not take proper action on this clear violation of privacy rights of individuals.

It is clear that Google can collect enormous amounts of data on individual users. These data are related to different web services provided by Google, but can be combined. The idea that individuals only have one identity which is applicable to the entire web is reflected by Google's new privacy policy, which came into effect on March 1st 2012.

4.2.1. Google Privacy Policy: one policy for the entire web

In 2012, Google took a new step concerning the privacy of internet users. Due to the diverse set of services and applications provided by Google, all with their own privacy policies, the way Google handles personal data of internet users had become very opaque. Google wanted to solve this problem by streamlining and simplifying its privacy policies. Google did so by releasing a new privacy policy: one single policy for all Google web services. This new policy was announced on January 24th and would enter into force on March 1st.

The new policy appeared to conflict with European data protection legislation on several points and, despite of the fact that Google publicly announced that the introduction of the new policy took place after extensively pre-briefing of the data protection authorities, there had hardly been any opportunity for the authorities to access the policy before the public release.[322] In particular, the CNIL[323] indicated that the new policy did not comply with the information obligations of Articles 10 and 11 of Directive 95/46/EC, and, moreover,

---

[320] Page 15 of the Notice.
[321] Page 23 of the Notice.
[322] Letter of the CNIL on behalf of the Article 29 Working Party and European Data Protection Authorities to Google, 27 February 2012. Online available at: <http://www.cnil.fr/fileadmin/documents/en/Courrier_Google_CE121115_27-02-2012-EN.pdf> (last accessed June 28, 2012).
[323] La Commission nationale de l'informatique et des libertés (CNIL) is the French Data Protection Authority.

"rather than promoting transparency, the terms of the new policy and the fact that Google claims publicly that it will combine data across services raises fears about Google's actual practices."[324] What data is combined between which services and for what purposes is extremely difficult to understand, even for privacy professionals.

The CNIL has requested Google to postpone the introduction of the new policy until the authorities had had the time to investigate the implications of the new policy. However, Google refused and launched the policy as of March 1st, 2012. The CNIL has sent a detailed questionnaire[325] to Google, including 69 questions on the new policy, and asked for answers until April 5th. The first response by Google only provided answers to a few questions, but on April 20th the response was updated and included the answers to the remaining questions.[326] The answers are not really satisfying and leave open a lot of issues. Nevertheless, some things have become clear already, including the basics of combining data by Google across services. When a user is logged in, Google calls this an authenticated user, whereas a logged out user is in a non-authenticated state. For authenticated users, data are combined across services, such as Search, Maps, YouTube and News. However, logging out does not make a real difference, since then still data are combined, albeit not based on the login status, but based on cookie identifiers.[327]

Since the introduction of the new policy, Google also automatically combines subscriptions for their users. An individual can choose to create a Gmail account for sending emails. The creation of such an account can also be necessary for the use of a mobile device based on the Android platform. Android is an operating system from Google, which is used on most smart phones and tablet computers, except those from Apple.[328] Applications can be downloaded and installed on the device with the use of the Gmail account. The purposes are clear. However, the creation of a Gmail account now implies a combined subscription. This can be derived from one of the first email messages that will be delivered to the newly created account, which welcomes the user to Google+, the SNS hosted by Google. The subscription to Google+ is not what the individual wanted to achieve and is not what the

[324] Letter of the CNIL on behalf of the Article 29 Working Party and European Data Protection Authorities to Google, 27 February 2012. Online available at: <http://www.cnil.fr/fileadmin/documents/en/Courrier_Google_CE121115_27-02-2012-EN.pdf> (last accessed June 28, 2012).
[325] Available at: <http://www.cnil.fr/fileadmin/documents/La_CNIL/actualite/questionnaire_to_Google-2012-03-16.pdf> (last accessed June 28, 2012).
[326] Available at: <https://docs.google.com/file/d/0B8syaai6SSfiSUhFMHVpMmhFUG8/edit?pli=1> (last accessed June 28, 2012).
[327] See the answer to question 29.
[328] Apple has its own operating system, which is used for iPhones and iPads: iOS.

142

individual consented to either. Moreover, the practice is not mentioned in the Policy of Google, so the individual cannot even be aware of this beforehand.

4.3. The combination of online and offline data[329]

While in a web context, most of the decisions taken based on digital personae or profiles concern the displaying of advertisements and the presentation of offers, digital personae can also be used in other commercial contexts for different purposes. An important point of attention in relation to contexts that are not essentially web based, is that digital personae can be built up from combined online and offline sources. A basic profile is enriched with other data that were not provided by the concerned individual, at least not to the specific party with whom the actual interaction takes place.

4.3.1. Credit rating agencies

A case in point concerns credit rating agencies. These agencies are frequently used by banks and retail companies in order to decide whether someone will receive a loan or mortgage. The exact workings of credit rating agencies are not always transparent, so problem may occur when the individual wants to know why a certain loan has been denied. An individual, who visits a store and wants to buy something, but not directly pay the full price, can be affected by this. It is a common practice that expensive products, such as cars or furniture, are bought with a loan. Dealers of the products function as an intermediary between the loan provider and the customer. The customer has to identify himself and the dealer then checks whether a loan is granted. The decision to grant the loan or not is made instantly, based on the records of the credit provider. Usually, this credit provider (automatically) consults a credit rating agency to check past payment performances of the customer. If there is too much risk of not receiving the money back, the loan will not be granted. The exact reason, however, is not communicated to the dealer. Normally, he only receives a 'yes' or a 'no' or a grade. A grade leaves the decision to the dealer, which integrates some human intervention in the decision making process.[330] However, a grade below a certain level will always lead to a decline of the loan. This can even be based on internal guidelines of the company.[331]

---

[329] The information in this section is gathered from talks and 6 semi-structured qualitative interviews with representatives from the credit rating and debt analysis industry, from an insurance company, and software developers and providers specialized in on-the-fly web personalization. The interviewees expressed their wishes to remain anonymous.

[330] This is the approach taken by Stichting PPS (Organization for the Prevention of Problematic Debts) in the Netherlands.

[331] Similar practices occured in relation to mobile phone subscriptions. See Wishaw 2000, p. 43.

In cases where an individual is routinely singled out, based on a profile, he may want to challenge the profile. Nevertheless, "there appears to be no way to do so unless the profile is revealed."[332] This practice also implies that the dealer cannot explain why a certain loan has or has not been granted. The customer can fight the decision, but the outcomes of the algorithm that made the decision are not stored and cannot always be reproduced.

While traditionally credit records were based on past performances only, such as other loans, debts, or delayed payments, a relatively new practice is the combination of online and offline sources and tracking technologies to take decisions. These decisions can even be taken 'on the fly'. Specialized companies, such as Experian, create detailed profiles at an individual or household level. These profiles are built up on the basis of numerous sources. These sources not only concern credit history, but also demographic data, information about employment, income, and interests. Other companies can obtain access to the databases of Experian and use this information for their own purposes. One important sector using this information is the banking and insurances sector.

4.3.2. Tracking and profiling by banks and insurance companies

Banks and insurance companies also make use of digital personae to take decisions, for instance on whether they grant a loan or whether someone is refused an insurance. The creation or obtainment of these digital personae can take different forms. Since banks and insurance companies do not have a position as advertising provider or other functionalities which enables them to monitor web activity, as is the case with Facebook and Google, they have to obtain their information from other parties or sources. Essentially, there are two options to do this: one is to cooperate with a technological partner that can do the tracking and monitoring, the other is to obtain offline information about individuals.

Cooperation with a technical partner can help companies to monitor browsing behavior of individuals. The use of Google analytics may be helpful in displaying targeted advertisements to individuals that have previously visited the company website next to, for instance, a YouTube video. Google can recognize the web user and make the connection. It is, however, also possible to monitor visitors' behavior on the specific company website and to combine this with information concerning the channel via which the visitor reached the site (direct URL, search engine) and what site the visitor goes to when leaving the company website. This kind of side-information is even used to decide on what content is displayed on a company website and in

---

[332] Solove 2011, p. 194.

what form. An often used way of collecting information on the browsing track an individual followed is by looking at the URL[333] and the referrer headers that are received by the website owner at the moment the individual visits a webpage.

As indicated, another type of information concerns the type of content via which an individual accesses a website. This type of information can be labeled as 'betraying elements'. For instance, an advertisement with an image of a good looking woman will be clicked more by men than by women. The information that can be analyzed can be divided into three types: explicit, organic, and implicit information. Explicit information can be found in the URL, which shows the path an individual took along a website. Other explicit information concerns the type of expression on which the individual clicked. Whether this was a piece of text (with title, content, and tags), an image, a banner, or a clear URL discloses information about the type of internet user the individual is. Organic information relates to the order and time of visits to a website and whether a visitor is a returning visitor or not. The last category, implicit information, is formed by the conclusions that are drawn from the explicit and organic information. This is the analytic part where products are matched to interests and where the individual is labeled as a specific type of customer.

Strategically placing advertisements can also provide information, even before the individual enters the website. For instance, when advertising on Facebook, specific categories of individuals can be indicated that should receive the advertisement (for instance, men of age 25-35). Facebook can target these individuals based on their profile information. An individual who visits a company website, because he clicked on such an advertisement, thus, certainly belongs to that category. The link, therewith, confirms the profile of the visitor.

Based on the combined information, the content of the visited website is tailored to the individual visitor. This can be done in real-time, where third party companies function as intermediaries and collect, combine, and apply the information. The tailoring of the website concerns the way content is displayed (text, images), but also the content itself. The presentation of the content can highly influence how the individual navigates over the website and what information receives the most attention. With regard to the content itself, specific products or serviced can be displayed and others can be left

---

[333] URLs can contain lots of information, sometimes, next to the web page, even including the name, postal code and bank account number of the individual visitor. If this information is accessible by third parties, very valuable personal information is inadvertently shared.

out. Finding alternatives is made difficult in this way. At the moment, there are no examples of companies that completely block the opportunity to find alternative products on their website, but this may be very well possible in the (near) future. Moreover, finding alternatives is made difficult and requires skills of the individual to cleverly navigate through the website. Options are implicitly limited, which can have important effects when it concerns, for instance, insurances. In the Netherlands, health insurance companies are obliged to offer basic insurance, but additional packages can be refused and this is to a large extent automated by this kind of web 'personalization'.

With the help of third parties who are able to combine online information with offline information, individuals can be identified even when they are not logged on to the website of, for instance, their bank or insurance company. Recognition can be based on the IP address, but via the third party several cookies can be identified and establish the link to the offline individual. Combining information offers new opportunities. It is, however, heavily debated whether it is allowed to enrich online information with offline data sets[334], for instance, when the individual has enabled DoNotTrack (DNT). The expressed wish not to be tracked may be respected, but still, additional information may be gathered from offline sources in order to extend the digital persona of a specific individual. The wish not to be tracked, however, indicates that the individual does not want to have an extensive profile built of his behavior and whereabouts. Doing so based on offline sources can, thus, be seen as disrespecting the wish of the individual. The individual is provided with an option, which is not a real choice. By analogy, in the context of cookie tracking, deleted cookies are respawned. Users "cannot fairly be said to have notice of these activities" and, "because [the cookies] are resistant to blocking, they rob consumers of choice."[335] Ultimately, the practices deny the opportunities for individuals to exercise autonomy.[336]

4.3.3. The shift from commercial contexts to administrative and law enforcement contexts

Finally, even though this study focuses on the commercial context, there is a trend towards governments increasingly accessing and using the information gathered by commercial companies. Profiles and digital personae created in

---

[334] As is, for instance, done by MindShare: <http://www.mindshareworld.com/who-we-are/news/@Mindshare_Launches_Core>, last visited 6 October 2012. In the case of MindShare, the link between cookies is provided by 24/7 Media. Companies in the Netherlands make the combination via Google (with a Google Analytics subscription) and Omniture.

[335] Hoofnagle a.o. 2012, p. 291.

[336] Hoofnagle a.o. 2012, p. 274.

the commercial context, including the analysis of the data and the attached conclusions, thus, also become input in the public administration and law enforcement sector.[337] A concrete example, with significant consequences, is the case where an individual can be registered in an administration of incidents related to criminal activities. A woman was registered because of suspicious activities on her bank account. There was a suspicion of fraud, but there has never been a conviction. Nevertheless, the woman's record can be kept for a maximum of 8 years. The register is consulted by all kinds of financial services, which are likely to refuse any service to the woman.[338]

Also decisions to exclude individuals from options for insurance, such as additional health insurance packages, or the rejection of insurance claims can have a severe impact. The lacking opportunity for an individual to properly insure himself may result in the absence of the financial means to undergo proper health care. A decision to exclude an individual is, thus, to a certain extent also a decision on the value of providing the opportunity for proper health care services. The question that arises is whether specific individuals are less worthy to be insured properly. Indirectly, these decisions may indicate that certain individuals have less human dignity as an intrinsic value.

5. Implications of digital persona and profile creation and use

The three examples discussed above show how data are collected and what kind of data it concerns. The collected data together form digital personae. In the case of Facebook, the digital persona can take different forms. Individuals who become a member of Facebook share information by adding this to their personal profile page. The personal profile is initially created by the individual himself and the information in the profile has been shared by this individual. This information is enriched with information derived from friends of the member, but also information obtained via address books of email accounts. Moreover, information concerning browsing behavior is collected and added to the digital persona. A digital persona in the form of a Facebook profile, thus, starts as a projected digital persona and almost directly becomes a hybrid digital persona.

---

[337] EDPS 2010, The Surveillance Policy in Europe, today and tomorrow. Speech by G. Buttarelli, Assistant Supervisor EDPS, at the Conference for the 30th Anniversary of the CRID, Namur 20-22 January 2010.

[338] See <http://www.solv.nl/weblog/veroordeling-door-strafrechter-niet-vereist-voor-opname-in-incidentenregister/18989>, last visited 6 October 2012, and Court The Hague, 31 May 2012, 407012 / HA RK 11-691, LJN: BX1743.

For individuals who are not a member of Facebook, a digital persona can be created as well. This digital persona mainly consists of browsing behavior information. Nevertheless, additional details can be collected when members of Facebook share information about other individuals or initiate Friend requests. When the invited individual clicks on the link in the invitation, the email address is connected to the tracking cookies and, thus, the browsing behavior of the individual. A digital persona concerning an individual who is not a Facebook member is, thus, usually an imposed digital persona.

In relation to Google, a digital persona usually consists of accumulated data collected from the (intended) interaction between the individual and one of Google's services. However, the individual can influence the contents of the digital persona by creating a Google account and adjusting preferences. Obviously, the consequence of this is that the individual actively identifies himself and, by signing up for the service, implicitly accepts the General Terms and Conditions of Google, which include giving consent for the processing of personal data. Moreover, signing up implies consenting to more services and processing than intended and it cannot be derived from the Terms what the exact scope of the consent is. The validity of this form of obtaining consent is, thus, questionable. This will be discussed more elaborately in Chapter 6 of this study.

Facebook and Google apparently have opposite approaches to online identity. Facebook facilitates the construction of an identity on its platform and encourages members to use this identity for other web services as well. In contrast, Google builds an identity composed of information obtained from the use of various web services by the individual. The common ground in both approaches is the idea that an individual has only one single identity which is applicable to every context. Both Google and Facebook have access to numerous digital personae. There may, however, also be cases where the individual cannot (yet) be identified, but is only recognized based on a cookie identifier. In particular, this is the case for users who do not have an account to access the services. In these cases, the data sets that are created are profiles. These profiles can also be used to influence individuals and to adjust web content.

In the case of Facebook as well as Google, the information of which the digital persona consists is used for purposes of selecting and advertising. Based on the data, the individual will be excluded from certain information, because information provided is mostly reconfirming earlier (alleged) preferences. Diverging content is filtered as irrelevant for the specific individual. Pariser calls this the 'Filter Bubble'.[339] The sorting of individuals into categories can

---

[339] Pariser 2011.

have a negative impact on privacy, and, even worse, monitoring and profiling can become a matter of social justice.[340]

Another approach to targeting individuals was shown in the example of combining online and offline data and the personalization of web content. The combination of data sources inevitably leads to problems in relation to contextual integrity. Not only online contexts, but also offline contexts are becoming intermingled and the individual cannot reasonably be expected to maintain control. Moreover, offline information becomes a decisive factor in what information is available online for a specific individual.

The technical means for individuals to prevent being monitored are limited and are fairly easy for companies to circumvent. Cookies can be blocked, but this may also negatively influence the performances of websites. Cookies are still a main factor in following individual users and an important tool to create profiles. Unfortunately, it seems that there is no real escape possible due to technological developments, which include, for instance, evercookies,[341] flash cookies[342] and HTTP cookie respawning.[343] Another problem is the circumvention of technological counter-measures, such as Google bypassing privacy settings of Safari browser users[344] and misuse of P3P policies by providing erroneous machine-readable policies[345] or by issuing third party tracking cookies as response to requests for the P3P policy of a website.[346]

However, more is going on. Over the last couple of years the use of SNS has increased enormously. The practice in these SNS is a good example of how a policy can lead to conflicting outcomes. It appeared that lots of personal information is disclosed on SNS and that people wanted to have an opportunity to switch to another SNS. Switching should not be too difficult and SNS implemented a system for the transfer of data between sites. As in other domains, interoperability of identities became a key aspect. Now, most

---

[340] Lyon 2006, p. 13.

[341] Evercookies are cookies that can hardly be deleted due to backup cookies and respawning: <http://samy.pl/evercookie/> (last accessed June 20, 2012).

[342] Soltani, Canty, Mayo, Thomas & Hoofnagle 2009; Ayenson, Wambach, Soltani, Good & Hoofnagle 2011.

[343] McDonald & Cranor 2011.

[344] Angwin 2012.

[345] Leon, Cranor, McDonald & McGuire 2010.

[346] This finding came out of my own (unpublished) research (on file with the author). The use of a privacy enhancing tool which maps third party content on websites and their privacy policies resulted on websites with a Facebook Like-button in a HTTP response from Facebook stating that Facebook did not have a P3P policy and including a tracking cookie which was then installed on the user's computer. My findings date from 23 November 2011 and the practice ('bug') has been fixed by Facebook after I reported the issue to the Facebook WhiteHat Program and email contact with Facebook engineers.

SNS include an option to import friends from other SNS accounts or from address books in mail accounts. This makes it easier to switch to another SNS without having to completely fill a new profile and making a new friend list. However, SNS also try to encourage users to import their address books and other data to integrate different services. Not switching, but combining data to come to a more complete profile is the aim. As a result, individuals are more and more combining and aggregating data themselves. The use of these data, and therewith the consequences, are often unclear. However, technically the users give their consent for the data processing.

Even when individuals are aware and careful in sharing or connecting their personal data, it seems inevitable to be tracked and traced in some way. An individual can have different partial identities related to different contexts. In order to keep these contexts separated, for each partial identity another avatar can be created. So, different user names and passwords are means to keep different data sets unlinkable. However, even then third party cookies or browser fingerprinting can lead to a connection. When separated data sets are combined the contexts to which the data belong collapse.

The collection of data and creation of digital personae and profiles is, to a large extent, meant to facilitate targeted advertisements. The more data are collected, the more accurate the representations can be. There are advertisement companies that function as intermediaries between the advertisers and the individual web users. In the UK, Xaxis claims to have built a database of individual profiles of over 500 million internet users across the world. The quality promised by the company is "an unprecedented level of precision" and "zero waste", with only people interested in the product seeing the advertisements.[347] It would, therefore, be expected that the quality of the presented advertisements is relatively high. Nevertheless, in practice, this seems not to be the case. Advertisements on Facebook show dating opportunities to people in a relationship, offer outings for hobbies the individual does not have, and credit card offers because Facebook friends 'Like' the credit card company.[348] This appears not to match with the interests of the targeted individual, so even though data collection is massive, the targeting still seems to be of low quality. Other forms of advertising are often experienced as annoying. For instance, looking at a pair of shoes on a webpage may result in seeing these shoes displayed on your screen over and over again, for days.

Facebook is one of the biggest companies involved in online targeted

---

[347] Foley 2011.
[348] D. Searls. After Facebook Fails. Doc Searls Weblog, 23 May 2012. Online available at: <http://blogs.law.harvard.edu/doc/2012/05/23/after-facebook-fails/> (last accessed June 22, 2012).

advertising. The data used for the targeting are collected via the Facebook 'Open Graph', which is a technical system that offers third party website functionalities to integrate with Facebook. Content on third party websites is real-time personalized based on Facebook content, such as Friends who liked a webpage. Facebook, on its turn, can distract all the data in a simple format which makes it readily for input in the data processing.[349] Due to the enormous web coverage Facebook is getting, Google is becoming nervous because of the competition it brings. Nevertheless, Google's ads are far better targeted, because they relate to the exact thing an individual is searching for at the moment the advertisement is displayed; something which is not the case on Facebook.[350] In the case of Facebook, the concerns in relation to targeted advertisements may, thus, be a bit overrated. In addition, Facebook uses privacy preserving technologies towards the users of its targeted advertisement system. For instance, in the reports on audience reach, Facebook uses differential privacy technologies, which means that "a database system [...] behaves similarly whether or not any particular individual is represented in the database, effectively producing anonymity."[351] A third party that receives a report from Facebook cannot see whether an individual to which an advertisement was displayed is identified or not.

Whilst the above may suggest that the impact of the use of digital personae for targeted advertising is relatively small, there definitely are concerns. First, it is important to distinguish between two separate parts of the targeted advertising system: the data collection and mining, and the displaying of advertisements. The fact that the advertisements are not very well targeted does not mean that there is not much personal data collected. Second, the practice of targeting seems to lead to more revenues. This is why the recent developments in relation to the duty to obtain prior informed consent before tracking cookies are placed have shown lots of worries from the advertising landscape.[352] Even though the targeting is of low quality, the revenues generated via targeted advertisements are still higher than without this targeting. Moreover, there has been quite some outrage as a response to Microsoft's announcement that in the new version of Internet Explorer the DoNotTrack feature will be enabled by default.[353] Advertisers are afraid that

---

[349] Metz 2012.

[350] M. Somers. Facebook Advertising is Fool's Gold. Behind Companies, 29 May 2012. Online available at: <http://behindcompanies.com/2012/05/facebook-fools-gold/> (last accessed June 28, 2012).

[351] Chin & Klinefelter 2012.

[352] S. Boone. EU Cookie Law Could Be the Death of Digital. AdAge Digital, 24 May 2012. Online available at: <http://adage.com/article/digitalnext/online-privacy-eu-cookie-law-death-digital/234950/> (last accessed June 22, 2012).

[353] M. Santos. Microsoft sets 'Do Not Track' as Default on IE 10: Ruffles feathers.

they will not earn as much money as with targeted advertisements and warn for the internet becoming too expensive to maintain.[354]

The targeting of ads can only be done if (extensive) data sets are created at an individual level. Regardless of whether these data sets are digital personae or profiles, the collection of the data can infringe informational self-determination and contextual integrity. As was shown by the case study of insurance companies and banks adjusting their offers based on a combination of online and offline information, the implications for the individual can be more severe when he is identified, so when the data set is considered a digital persona. The increased difficulty to find certain information can have discriminatory effects. In particular, since it is not clear that an individual is excluded from certain information, or at least has to take additional efforts to find it, the individual will usually not find the information. The practices can, thus, steer behavior and limit opportunities at an individual level.

The fact that there is a very limited number of companies that is able to influence web content on a large scale also implies that the profiles and digital personae can be applied on a very broad scale. The lack of competition limits the opportunities to choose for an alternative service, but also has the result that many services will make use of the same big company as a provider of information concerning individuals. Google and Facebook have a very powerful position on the internet and many other services use the information these two companies have to base their decisions on. Individuals become largely dependent on a few companies, without having appropriate control over the data collection and without having good options to keep contexts separated. The information owned by these companies becomes decisive and the individual is limited in its free construction of an identity and in its freedom to pursue its own wishes and desires. Individual autonomy is affected and, in cases where structural exclusion has the effect of (indirect) discrimination, dignity is affected.

From the examples given above, it has become clear that the creation and use of digital personae has severe implications for individuals. In particular, conflicts occur with regard to respect for informational self-determination, contextual integrity, identity, and privacy. Ultimately, there is an impact

---

EnGadget, 1 June 2012. Online available at: <http://www.engadget.com/2012/06/01/do-not-track-is-default-on-ie10/> (last accessed June 22, 2012).

[354] Digital Advertising Alliance (DAA). Digital Advertising Alliance (DAA) Comments on Microsoft Decision to Embed Do Not Track in IE 10 Set "on" by Default. Press Release 31 May 2012. Online available at: <http://www.businesswire.com/news/home/20120531006914/en/Digital-Advertising-Alliance-DAA-Comments-Microsoft-Decision> (last accessed June 22, 2012).

on individual autonomy and human dignity. The exact implications will be described in the next chapter.

Chapter 6
Shortcomings in Data Protection Regulation: The Practical Level

1. Introduction

In the foregoing chapters, the main rights and values that need to be respected in relation to human dignity have been described and examples have been given of the creation and use of digital personae in practice. In this chapter, these findings will be combined by looking at the protection offered by the Data Protection Directive (DPD) and the extent to which digital personae are covered by the DPD regime. Moreover, profiles, as data sets that may become digital personae, will be discussed. Subsequently, the findings will be connected to the principles of privacy, autonomy, and identity in order to assess whether the DPD offers sufficient protection to ultimately protect human dignity and related values of the individual.

The relation between digital personae and profiles, as well as the types of identifiers discussed in chapter 2 of this study, will be at the core of this chapter. The problems that will be described are strongly related to identification and identifiablity and the applicability of the DPD to different data sets. Moreover, even in cases where the DPD is applicable specific problems appear to remain.

In this chapter, first the digital persona will be discussed in view of the DPD (section 2). This will provide the background for an analysis of shortcomings in data protection regulation. Also the requirements and rights from the DPD will be discussed. Then, in section 3, the applicability of the DPD to profiles will be assessed. In particular, the concept of identifiability will be discussed here, because this is essential in making the distinction between digital personae and profiles. In order to assess identifiability, all means likely reasonably to be used by the data controller or any other person have to be taken into account. Depending on the means available to someone who has access to a data set, identification of an individual is more or less likely. This will be the subject of section 4 of this chapter.

In section 5, problems occurring when the DPD is applicable to data processing will be described. These problems will be related to the main rights and values to be protected in section 6. Finally, in section 7, the exact problem of this study will be defined.

2. Digital personae in view of the DPD

In the information society, numerous data sets are created. These data sets are sometimes necessary for executing a process and are sometimes unintended. Most of the times the creation of data sets is intentional and serves a specific goal. Data sets can take several forms, depending on the technical process involved and the functionalities as desired by the party who collects or creates the data. Not all data sets are digital personae; only data sets that form a representation of an individual natural person and that can be linked to the represented individual are. The exact way of linking the data set to the individual is not the most important aspect, but the fact that a link can be made and that an individual can be affected by decisions taken based on the digital representation is.

This gave rise in Chapter 3 to the following definition:

A digital persona is a digital representation of a real-world individual, which can be connected to this real-world individual and includes a sufficient amount of (relevant) data to serve as a proxy for the individual within the context and for the purpose(s) of its use.

In this definition, the connection between the real-world individual and the digital persona was stressed, as well as the representational function of the data set. Representation is connected to context and purpose of the digital persona, which emphasizes the fact that data in the representation are context-bound and the creation of the digital persona is related to an intended purpose or purposes. The amount of data needed for the representation depends on the context and purpose of the intended use of the digital persona. However, in the previous chapters it has also become clear that the purpose is not always present before the creation of the digital persona is taking place. Data can also be collected to build a profile of which the possible application is not foreseen yet.

In the following sub-sections, digital personae will be discussed in view of the DPD. The DPD has not been written with the concept of digital personae in mind and at the time of drafting many opportunities and risks brought by technological developments concerning data processing were unforeseen.

2.1. Identified or identifiable

A first question that needs to be addressed is whether the DPD is applicable to digital personae. In order to assess this applicability, it is necessary to look at the concept of personal data. The qualification of data as personal is decisive in whether the DPD is applicable to the processing of the data.

The concept of personal data is defined in Article 2(a) of the DPD as "any information relating to an identified or identifiable natural person ('data subject'); an identifiable person is one who can be identified, directly or indirectly, in particular by reference to an identification number or to one or more factors specific to his physical, physiological, mental, economic, cultural or social identity." In Chapter 4, identifiability was briefly discussed on the basis of the Article 29 Working Party Opinion on the concept of personal data.[355] The Working Party adopts a broad interpretation of personal data. In particular, with regard to identifiability of a person, the Working Party took the ability to 'single out an individual in a group' as the main criterion. This means that it is not necessary to have an individual's name. Merely the indication to what individual in a group data relate is enough to qualify the data as personal.

Identification, as understood by the Article 29 Working Party, is not taking place when data from a group profile are applied to a number of individuals. In order to qualify the data as personal data, they have to be individualized; the data have to relate to an identified or identifiable individual. Applying the general characteristics of a group to a number of individuals can be compared to the traditional practice of targeting an audience for advertisements or selecting a group of people who have to pay a higher insurance premium, based on postal code and the information that in most cases applies to the people who live in a certain area.[356] However, in contrast with the offline practice of postal code selection, in online environments the link between the individual and the selection may be less clear to the individual.[357] Basically, it is more difficult for the individual to know the other people in the group. It may even be unclear that the selection concerns a group at all. Nevertheless, the data remain data concerning a group of individuals, a group profile. Adding an R-identifier, such as a cookie, to recognize an individual within the group makes the profile an individual profile.[358]

The crucial distinction between individual profiles and digital personae relates to the identifiers that can be part of the data set. As was indicated in Chapter 2 of this study, while profiles may contain an R-identifier (or

---

[355] Article 29 Working Party 2007.
[356] The process of postal code differentiation is often even unlawful, for instance when this has the effect of indirect discrimination based on race. See: Factsheet 'Postcodediscriminatie' 2009/2, Bureau Discriminatiezaken Hollands Midden en Haaglanden, online available at: <http://www.discriminatiezaken.nl/doc/Factsheet%20postcodediscriminatie.pdf>.
[357] With reference to Stepanek 2000, Lyon describes the shift from traditional postal code selection, called 'redlining', to 'weblining' through geo-demographic discrimination: Lyon 2007, p. 102.
[358] Leenes 2008. See also Chapter 2 section 4.3.

sometimes no identifier at all), digital personae by definition contain an L-identifier.[359] This means that in the case of digital personae the individual can be identified by looking up identifying data related to the L-identifier. For instance, concerning IP addresses, the Article 29 Working Party is of the opinion that for ISPs these are in most cases personal data - they are L-identifiers -, since the necessary data of the user(s) of the IP address will be available.[360] So, "unless the Internet Service Provider is in a position to distinguish with absolute certainty that the data correspond to users that cannot be identified, it will have to treat all IP information as personal data, to be on the safe side."[361] Equal application of these considerations is present for search engine operators.[362] Commercial companies, however, often state that IP addresses are not personal data, because it is not known to them who the individual behind the IP address is; it is an address of a device and this device may be used by several individuals. In these cases, the IP address is an R-identifier, while for ISPs it is an L-identifier[363] and the data set is a digital persona. Nevertheless, it has to be taken into account that an IP address as an R-identifier facilitates the linking of data as belonging to the same person. An accumulated set of data, constructed in this manner, may contain information that, in combination, allows for identification.[364]

Another example is the account name of an individual with which he signs in to a web service connected to an individual subscription. This is, for example, the case when an individual has a health care insurance and can check or update his insurance information online via a web portal of the health care insurance provider. Signing in to the web portal can be based on the insurance number and a password. The insurance number is an L-identifier, since the insurance provider can look up the corresponding name of the insured individual. As an implication of the L-identifier, the data that constitute the digital persona relate to an identifiable natural person and, thus, qualify as personal data. Because digital personae consist of personal data, the DPD is applicable to the processing of digital personae. This also means that all the requirements for lawful processing of personal data and all safeguards for data subjects as provided by the DPD are applicable to the use of digital personae.

---

[359] Types of identifiers cf. Leenes 2008.
[360] Article 29 Working Party 2008b.
[361] Article 29 Working Party 2007.
[362] Article 29 Data Party 2008a.
[363] Note that the user information an ISP has usually identifies the subscription holder and not necessarily the specific user (or users) of the IP address. Using the IP address as an L-identifier may, thus, result in false connections between data set and individual. This is why for most purposes, ISPs will use IP addresses as R-identifiers and not as L-identifiers.
[364] This will be discussed in the context of quasi-identifiers (section 3.2 below).

2.2. Requirements from the DPD: data controllers

As was shown above, the DPD is applicable to the processing of digital personae, which means that any processing of these data, including mere collection or storage, has to be in accordance with the rules laid down in the Directive. There is a data controller, who is responsible for the processing of the data, and probably one or more processors of the data. The requirements of purpose binding, data minimization, and a legitimate ground for the processing have to be fulfilled and the information duties apply.

The processing must be for specified, explicit and legitimate purposes.[365] The data controller has to specify the purpose of the collection of the data beforehand and all further processing has to be in accordance with this purpose. A soon as another purpose incompatible with the initial purpose of the processing is at stake, the requirements have to be met again and there has to be a legitimate ground for the (new) processing. In line with the data minimization principle, the data must be adequate, relevant and not excessive in relation to the purposes for which they are processed.[366]

2.2.1. Grounds for legitimate data processing

As indicated, all data processing activities have to be based on a legitimate ground for the processing. The legitimate grounds for processing are mentioned in a limitative list in Article 7 of the DPD:
Member States shall provide that personal data may be processed only if:
(a) the data subject has unambiguously given his consent; or
(b) processing is necessary for the performance of a contract to which the data subject is party or in order to take steps at the request of the data subject prior to entering into a contract; or
(c) processing is necessary for compliance with a legal obligation to which the controller is subject; or
(d) processing is necessary in order to protect the vital interests of the data subject; or
(e) processing is necessary for the performance of a task carried out in the public interest or in the exercise of official authority vested in the controller or in a third party to whom the data are disclosed; or
(f) processing is necessary for the purposes of the legitimate interests pursued by the controller or by the third party or parties to whom the data are disclosed, except where such interests are overridden by the interests for fundamental rights and freedoms of the data subject which require protection under Article 1 (1).

---

[365] Article 6(1)b of the DPD.
[366] Article 6(1)c of the DPD and Preamble at 28.

The most prominent ground is the consent of the data subject. The reason for this is directly related to individual autonomy. Obviously, when there is consent, the data subject is aware of the data processing and has given his permission. However, the exact meaning of consent and in what circumstances consent can reasonably be considered to be given in an informed manner is debatable.[367] Obtaining consent provides the individual (data subject) with a certain degree of control over the processing that is taking place.

There are, however, two other grounds in the list that are of specific importance when it concerns legitimizing processing in light of the privacy of the individual.[368] These grounds are under (b) and (f) respectively. Under (b), the performance of a contract is mentioned as a ground for legitimate processing. Many services apply General Terms and Conditions which have to be accepted prior to using the service. The terms and conditions may contain several provisions concerning data collection, also in the light of improving the service. Depending on the service and what can be improved, data collection and, for instance, web monitoring can be very extensive. Many web services, including Facebook and Google, require users accept General Terms and Conditions in order to use the service. In the case of Google, this is done automatically, by stating that by using the service you agree to the Terms of Service of the company.[369] The 'acceptance' of the contract includes providing consent for several data processing activities that are not necessary for the contract itself. Simply visiting google.com, the homepage of the search engine, is considered to be using the service by Google, regardless of whether the individual actually enters a search term and asks for results by pressing 'search'. Facebook requires users to agree to the Terms when signing up. Clicking 'Sign up' implies that you agree to

---

[367] See below, section 6.

[368] The grounds under d and e are not considered problematic by me, since they are either directly in the interest of the individual himself (vital interest, such as medical emergencies) or in the public interest (such as municipal administrations). Even though the public interest may seriously conflict with individual autonomy, this ground has been accepted in most legal documents, including the ECHR. Not accepting this ground as an exception to consent of the individual would impose too heavy restrictions on the room to maneuver for public authorities in urgent cases for national health or safety. Obviously, in less urgent cases, the performance of a task in the public interest can have an impact on individual autonomy as well, but, though relevant, these tasks are specifically related to government-citizen relationships, which are out of the scope of this study. Under c, the processing is based on a legal obligation (such as taxation purposes) and can be considered to be based on a democratic legal process.

[369] This is even included in the Terms of Service itself, as "By using our Services, you are agreeing to these terms." See: <http://www.google.com/intl/en/policies/terms/>, last modified March 1st 2012. The use of the service is supposed to be a declaration of the will to enter into a contract for using the service.

the Terms.[370] For both companies, the terms include several provisions on the collection and processing of personal data. Moreover, it is not possible not to agree with the Terms as used by these companies, except by leaving the site.[371] There is no need to actively tick a box stating that you agree to the Terms and there is no button to decline. Active buttons indicating 'agree' or ticking a box is, however, common practice when signing up for services on the internet. However, also in these cases, the user is forced to accept the Terms, because not accepting the Terms means no access to the service. The choice is therewith not a choice to accept the Terms, but a choice to access the service. Signing up for a service, or using a service, implies that a contract is established between the service provider and the individual. When the establishment of the contract includes General Terms and Conditions, these become part of the contract. Moreover, agreeing on the Terms can be explained as giving consent for the practices indicated in these Terms. The way Google and Facebook obtain agreement of the user to the General Terms and Conditions is legally not unproblematic. It is often not clear that a contract is entered,[372] and provisions in the terms allowing for unilateral modification will possibly not result in a valid contract.[373] Entering into a contract requires that the party who offers a service, i.e. Google or Facebook, provides clear information about what the service entails and, if General Terms and Conditions apply, what these terms are. The mere presence of a hyperlink to the terms does not provide certainty about the user accepting these and, thus, making them become part of the contract.[374] Verhelst analyses the legal possibility of entering into a contract concerning the processing of personal data and, based on discussion of the viewpoints of Cuijpers[375] and Purtova,[376] concludes that the conclusion of such a contract is allowed as long as there is no conflict with the minimum level of protection as provided for by the DPD.[377] When the information obligations are not met, as seems to be the case with Google and Facebook, this minimum level of protection is absent. However, in the US, Courts are generally accepting and enforcing 'browsewrap' contracts, sometimes even based on the assumption that "people should generally be aware that TOS exist and therefore everyone has 'constructive' notice that the terms are there

---

[370] See: <www.facebook.com>.
[371] Nevertheless, in the case of Google the visit to the homepage already implied acceptance of the Terms.
[372] Preston & McCann 2011, p. 22.
[373] In this respect, a solution is to explicitly ask for a user to agree again when the Terms will be modified. For instance, Apple iTunes always provides an overview of the changes to the Terms of its services and asks for the user's consent.
[374] Van Esch 2004, p. 182.
[375] Cuijpers 2007.
[376] Purtova 2011.
[377] Verhelst 2012, p. 72.

somewhere."[378] Obviously, this does not meet the requirement of clear and prior information from the DPD. The requirement also has to be met by companies from outside the EU that offer services to EU citizens by means of equipment on the EU territory.[379] Not meeting the requirement implies that the data controller has not fulfilled his information duties from the DPD.

Under (f), the legitimate interest of the controller or of third parties who receive the data is provided as a ground for legitimate processing if this interest prevails over the privacy interest of the data subject. This ground for processing data is a rest category and can be used in numerous cases. The interest of the data controller can be almost anything. For instance, for advertising companies who collect data as third parties, the interest may be completely commercial. They want to earn money and they can earn more money if they use targeted advertisements, so it is in their legitimate interest to process personal data to achieve that extra benefit.

In practice, it is not that difficult to bring forward a legitimate interest for the processing of personal data. A commercial business interest (making money) is recognized as a legitimate interest. This implies that the grounds for legitimate processing can have a broad reach and legitimize most data processing. This is also what was allowed for by the DPD. Personal data and the rights of the data subject have to be protected, but the DPD clearly facilitates the processing of personal data because of economic incentives. The weighing of interests is, thus, more a safeguard on paper than in practice, since in practice the data controller weighs the interests and is likely to have their own (commercial) interests prevail. Even more, a notification to the data protection authorities of a company that processes personal data is sufficient to have the processing approved. There is no prior check by the authorities on whether the processing is legitimate and certainly no active weighing of the interests at stake. As a result, as long as a company has a legitimate interest and can argue that this interest prevails[380] over the privacy interests of the individuals concerning whom the company processes personal data ground (f) can be applied successfully.

---

[378] Preston & McCann 2011, p. 30.
[379] Cf. Article 4 of the DPD, which also applies when, for instance, "cookies or similar devices" are used to access the terminal equipment of a user: Information Commissioner's Office (ICO) on the new EU cookie law (e-Privacy Directive): <http://www.ico.gov.uk/for_organisations/privacy_and_electronic_communications/the_guide/cookies.aspx>, last accessed August 3, 2012.
[380] This can be contested by the data subject, assuming that the data subject is informed about the processing.

2.2.2. Information duties

With regard to the information duties of data controllers, there is a slight difference between the information that has to be provided when the data are obtained from the data subject (Art. 10 DPD) and the information that has to be provided when the data have been obtained otherwise (Art. 11 DPD). In both cases, the identity of the data controller and his representative (if any) has to be provided (Artt. 10 (a) and 11(a)), together with the purposes of the processing (Artt. 10(b) and 11(b)) and the recipients or categories of recipients of the data (Artt. 10(c) and 11(c)). Both articles sub (c) also indicate the duty to inform the data subject about his rights. The difference is under the remaining parts of subs (c). Article 10 requires information on whether replies to questions are mandatory or voluntary and what the consequences of failure to reply are. This indicates that there is an explicit request for data from the individual. Article 11 requires information about the categories of data concerned. This is something the individual cannot derive himself, since the data are not obtained from him. In all cases, the information has to be provided as far as necessary, and including additional information when appropriate, in order "to guarantee the fair processing of information in respect of the data subject." Since fair processing is the overarching concept determining what information has to be provided, the difference between the two articles is not that big, even though, in practice, determining what article is applicable may be problematic. While article 10 applies to situations where the data are obtained from the data subject and gives the example of a questionnaire, the question arises whether data relating to online behavior are obtained from the data subject. The data have not been obtained from a third party, but the individual is not as actively (and consciously) involved as in the case of filling out a web form. The problem here is that the distinction between the articles seems to be based on the source of the data, while conscious involvement of the individual in the data collection may appear to be a more proper distinction. Even though tracking of web behavior seems to concern data obtained from the individual, because there is no third party involved between the data controller and the individual, information about the categories of data that are processed is probably the most appropriate information to provide in combination with the identity of the controller and the purpose of the processing. The distinction between articles 10 and 11, thus, can be problematic when it has to be decided which of the two applies to a data processing practice. In any case, the data subject has to be informed properly about the data processing and the purposes of this processing.

In the context of online services, a common practice for the provision of this information is the use of general terms and conditions or a privacy policy.

Often, finding these terms or policies requires an active search[381] and huge amounts of reading efforts are expected from the data subject to understand the contents.[382] The data subject, thus, has to inform himself instead of being informed by the data controller. When there is no explicit contract[383] established, the individual may have a suspicion that data are processed, but is not informed by the data controller. In that case, data are shared with or collected by others who decide what data they want to receive. Digital collecting and processing of data makes it possible to collect more data and to analyze these data revealing more knowledge[384] than was available initially.

2.3. Rights from the DPD: data subjects

The duties described in the previous subsection apply when digital personae are processed. As a counterpart, the individual has rights that are important to stimulate data controllers to be compliant. Otherwise, individuals can have their data deleted, which results in the data controller having no legitimate opportunity left to process the data, unless a new legitimization is found. Evidently, when the data are essential for the commercial purposes of a company, this should be a strong mechanism to enforce compliance. Obviously, exercising the rights individuals (data subjects) have, to a certain extent, depends on the compliance of data controllers with the DPD and the performance of their duties. In this respect, the most important duty for data controllers is to provide information about the processing and the purposes of processing. Without this information being provided, the individual may be unaware of his data being processed and is, thus, not able to exercise his rights.

Properly providing the necessary information is essential to facilitate the exercise of data subject rights. As indicated, the information that has to be provided concerns a number of specific issues. The identity of the data controller and his representatives is essential to enable the individual to contact the data controller to exercise his rights. Contact details have to be included in the information.

---

[381] Verhelst 2012, p. 208.
[382] Privacy policies are often very extensive and basically have the individual withdraw all his rights relating to data or content provided to or collected by the visited website. See, for instance, the research project Accept or Decline executed in April and May 2011: <http://www.bright.nl/files/brght39_accept.pdf>.
[383] By explicit contract I mean that the individual has explicitly expressed his will to enter into a contract, instead of being automatically bound to a contract because of the use of a service, without further notification of this contract being in place.
[384] Schermer 2011.

The indication of the purposes of the processing is necessary to allow the individual to decide whether he feels comfortable with the processing or not. The requirement directly relates to the purpose binding principle and the duty to only collect data for specific purposes that have been defined beforehand.[385] The processed data have to be relevant for this purpose and not excessive to this purpose,[386] which also explains why categories of data to be collected have to be disclosed by the data controller. The purpose is also relevant in relation to the ground for legitimate processing, which will be discussed below (section 6).

Another point of discussion, but relatively less present in academic and public debate,[387] concerns Article 15 of the DPD. The Article and its conditions for applicability have been scarcely mitigated by the recitals or travaux préparatoires of the DPD,[388] but is at the core of contemporary data processing activities. This Article prohibits taking decisions concerning an individual by fully automated means. That is to say: at some point in the decision making process a human being has to be involved.[389] The provision is closely related to profiling practices.[390] The Article reads as follows:

Automated individual decisions
  1. Member States shall grant the right to every person not to be subject to a decision which produces legal effects concerning him or significantly affects him and which is based solely on automated processing of data intended to evaluate certain personal aspects relating to him, such as his performance at work, creditworthiness, reliability, conduct, etc.
  2. Subject to the other Articles of this Directive, Member States shall provide that a person may be subjected to a decision of the kind referred to in paragraph 1 if that decision:
  (a) is taken in the course of the entering into or performance of a contract, provided the request for the entering into or the performance of the contract, lodged by the data subject, has been satisfied or that there are suitable measures to safeguard his legitimate interests, such as arrangements allowing him to put his point of view; or
  (b) is authorized by a law which also lays down measures to safeguard the data subject's legitimate interests.

---

[385] Article 6(b) of the DPD.
[386] Article 6(c) of the DPD.
[387] The issue has been taken up, however, for instance by Hildebrandt: Hildebrandt 2008b, p. 65.
[388] Bygrave 2001.
[389] See also: Custers 2004, p. 150.
[390] Which is strongly emphasized in the new Data Protection Regulation Proposal (see Chapter 7).

With regard to the ratio of the Article, three aspects can be distinguished.[391] First aspect is the protection of the interest of the data subject to participate in the process of taking decisions that are important to (affect) him. The second aspect is providing counterweight to the risk of a 'human decision-maker' attributing too much weight to the apparently objective result of automated data processing by the machine, therewith neglecting his responsibilities. And, third, the provision has to provide counterweight to the threat automated decisions form with respect to human dignity.

Article 15, thus, provides that for decisions concerning an individual that have either a legal effect or significantly affect the individual some form of human involvement has to be present in the decision making process. There are lots of industrial opportunities for automated decisions, but "[e]ven when fully automating a decision process is possible, fiduciary, legal or ethical issues may still require a responsible person to play an active role."[392] What kind of human involvement is required and how big this involvement should be, however, remains unclear.[393] A routine human intervention may be enough to make the Article inapplicable.[394] However, as indicated above, too much routine and relying on the machine has to be avoided, so the human being has to perform active influence in the reaching of the outcome of the decision making process.[395]

2.3.1. Data subject access rights

When the individual is informed about the processing and the identity of the data controller, he can exercise his access rights. These rights are set out in article 12 of the DPD:

> Right of access
> Member States shall guarantee every data subject the right to obtain from the controller:
> (a) without constraint at reasonable intervals and without excessive delay or expense:
> - confirmation as to whether or not data relating to him are being processed and information at least as to the purposes of the processing, the categories of data concerned, and the recipients or

---

[391] Groothuis 2004, pp. 60-61.
[392] Davenport & Harris 2005.
[393] For this reason, the Article is sometimes referred to as the "Kafka-Article" by privacy activists and automated processes are sometimes called "Kafkaesque" with reference to Kafka's book 'Der Prozess', Kafka 1925. See, for instance: Winkelhorst 2005, p. 149.
[394] Hildebrandt 2008b, p. 65.
[395] Groothuis 2004, p. 63.

    categories of recipients to whom the data are disclosed,
- communication to him in an intelligible form of the data undergoing processing and of any available information as to their source,
- knowledge of the logic involved in any automatic processing of data concerning him at least in the case of the automated decisions referred to in Article 15 (1);

(b) as appropriate the rectification, erasure or blocking of data the processing of which does not comply with the provisions of this Directive, in particular because of the incomplete or inaccurate nature of the data;

(c) notification to third parties to whom the data have been disclosed of any rectification, erasure or blocking carried out in compliance with (b), unless this proves impossible or involves a disproportionate effort.

The first part of this article corresponds with the information obligations. It is the counterpart of the information duties, which now gives the individual the right to obtain the information from the data controller. Moreover, the data subject has the right to receive the data that are being processed concerning him in an intelligible form as well as, in cases of automated processing, the logic involved in the processing. When the processing does not comply with the provisions of the DPD or the data are incomplete or inaccurate, the individual can ask for rectification, erasure or blocking of the data.

With regard to data processed for fully automated decisions, in the meaning of Article 15 of the DPD, the individual also has the right to know the logic involved in the processing.[396] This may not provide real protection in practice, however, since the individual has to be able to understand the algorithms to have an idea of how a decision is taken. For instance, an algorithm that selects website visitors which use a Mac computer and then suggests more expensive hotels may be difficult to understand for a layman. The simple explanation that an individual is offered more expensive hotels than PC users, because he uses a Mac computer and Mac users generally spend more money on hotel rooms is easier to understand.[397] The effect on the individual using a Mac is that it requires more effort to find a cheap hotel. This may not seem a significant effect, but can become one once it is made impossible to find and book cheaper hotels by blocking access to these for Mac users. The effect may also become significant when the selection for more expensive products is widely exploited, which implies that the extra effort required to find cheaper products becomes very substantial. A comparable hypothetical practice was described in the case study in relation to banks and insurance

---

[396] Article 12(a) of the DPD.
[397] Mattioli 2012.

companies in Chapter 5. The choice left, then, is either to invest much more time, or to take the loss and buy more expensive products. In effect this is price discrimination.

If a data controller has not fulfilled the requirements for proper information provision towards the data subject and is not corrected in this, there is an enforcement problem. Data protection authorities do not have the means to verify compliance with the DPD of every company. In practice, data controllers can be non-compliant without effect. If a DPA starts an investigation concerning compliance of a company with the DPD, this is often instantiated by an incident, such as data leakage. In these cases, there is a clear indication that there may be problems with the way the company processes data.

However, even when the information duties are fulfilled there may be problems. Basically, it may be problematic to provide clear and comprehensive information when it is not that clear what the impact of the processing may be for the individual. This will be discussed more elaborately below, in section 5.

3. Profiles in view of the DPD

In the previous section it was shown that digital personae consist of personal data and that the DPD is applicable to the processing of the data. Another category of data sets that is of importance in relation to the subject of this study are profiles. As indicated in Chapter 2, profiles can become digital personae at some point in time. With regard to legal certainty, it is important to know whether the DPD is applicable to profiles as well and under what conditions. This is the topic of this section.

There are a number of options concerning profiles and the (potential) applicability of the DPD to the processing activities related to these profiles. The key concept in determining whether the DPD applies is the concept of personal data. In commercial contexts,[398] if data qualify as personal data and the processing falls under EU jurisdiction, the DPD applies. The essential issue is, thus, whether the data in the profile are to be considered personal data. Personal data are data that directly or indirectly relate to an identified or identifiable natural person. Identified and identifiability will be discussed here separately.

---

[398] When data is processed for commercial purposes, the household exemption will not apply. This is generally also the case on SNS (see: Article 29 Working Party 2009a; Marbus, Fennell-van Esch & Roosendaal 2009).

Whether the individual is identified or not is relatively easy to assess. If the data set contains a direct identifier, such as a name, the individual is identified.[399] The same is the case if the data set contains an L-identifier and this identifier is connected to a direct identifier by combining available data sets. The data set now qualifies as a digital persona and the DPD is applicable. If the data set contains no direct identifier or L-identifier, the individual is not identified or identifiable[400] and the data set is a profile instead of a digital persona.

An individual profile can contain an R-identifier, such as a cookie or an IP address. With an R-identifier, the individual is not identified. In online contexts, the R-identifier is connected to the device used by the individual.[401] The likeliness of a device being used by one single individual is growing, because the increasing use of mobile (smart) phones and laptops makes that devices are ever more personal. Besides, according to McIntyre "the IP address can go beyond identification and actually associate a person with the content of his online activity,"[402] so the IP address directly connects the identity of the individual to other data. McIntyre[403] argues for recognizing IP addresses as personally identifiable information (PII, the US equivalent of personal data[404]) by showing that IP addresses can be traced back to individuals, even when the addresses are dynamic or are used in private networks. The key entity in this respect is the ISP. It has become commonplace for litigants to subpoena ISPs to reveal the subscriber's identity related to an IP address. ISPs have no direct reason to fight these subpoenas, which has the result that usually the requested identifying data are provided to the litigants.[405] Even though the argument as such may be valid, there is an important difference with the line of argument in this study. As indicated, an IP address is an R-identifier for certain parties, so based on the IP address the individual is not identified as McIntyre states. However, for ISPs, the IP address is an L-identifier and by combining the data the individual is identified. The identification is based on the name or bank details of the individual which is available in the databases of the ISPs and not on the IP address as such. So, when a profile contains no identifier at all or only an R-identifier, the

---

[399] Unless the name is present several times in the set of individuals and as such cannot single out which individual within the set it concerns.

[400] The L-identifier in fact facilitates identifiability and, therewith, makes the DPD applicable. If the L-identifier is connected to identifying data, the individual is identified. In any case, a profile does not contain an L-identifier.

[401] Or to a pseudonymous or anonymous account.

[402] McIntyre 2011.

[403] McIntyre 2011.

[404] Albeit more restricted, because it covers only some direct identifiers, such as name and Social Security Number.

[405] McIntyre 2011.

individual is not identified. This contradicts the viewpoint of the Article 29 Working Party, which states that "web traffic surveillance tools make it easy to identify the behaviour of a machine and, behind the machine, that of its user."[406] This singling out via the contact point of a computer is deemed equal with identification of the individual.[407] I disagree, since it is not possible to single out the individual *natural person* based on an R-identifier in a data set, even though it is possible to categorize the individual based on attributes and take decisions that may influence the individual. Not the identifiers (IP addresses or cookie identifiers) as such are always to be considered personal data, but the fact that these allow for combining information in data sets (profiles) makes them a specific point of attention, since this can lead to the creation of an extensive profile which can be related to an identifiable natural person at some later point in time. In the wordings of the European Commission: "When using online services, individuals may be associated with online identifiers provided by their devices, applications, tools and protocols, such as Internet Protocol addresses or cookie identifiers. This may leave traces which, combined with unique identifiers and other information received by the servers, may be used to create profiles of the individuals and identify them."[408] So, the combination of data and data sets by the use of identifiers can make the data personal data. The crucial point seems to be that the Article 29 Working Party does not connect the element 'natural person' from the definition to 'identified or identifiable' when discussing R-identifiers, but merely explains natural person as a means to exclude dead or unborn people and legal persons (companies). For the distinction between a digital persona and a profile, the element of the natural person connected to the data set is a central part. In the case of digital personae, the individual is identified or identifiable, so the combined set of data as a whole should be considered personal data and processing is subjected to the DPD.

If the individual is not identified it may be the case that the DPD is not applicable, but only if the individual is not identifiable. This is a more problematic issue, which can take different forms. First, it can be the case that the individual is not identifiable at all; second, the individual may be identifiable, but the data are not recognized as identifiable in practice, and; third, the individual may be identifiable in the future as a result of new data combinations or additional data or technologies that become available. These three options will be discussed in the following subsections.

---

[406] Article 29 Working Party 2007, p. 14.
[407] Article 29 Working Party 2007, p. 14.
[408] European Commission, Proposal for a Regulation of the European Parliament and of the Council on the protection of individuals with regard to the processing of personal data and on the free movement of such data (General Data Protection Regulation), Preamble at 24.

3.1. The individual is not identifiable

An individual is not identifiable if a profile contains no identifying information at all. For instance, consider the case where Google is collecting data on browsing behavior of an individual by means of a tracking cookie. At some point, the ID of the tracking cookie is deleted from the data set. The tracking cookie on the user's machine was an R-identifier, but now the data set at Google contains no identifier to make the link to the tracking cookie. As a result, there is no option to link the profile to an individual, so the individual whose data was aggregated cannot be identified (recognized) anymore. Because the individual is not identified nor identifiable, the DPD is not applicable to the data set and the set is or rather, has become an anonymous profile.

There are two important remarks to be made on this scenario. First, the deletion of the cookie can also be done by the individual. The tracking cookie is, then, no longer available on the device of the individual and the device cannot be recognized by Google. Even though the ID of the cookie is still present in the data set Google has, it cannot establish a link to the device. The R-identifier has become void. The data in the profile no longer point to a recognizable or identifiable person and the DPD is still not applicable, albeit for a reason Google may not be fully aware of.

The second remark challenges the inapplicability of the DPD. While the starting point in this scenario is an R-identifier, or the absence thereof, the applicability of the DPD strongly depends on the other data in the profile. Even without an R-identifier, at some point the data set may become so rich, or contain such specific data, that it is possible to indirectly identify the individual. The set as a whole, then, contains information that in combination is unique and facilitates identification. This is also the most important counter-argument against Google's statement[409] that it only processes anonymous data, because the IP addresses are deleted from the profiles. In particular, the data collected via the Google search engine can form a unique profile when accumulated. Moreover, there are so-called vanity searches,[410] which in fact directly disclose the name of the individual belonging to the profile in a search term. "[A] mere hypothetical possibility to single out the individual is not enough to consider the person as 'identifiable'."[411] However, accumulation of data in profiles or the combination of data with a direct identifier or L-identifier may not always be very hypothetical. Where

---

[409] Whitten, A. (Google Software Engineer), Are IP Addresses Personal?, on Google Public Policy Blog, 22 February 2008. See: <http://googlepublicpolicy.blogspot.nl/2008/02/are-ip-addresses-personal.html>.
[410] Soghoian 2006.
[411] Article 29 Working Party 2007, p. 15.

to draw the line is difficult to say. This has to be assessed in relation to the means likely reasonably to be used for identifiability, which will be discussed below in section 4. In any case, in this scenario the profile may seem to be anonymous, but in fact the related individual may be identifiable, which is the second option and will be discussed below.

3.2. The individual may be identifiable

A second option is that the individual is not identified, but may be identifiable (even though he is not identified in practice). The formulation 'may be' indicates that identifiability is uncertain, as opposed to the identifiability of digital personae based on an L-identifier. As Koot states: "[a]nonymity is not a binary property; it is not either present or absent. Rather, a subject is more easily or less easily identifiable at any given time, and anonymity is a point on a scale."[412] The gradual difficulty to identify an individual is exactly what makes it difficult to make clear distinctions between data sets in the context of whether they contain personal data or not. Anonymity is the opposite of identifiability, which can clearly be derived from the definitions proposed by Pfitzmann and Hansen.[413] According to them, "[a]nonymity is the state of being not identifiable within a set of subjects, the anonymity set."[414] Identifiability is defined as "the possibility of being individualized within a set of subjects, the identifiability set."[415] Identifiability is, thus, a possibility and the likeliness of the possibility taking place depends on the data set. The size of the data set is important, as well as the overlap of data between subjects.

Typical issues relate to the endeavor of companies to maintain anonymous data sets. Basically, the DPD is not applicable to "data rendered anonymous in such a way that the data subject is no longer identifiable."[416] In order to achieve this anonymity, "a common practice is for organizations to release and receive person-specific data with all explicit identifiers, such as name, address and telephone number, removed."[417] Nevertheless, the remaining data in the set can often be used for re-identification of individuals. To re-identify, the data can be linked or matched to other data, or unique characteristics can be found in the data which leads to identification.[418] So, even though no identifiers are present in the profile, the combination of the

---

[412] Koot 2012, p. 13.
[413] Pfitzmann & Hansen 2008.
[414] Pfitzmann & Hansen 2008, p. 3.
[415] Pfitzmann & Hansen 2008, p. 12.
[416] Preamble of the DPD, Recital 26.
[417] Sweeney 2002, p. 558.
[418] Sweeney 2002, p. 558.

data in the set or linking the data to other data sets can make the individual identifiable.

A set of attributes that are individually anonymous, but can uniquely identify an individual when combined, is called a quasi-identifier.[419] For instance, anonymous data, such as gender, date of birth, and postal code, cannot uniquely identify an individual, since potentially there are several individuals sharing these attributes. However, in the data set there should be enough individuals with similar characteristics in order to prevent identification. For instance, if there is a group of ten individuals composed of nine females and one male person, the attribute 'gender' is identifying for the man. Would the group consist of five females and five males, identification based on 'gender' solely would not be possible. If combinations of data are made, the likeliness of identifiability increases. For instance, an empirical study showed that in a sample of nearly 2,8 million Dutch citizens, approximately 99,4% of the people in the sample could be identified based on the combination of gender, date of birth, and full postal code (in the Netherlands this is 4 numbers and 2 letters). When only using the four numbers of the postal code, in combination with gender and date of birth, the identification rate was still 67,0%.[420]

The problem of identifiability described above can be avoided by a mechanism called k-anonymity.[421] k-Anonymity means that each release of data is such that every combination of values of quasi-identifiers can be indistinctly matched to at least k respondents.[422] The combination of data within a set should, thus, never be unique. "It remains a matter of policy what value of k can be considered *sufficiently strong* anonymity for particular personal information."[423]

In any case, the important issue is that profiles may seem to be anonymous and the individual is not identifiable. However, the presence of so-called quasi-identifiers can make the individual identifiable. In line with this, the earlier mentioned Google profile, which does not contain an IP address or cookie identifier, can concern an identifiable individual when the combination of attributes in the profile is unique. The attributes together form a quasi-identifier. So, even though companies try to anonymize the profiles they have, the profiles may still be personal data in the meaning of the DPD. Companies can be perfectly unaware of this, or just ignorant. In any case, there seems to be a discrepancy between theory and practice here.

---

[419] Koot 2012, p. 23.
[420] Koot 2012, p. 35.
[421] Sweeney 2002.
[422] Ciriani, De Capitani Di Vimercati, Foresti & Samarati 2007.
[423] Koot 2012, p. 40 (Emphasis in original).

Uncertainty about the possibility of identifiability makes that the DPD is not applied to the profiles, while it may very well be the case that the profile relates to an identifiable individual and is, in fact, a digital persona, because of the presence of quasi-identifiers. The combination of data is identifying information, which can function in a comparable manner as an L-identifier. The identity of the individual may be looked up by comparing the data, for instance, with accounts on an SNS[424] or with a register, such as a telephone book.[425] The DPD should be applied to these profiles.

3.3. The individual may be identifiable in the future

Any data set may pertain to individuals who may be identifiable in the future. The profile as such does not contain an L-identifier or quasi-identifiers and can be considered anonymous at some point in time. It may, however, be the case that at a certain point the profile becomes so rich that it can be related to an identifiable person. It may also happen that the profile itself does not change, but can be connected to another database that becomes available to the data controller. And, there is the option that an individual 'claims' to be the profiled person and, therewith, identifies himself or adds an L-identifier to the profile.

As an example, consider the Google profile again. By means of a tracking cookie, a profile has been built concerning the browsing behavior and search terms of an individual. The profile is quite rich, but not unique in the sense that it contains quasi-identifiers. Based on the profile, targeted advertisements are presented to the individual when he visits websites which have Google AdSense implemented. Moreover, search results are 'personalized'. The individual, however, is annoyed by the bad quality of some advertisements and suggestions, because they do not meet his interests, but continue to show up. For instance, as a male person, age 54 and fired for the third time in two years, he is not interested in expensive cars. And by the way, he does not wear bikinis. Nevertheless, Google appears to think that he is interested in bikinis and BMWs. To solve this problem, Google offers the individual the opportunity to correct his profile. This can be done by adding or removing interests on the Google Dashboard.[426] To use this dashboard functionality, it is required to sign in with a Google account or create one. For this purpose, the individual may use an email address which contains identifying information and, therewith, either directly identify himself

---

[424] Google even has its own SNS, Google+, on which the company can access all data provided by the users.
[425] Koot 2012 refers to public administration records, but these will usually not be available to commercial companies.
[426] See: <https://www.google.com/dashboard>, (last accessed: June 27, 2012).

(e.g. ArnoldRoosendaal1979@email.com) or provide an L-identifier (e.g. LawSchoolDean@tilburguniversity.edu). The first contains a full name and year of birth and the second contains information about a unique function and affiliation. At the moment of creating the account, the individual identifies himself and the profile becomes a personal profile (a digital persona) instead of an anonymous profile.

The future event that facilitates identifiability may, thus, originate from different sources. Either the data controller himself adds data to the profile or adopts new technologies, which makes the profile containing identifying information, or an external party facilitates the additional information that enables (possible) identification. As soon as the profile can be related to an identified or identifiable natural person, the DPD is applicable. The problem is that it may be very uncertain whether a future event will happen that leads to identifiability of the individual to whom the profile relates.

4. Means likely reasonably to be used for identification

The second and third scenario described in the previous section concerned a probability that the individual may be identifiable, now or in the future, based on the data in the profile. As indicated, in these cases it is not always clear whether the DPD is applicable to the processing of the data. The basic requirement for applicability is the identifiability of the individual. However, whether an individual is identifiable can depend on internal or external factors. It is, thus, difficult to quantify the probability that identifiability is possible or will become possible.

According to the Preamble of the DPD, "to determine whether a person is identifiable, account should be taken of all the means *likely reasonably to be used* either *by the controller or by any other person* to identify the said person."[427] Two parts of this sentence are important here: 'likely reasonably to be used' and 'by the controller or by any other person'. Both will be discussed below.

4.1. The controller or any other person

To start with the latter, identifiability is present when the controller or any other person is able to identify the individual. The presence of quasi-identifiers in the data set may make the data personal data, even though the data controller may be unaware of the identifiability of the individuals in the data set. The data controller will classify the data as anonymous and it may

---

[427] Recital 26, my emphasis.

not be likely that he will apply means to identify an individual in practice. As the data controller is unaware of the possible identifiability, he will probably not be aware of this identification taking place when 'any other person' obtains access to the data. It may also be possible that a profile becomes identifiable in the future, due to the application of new technologies, the combination of data, or because an individual identifies himself in relation to the profile. Even though the DPD should be applicable to the processing of the data in those cases, the data controller fails to take the actions prescribed by the DPD and hence does not comply with the DPD.

Also the interpretation of 'any other person' is important here. Most likely, this is meant to be any other person that has legitimate access to the data. These are, for instance, data processors who work under the responsibility of a company (the data controller), either within the company or in another company based on an outsourcing agreement. It is, however, also possible that access is obtained by someone outside of the organization. Legitimate access in this category can be obtained by law enforcement.[428] Whether a law enforcement agency is able to identify someone based on the profile in combination with other available data is unclear to the company, because the company has no insight in the available data at the law enforcement agency. Identifiability may be likely, however. Consider the case of illegal web content such as child pornography. Google may be requested to deliver an overview of the search and browsing history related to an IP address and the police may have received the identifying data belonging to the IP address from an ISP. The police can, then, connect the profile to the identifying data, which makes the anonymous Google profile personal data for the police. The police falling in the category of 'any other person' makes that the data controller has to process the data as personal data, even though the controller himself may not be able to identify the individual.

Other persons may also be involved directly in cases where processing of data involves numerous parties. As was described earlier in Chapter 5, web interactions usually involve several parties. Next to the party the data subject is interacting with consciously and intended, there are interactions with third parties. These can, for instance, be content providers, delivering pieces of content for a web site, tracking companies, who follow the internet browsing behavior of individuals over the web,[429] or third parties who are involved in making the interaction possible by providing platforms or technologies for communication and storage of data. For the individual

---

[428] See, for instance, Hustinx 2009, who explicitly mentions law enforcement officials as an example of any third party.

[429] Turow refers to the phenomenon of connecting as many devices and locations as possible as the "long click": Turow 2011, p. 139.

it may be difficult to distinguish between first and third parties. However, the individual may think not to be identifiable to the first party, but may be identifiable by a third party of which he is not aware that he is involved in the interaction. The distinction between first and third parties can be based on user expectations: an entity acts in a first-party capacity if a user reasonably expects to interact with it; it acts in a third-party capacity if a user does not expect this interaction.[430] The user expectation can be influenced by factors such as domain names, branding, and business relationships. Even when advertisements are displayed, the user may not expect to interact with other parties than the domain name owner, because the advertisements may be placed by the domain name owner, like is the case in a newspaper. The advertisers have bought advertising space, but do not receive information from the readers. Mayer and Narayanan give some examples:[431]

- A user visits The New York Times' website; Google's Doubleclick ad network collects user data. Google is a third party because it operates at a different domain, uses a different brand, and only has an advertising relationship with The New York Times.
- A user visits Amazon.com; data is collected with the Amazon Web Services platform, located at amazonaws.com. Here Amazon Web Services is a first party because, though domain names differ, Amazon Web Services is functionally a business unit of Amazon.com and is branded as an Amazon.com product.
- A user visits the ESPN website at espn.go.com; Omniture, an analytics provider, collects data at the domain w88.go.com. Omniture is a third party because, though it shares a second-level domain, it is branded independently and only has an advertising relationship with ESPN.

The examples above clearly distinguish between first party and third party cookies, based on user expectations. In practice, however, companies sometimes argue that they should be treated as first parties, while an objective viewpoint from the user perspective would classify them as third parties. For instance, Google and Facebook provide plugins, such as Maps or YouTube player, or Like buttons and Comment fields. They argue that the website owners have implemented their features in the core code of the website, which makes them part of the first party website.[432] Objectively, this argument does not hold, since the user instigates an interaction with

---

[430] Mayer & Narayanan 2011, p. 4.
[431] Mayer & Narayanan 2011, p. 4.
[432] Discussed with Chris Hoofnagle, Ashkan Soltani, and Aleecia McDonald at Workshop DoNotTrack organized by Berkeley Law and Technology Center and Institute for Information Law (IViR Amsterdam) with cooperation of EU Commissioner Kroes and FTC Commissioner Brill, Brussels, June 23, 2011.

the website connected to the URL he is visiting. That is the only first party and all other actors on the website are third parties. In some occasions, the distinction becomes very fuzzy. For instance, on techcrunch.com Facebook provides the Comment Field. This Field is not a feature as part of the core website, but is completely hosted by Facebook. This implies that, when a visitor of techcrunch.com wants to leave a comment to a news story, the comment is directly typed in a part of the website that is actually a facebook. com domain. Facebook, on its turn, provides the comments to Techcrunch and displays the comments on the techcrunch.com webpage. Facebook acts as a first party in this scenario, because the data are directly sent to Facebook, even though the visitor is at the techcrunch.com webpage and leaves a comment to a news story provided by Techcrunch. The user, thus, expects Facebook to be a third party, which is in fact, based on the URL of the visited webpage, a more valid interpretation. Difficulties in assessing the possibility of being identified from the perspective of the user are, thus, relevant as well, even though in these cases the data have to be treated as personal data by the third parties who can identify the individual.

Similar difficulties concerning responsibilities and the role parties play in the processing of data show up in the context of information enrichment in data flows. At each step of the data flow model, different parties can be involved.

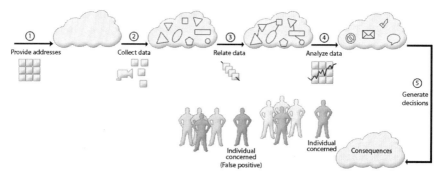

Figure 16. Data flow model. Source: Hansen 2008.

In the chain of information flows (see figure 16 above), collaborating parties usually work on the basis of contracts. Parts of the work can be outsourced to others. In the light of data handling, it is required to include clear agreements on how data should be handled and who has access and who should not have access, in order to have responsibilities clear between the different actors involved. Nevertheless, the complex chain may lead to situations where there are proper agreements between the first parties in the chain, but where at some point a contract between two parties does not contain provisions on, for instance, disclosure or use of the data. In that case, the entire chain has become ineffective as regards the protection of the data. This is a specific risk related to the complexity of information ecosystems. As the adage says: a chain is as strong as its weakest link.

The important issue concerning the involvement of multiple parties in data processing, as first or third parties on a website, or as part of an information chain, is the difficulty to indicate for whom the processed data are personal data. An anonymous visitor of a website may very well be identified or identifiable for a third party who delivers content on that website. For the website holder, the DPD does not apply, but for the third party it does. It also means that the website holder may provide information to the third party. Because for the third party (any other person) the data concern an identifiable individual, the first party website holder, for whom the data are anonymous, has to treat the data as personal data. The DPD is, then, applicable even though this may be unexpected or unclear to the website holder, and sometimes even unreasonable. The same problem arises in information chains where at some point one of the parties in the chain may be able to relate the data to an identified or identifiable individual.

Illegitimate access to the profiles is possible as well. Databases can be hacked or data can be leaked. In the DPD it is required to take appropriate organizational and technical measures to prevent this. Moreover, data should be protected in such a manner that, if they are inadvertently leaked, the data are unintelligible. This means that, for instance, encryption technologies should be used. However, when data are considered anonymous, the DPD does not apply and there is no duty to comply with its requirements. This is the start of an *a contrario* circular argument. The DPD is not applicable to anonymous data, but to consider the data anonymous the requirements on technical and organizational measures from the DPD have to be met. These measures, however, apply to data that were personal data and were made anonymous, so in a stadium where the DPD was already applicable to the processing. In this respect, the Article 29 Working Party indicates that the implementation of appropriate technical measures is not the consequence of the legal obligation from the DPD,[433] but rather a condition for not considering the data to be personal data of which the processing is subjected to the DPD.[434] The DPD is not applicable, but only if a number of requirements from the DPD are met. How far the category of 'any other person' reaches is unclear, but the Article 29 Working Party seems to include any possible person that might obtain access to the data at a given time. The result of this interpretation is that in fact all data sets about individuals fall under the DPD, because there may always be a person that is able to make

---

[433] Provided for in article 17 of the DPD.
[434] Article 29 Working Party 2007, p. 17.

the individual identifiable by combining the data with other data or by applying other techniques. In particular, due to the fact that the future has to be taken into account, it is impossible to foresee what technologies may be available to any other person that may lead to identifiability of the data set. If the data are "intended to be kept for 10 years, the controller should consider the possibility of identification that may occur also in the ninth year of their lifetime."[435] Nevertheless, the Working Party also indicates that, as these developments may happen, the systems of the data controller should be able to adapt to these developments and to "incorporate then" the appropriate technical and organizational measures in due course.[436] The unforeseeability is, thus, understood, but the Working Party also seems to believe that the possibilities any other person may have which may facilitate identifiability, can always be foreseen by the data controller before the data are obtained by this other person. Moreover, it has to be somehow likely that this other person wants to employ his means to identify the individual (see next subsection). In practice, however, this is impossible to foresee and may lead to unreasonable requirements for data controllers in the sense that the DPD always has to be applied to anonymous data as well.

4.2. Likely reasonable means

The first part of the sentence explaining identifiability is even more interesting: what are means likely reasonably to be used? This may depend on the function and competences of the data controller. A commercial company will, usually, not gain access to governmental administrative records, such as citizen records of the municipality, while an enforcement body will have this access. Returning to the example of IP addresses, an enforcement body may claim the identifying data belonging to the user of an IP address from an ISP. A commercial company will not receive this data and will have to submit a subpoena to the ISP. As indicated earlier, ISPs are likely to provide the data in such a case.[437] However, it is not very likely that a commercial company will submit a subpoena concerning each IP address in their profile databases in order to identify individuals. This is far too costly and too much of a burden. Moreover, it will usually not be possible to legitimize all these subpoenas by supporting them with an unlawful act.

Combining different databases, by buying additional databases from data brokers or obtaining them by buying other companies, however, is a more likely scenario in a commercial context. It is even a common practice.[438] "[I]

---

[435] Article 29 Working Party 2007, p. 15.
[436] Article 29 Working Party 2007, p. 15.
[437] McIntyre 2011.
[438] In the US, Acxiom processes more than 50 trillion data transactions a year in their

nformation or data brokers are private corporations which make it their sole business to collect, analyze, and sell personal information. In many ways, their presence and value represent the embodiment of the information society."[439] Another option is for companies to make use of so-called list brokers. These are specialized parties who 'rent' address lists which can be used to target specific audiences. The lists are 'hired' for single use, so only when an individual responds to a message, his details are added to the data set of the company.[440] Finally, there are Information Agencies and Credit Bureaus which are specialized in obtaining information from several sources concerning specific individuals, for instance to provide information about their financial situation and creditworthiness.[441] One relevant factor in assessing the means likely reasonably to be used by companies will be the purpose of the processing of the data. If the processing is aimed at identification of individuals, it is more likely that specific means will be used.[442]

If all means have to be taken into account, including future means, this may imply that possibly all profiles have to be considered data concerning a (potentially) identifiable individual. As a result, the DPD would be applicable to every data set concerning an individual or that may become a data set related to an individual. The entire applicability of the DPD is, then, based on probability. For data controllers, this may provide legal certainty, because the DPD is always applicable. However, this approach seems unreasonable and impracticable, because it requires data controllers to perform, for instance, information duties towards, currently, non-identifiable individuals. Moreover, the legal obligation to perform all duties from the DPD in case any set of data is processed would impose too much of a burden on data controllers, in particular when they do not intend to relate the data to an identified or identifiable individual.

The remaining problem is that if a less stringent approach is taken, the DPD is not applicable to profiles as long as they cannot be related to an identified or identifiable natural person. In online communications, however, the profile can be used to affect the individual, because it is possible to direct communications towards the individual, for instance based on an R-identifier. Even though the data relate to an individual and this individual can be affected by the use of the profile, the fact that the individual is not (yet) identifiable means there is no legal protection offered by the DPD. When it

---

activities to mine and analyze consumer data. See: Singer 2012.
[439] Van der Meulen 2010, p. 205.
[440] Schermer & Wagemans 2009, pp. 24-25.
[441] Schermer & Wagemans 2009, p. 30.
[442] Article 29 Working Party 2007, p. 16.

is assumed that identifiability is possible by use of means likely reasonably to be used, or when a data set (digital persona) contains an L-identifier, the DPD is applicable because the data are considered to be personal data. Now it is clear when the DPD is applicable, the next question is what this means with regard to the protection of the individual. This will be discussed in the next section.

5. Problems when the DPD is applicable

Also when there is no doubt that the DPD is applicable to the processing of data, as is the case with the use of digital personae, problems exist. The major advantage is, of course, that the protection of the data subject offered by the DPD is present and that the duties of data controllers are clear. Nevertheless, it may be very difficult to fulfill the duties and to properly balance the interests of the individual with the interests of the data controller.

A first problem concerns the information duties. As indicated earlier, the information duties may not be fulfilled by the data controller if the data controller is not compliant with the DPD. This may be related to an enforcement problem when the information is simply not provided. It may, however, also be caused by difficulties to indicate the exact purpose of the processing. The purpose has to be strictly defined beforehand. Current practices, however, indicate that purposes may sometimes change over time, simply because new applications of the data are found. Innovation and function creep may result in processing for purposes that were not yet taken into account. If the purposes are incompatible, this requires a new notification of the processing, a new legitimate ground, and fulfillment of the other duties from the DPD, but a more current practice is to use a relatively general description of the purpose which covers most of the possible future use as well. For instance, a purpose that is often mentioned is the 'improvement of the service'.[443] This can be basically anything, from improving the user-friendliness of a service by changing the layout of a website to maximizing commercial benefits from targeted advertisements. If an individual has to give his consent for the processing, 'improvement of the service' is insufficient to serve as a specified purpose which can serve as a basis for the informed consent of the individual.

---

[443] See, for instance, Facebook: <http://www.facebook.com/about/privacy/your-info#howweuse> (last accessed June 20, 2012), or Amazon: <http://www.amazon.com/gp/help/customer/display.html/ref=footer_privacy?ie=UTF8&nodeId=468496> (last accessed June 20, 2012) which even uses the terminology: "We use the information that you provide for such purposes as…" This seems to be meant as non-limitative.

The lack of clarity and certainty with regard to the processing activities and the impact it may have on the individual also leads to problems concerning the legitimate grounds for processing. In particular, the ground of consent and the legitimate interest of the data controller are relevant in this respect. Both will be discussed more elaborately below.

5.1. Consent

According to Article 2(h) of the DPD, the data subject's consent means "any freely given specific and informed indication of his wishes by which the data subject signifies his agreement to personal data relating to him being processed." Thus, the indication of wishes has to be 'specific', meaning that the indication has to relate to a specific set of personal data being processed for a specific purpose. This requirement relates to the purpose-binding principle. The indication also has to be 'informed', meaning that the data subject has to know what the processing entails and what the purposes of the processing are. This requirement closely relates to the information duties of the data controller.

A specific point of attention concerns the issue that the indication signifies the agreement to the processing of personal data relating to the data subject. When an indication signifies an agreement is debatable. For instance, in cases concerning the use of cookies to track and trace web users and to place targeted advertisements, it is heavily debated whether (default) browser settings can form an indication signifying such an agreement. The Article 29 Working Party is of the opinion that in general "providing information and, to some extent, facilitating the user's ability to reject cookies (by explaining how this can be done) cannot generally be deemed as informed consent *ex* Article 5(3) of the ePrivacy Directive and also in light of Article 2(h) of Directive 95/46/EC."[444] The European Commission has also asked for clarification of the conditions for consent "in order to always guarantee informed consent and ensure that the individual is fully aware that he or she is consenting, and to what data processing, in line with Article 8 of the EU Charter of Fundamental Rights."[445] As Kosta indicates, the focus of the Article 29 Working Party as well as the European Commission is on the definition of consent and on how it should be implemented in a harmonized way, "leaving outside from the discussion whether the consent of the data subject in the way it is treated today serves the role that it was intended to."[446] The intended role was strictly related to individual autonomy and informational self-determination. The current review of the EU data

---

[444] Article 29 Working Party 2010, p. 15.
[445] European Commission 2010, p. 9.
[446] Kosta 2011, p. 29.

protection framework gives an opportunity not only to look at the definition of consent, but also at its primary function in specific contexts.[447]

With regard to cookies and giving consent to the placing and use of cookies by other parties there are some important recent developments. Directive 2009/136/EC has amended, amongst other things, Directive 2002/58/ EC. One of the main points of discussion here was the means for giving consent to cookie use. As discussed above, the question arose whether browser settings could indicate such consent. By discussing the means for expressing consent in the context of the ePrivacy Directive, apparently the European Commission has taken the viewpoint that it considers the content of cookies to be personal data and that data protection legislation applies to the setting and reading of these cookies. In the discussion on the scope of the definition of personal data, this point has remained rather implicit. If a third party wants to place and use cookies[448] on the user's computer, he has to provide information about this and offer a right to refuse. "Exceptions to the obligation to provide information and offer the right to refuse should be limited to those situations where the technical storage or access is strictly necessary for the legitimate purpose of enabling the use of a specific service explicitly requested by the subscriber or user."[449] So, in case of a subscription or request for a specific service, the ground for legitimate data processing is based on Article 7(b) of Directive 95/46/EC: the performance of a contract. In all other cases, consent to the processing has to be obtained from the user.[450] When technically appropriate, meaning that a clear and comprehensible system is available, this consent can be expressed by browser settings. Even the advertisement industry firmly took the viewpoint of browser settings as sufficient means for establishing consent, instead of, traditionally, arguing that personal data are not processed in the first place. Adjusting the settings

---

[447] Kosta 2011, p. 316.

[448] Or wants to use other types of information, such as information about the device which can be used for device fingerprinting.

[449] Directive 2009/136/EC of the European Parliament and of the Council of 25 November 2009 amending Directive 2002/22/EC on universal service and users' rights relating to electronic communications networks and services, Directive 2002/58/ EC concerning the processing of personal data and the protection of privacy in the electronic communications sector and Regulation (EC) No 2006/2004 on cooperation between national authorities responsible for the enforcement of consumer protection laws, Preamble at 66.

[450] Directive 2009/136/EC of the European Parliament and of the Council of 25 November 2009 amending Directive 2002/22/EC on universal service and users' rights relating to electronic communications networks and services, Directive 2002/58/ EC concerning the processing of personal data and the protection of privacy in the electronic communications sector and Regulation (EC) No 2006/2004 on cooperation between national authorities responsible for the enforcement of consumer protection laws, Preamble at 66.

as to accept all third party cookies can, however, hardly be explained as specific consent.

Another aspect relates to the duration of consent. User control is one of the core principles of data protection regulation, so giving consent to an organization to use personal data must be understood to be restricted to the specific purpose of data processing for which consent was given and in the sense that consent may be limited in time (in relation to the purpose) or can be revoked. When taking a right-to-control as a starting point, the individual retains ultimate control over his data in spite of consenting to its use by some organization. "Consent *does not* give the organization ultimate control over personal information in perpetuity."[451] From this perspective, individuals have the right to withdraw their consent and therewith stop organizations from further processing the individual's personal data. In other words, "the *continued use* of an individual's personal information must be understood as a necessary consequence, not of the initial consent to collect the information, but rather of that person's *continuing consent* to the organization to use that information."[452] In this approach there is recognition of the fact that individuals may be subject to change concerning their desires and preferences. Taking the dynamics of individuals into account then automatically means that consent can only be given for specific data processing activities and only for the period of time that the individual actually agrees with this processing. Indicating that period beforehand, or even consenting to an unlimited timeframe, appears to be difficult, if not impossible, then. At this moment, a consent given is restricted only by the purposes for which the data are processed.[453]

The limits of consent are subject to interpretation. The more direct problem with consent, however, is related to what consent means. As indicated, it is a *freely given* specific and *informed* indication of the *wishes of the data subject*. What the indication (the *expression* of the will) looks like can be difficult, as was seen above in relation to browser settings, but it is clear that the data subject has to do something actively. A tick box indicating consent, for instance concerning the acceptance of general terms and conditions, has to be ticked by the data subject and may not be ticked by default. An active form of expression is preferred in a web context, since other indicators, such as body language, are absent. Moreover, if the individual ticks the box himself, this is beneficial for companies as well, because it makes it easier to prove

---

[451] Barrigar, Burkell & Kerr 2006 (emphasis in original). This article is written from a Canadian perspective, but the doctrine of ongoing consent is relevant for data protection laws in general.

[452] Barrigar, Burkell & Kerr 2006 (emphasis in original).

[453] Clauß, Hansen, Pfitzmann, Raguse, & Steinbrecher 2009.

that consent has been obtained from the individual. The other parts of the definition (emphasized above by my italics) relate to the practicalities of expressing a *will*.

Consent has to be *freely given*. This is directly related to individual autonomy. The data subject has to decide for himself whether he wants to consent to certain data processing activities or not. In cases where the individual wants to use a service or wants to have access to specific content, and this use or access is subjected to general terms and conditions, not accepting the terms implies not having access. This may be reasonable, for instance, when the terms relate to the content itself and the use of it. Content that is copyright protected, for instance, may not be copied or made public. Terms can explicate this and acceptance of the terms means that the individual expresses his will to obey these terms and not to engage in unlawful or criminal behavior. There is a logical and direct link between the service and the terms. However, if the terms for access to copyrighted materials also contain provisions in which it is indicated that the data subject may be tracked and monitored and that his data may be processed for targeted advertising and probably be sold to other companies, the link between the service and the terms is absent. Consent thus not freely given, but forced by the choice of having access or not.

In the above example, two things are of particular importance. First, the acceptance of the terms and conditions entails a concrete action to be taken by the individual and, second, it can be argued that there is a contract of which the general terms and conditions are part. The latter, however, does not hold. Indeed, there may be a contract including terms and conditions. This does, however, not imply that the processing is lawful. As was described earlier in this Chapter (section 2.2.1), the DPD indicates as a legitimate ground for processing that the processing takes place on the basis of a contract. This ground, however, only applies to the parts of the processing that are necessary for the performance of the contract. All other processing has to be based on consent.[454] The direct connection between processing in relation to the contract and other processing activities, by putting them in one document with terms and conditions, takes away the free choice of the individual. The individual cannot decline further processing, but accept processing that is necessary for the performance of the contract.

---

[454] This is also recognized by European Social Networks, an organization representing 9 EU based SNS. However, instead of emphasizing the importance of consent, they asked the European Commission to make profiling and targeted advertising being recognized as necessary for the performance of the contract, based on the argument that these practices generate the income to finance the services they provide. See: European Social Networks 2011, p. 5.

Another situation where the problem is even clearer is the assumed acceptance of all terms by merely using a service, as is the case with Google. When visiting a web page implies, according to terms and conditions, that you have accepted these, there is no freely given consent. The choice has not even been present. Moreover, recent changes within Google's practices have the result that the creation of a new Gmail account now implies membership of the SNS Google+, of which the welcoming message is one of the first messages you will receive in your Gmail inbox. Not having the option to choose is clearly problematic and is a direct restriction on the free will of the individual. Moreover, the implied membership of the SNS is not mentioned in the terms and conditions, so the individual cannot be aware of this beforehand. Here, individual autonomy is affected.

Another condition of consent is that it has to be *informed*. This means that the individual has to have a good understanding of what the processing entails. However, it is hard for the individual to understand the impact of the processing activities. On the one hand, it cannot be expected that the individual predicts all the effects related to the processing of his personal data. On the other hand, this is often even impossible for the data controllers to predict, because they may find new applications of the data or gain new, unexpected insights by applying data mining techniques. In the area of commercial data processing, consent can, thus, often not be informed.

Finally, the consent has to reflect the *wishes of the data subject*. As indicated above, the wishes of the data subject do usually not relate to consenting to monitoring and profiling, but to accessing a service against reasonable terms. Consent, in this case, reflects the wishes of the individual with regard to the use of the service, but not with regard to the tracking practices. The tracking is included in the Terms and cannot be denied while still gaining access to the service. Only because there is no option to choose or to accept only a part of the terms and conditions, the individual agrees to the terms.

To conclude, consent as a legitimate ground for processing as such is not problematic. The problem, however, is more of a practical nature. Consent is often not given explicitly for a specific type of processing for a specific purpose, but as connected to the entering into a contract or without any request to the individual. Even though data controllers can argue, based on a ticked box, that the individual has explicitly expressed his wishes, the individual does not have an option to choose, cannot understand the impact, and did not express his wishes concerning all the processing of personal data included or implied in the Terms and Conditions. The only option for individuals to avoid this is by not visiting certain websites or by not accepting the terms in general, therewith not being able to make use of the service. In some cases, such as services provided by Google, this is becoming problematic, since

Google has so many services that became part of everyday life that it may be difficult to circumvent these and it may happen relatively easily that, even if an individual wants to avoid this, he still visits a Google website by accident. The argument of leaving a website and choosing for another service is, thus, not as straightforward as it may seem. In particular in a web context it may become very difficult to avoid interaction with specific parties.

5.2. Weighing of interests

The other legitimate ground for processing which may lead to problems in practice is the legitimate interest of the data controller, which has to be weighed against the interests, in particular the privacy interest, of the individual. The weighing of these interests can be very difficult, because it is not always possible to have a good overview of the interests of the individual and to attribute weight to these interests. The fact that the data controller makes the weighing without necessarily involving the individual contributes to this difficulty. For instance, consider the case where a third party collects and processes individual data for advertising purposes. The commercial interest of the third party may legitimize the processing. However, when, as a result, the individual is confronted with less convenient advertisements there is a privacy problem. Imagine a case where displayed advertisements reveal searches for wedding rings and the 'wife-to-be' sees these advertisements, which implies that the 'husband-to-be' cannot have a secret. Another example is when data collected on individuals are compared with others and the individual is negatively impacted because of the behavior of others. This is what happened in relation to a credit card company. The company (American Express) collected information on visited shops where their customers paid with their credit card. It appeared that some customers who visited certain Wal-Mart stores had a poor repayment history. As a result, customers with a high credit rating were also lowered in their credit limits.[455] The interest of the credit card company was to reduce risk, but the individual has an interest of not being inappropriately indicated as a 'risky customer'. This kind of processing and decision making without involving the individual leads to unreasonable decisions and negative effects for the individual. The interest of the credit card company is overrated by applying an attribute of a group of customers to all customers, without assessing the interests of the data subjects. Privacy problems may, thus, occur in cases of unlawful processing of data, but also in cases of lawful data processing.

A comparable issue concerns the balance in trade-offs for pay-with-data exchanges. Numerous web services are 'free', which in practice means that the

---

[455] See: <http://abcnews.go.com/GMA/GetsAnswers/Story?id=6747461#.UGn0kE3hKX->, last visited 1 October 2012.

individual does not have to pay a certain amount of money or a subscription fee. The use of disclosed personal data, for instance for advertising purposes, finances the service. In traditional (offline) interactions, the individual makes a trade-off of what data to share and, in the interaction with the seller of a product or service, role-appropriate norms are developed. For this to happen, the individual has to be able to ascribe weights to the things being balanced. The problem is that role-appropriate information is lacking, in particular in pay-with-data exchanges, which makes it impossible to make a proper balance between disclosure of information and the received service.[456] The individual does not have a proper option to balance interests and to provide the data controller with appropriate information concerning his interests. So, in practice the decisions do often not involve the individual at all. However, the interests of the individual have to be taken into account in order to make a proper weighing of interests.

5.3. Consequences for the individual

The practices indicated above can be translated into a number of specific threats related to profiling practices and the use of digital personae as a basis for decisions. These threats are:[457] the surreptitious influencing, formatting and customization of individual behavior,[458] threatening individual autonomy;[459] knowledge asymmetries leading to power inequalities;[460] wrong decisions as a result of false positives[461] and false negatives and a threat to due process;[462] unfair decisions based on correct profiles that allow for unwarranted and invisible discrimination;[463] the taking of unmotivated and unilateral decisions about individuals.[464] People become vulnerable due to the "lack of any meaningful form of participation in the collection and use of their personal information."[465] All of the mentioned threats will be discussed more elaborately below.

---

[456] Warner & Sloan 2012.
[457] Gutwirth & Hildebrandt 2010, p. 34; Hildebrandt & Van Dijk 2010, pp. 70-72; Hildebrandt 2008b, p. 64.
[458] Lessig 1999, pp. 153-154; Hildebrandt 2008a, p. 307; Zarsky 2002-2003, at pp. 38-40; Zarsky 2006.
[459] Hildebrandt 2008b, p. 63.
[460] Lyon 2007, p. 101, with reference to a new conceptualization of the 'digital divide'.
[461] False positives or false negatives can also result from a problem Garfinkel calls the 'False Data Syndrome', which means that "[b]ecause much of the information in the data sea is correct, we are predisposed to believe that it is all correct." See: Garfinkel 2001, p. 74.
[462] Steinbock 2005.
[463] By Turow referred to as "*narrowed options* and *social discrimination*" (emphasis in original): Turow 2011, p. 89.
[464] Lyon 2007, p. 101.
[465] Solove 2004, pp. 47-48.

The surreptitious influencing, formatting and customization of individual behavior is taking new forms with the advent of real-time web personalization.[466] Websites can have different content and different types of displaying content, depending on the individual visitor that passes by. The more a website is tailored to the individual, the better it can influence the individual in clicking certain links or advertisements. It not only concerns the products advertised based on the interests of the individual derived from an analysis of web behavior, but also the way the advertisements or information is displayed. Whether something is presented as a picture, a piece of text, or a banner makes a difference and different individuals have different preferences. It can, thus, be assessed what type of presentation is the most attractive for an individual. By choosing how to display different content parts on a website, the individual can be surreptitiously influenced to click on a specific part of the web page. The next step, once the individual has clicked on a piece of content, is to decide what options are presented to the individual. For instance, banks and insurance companies, based on this type of behavioral analysis, choose what options for insurances or money saving or loans are presented. Alternative options may still be available by browsing the website, but are much harder to find and much less likely to be chosen due to their presentation form. A side step from the paved way is discouraged and even made harder in a practical manner. This highly influences individual behavior and the limited options and indirect exclusion threaten individual autonomy, in particular when there is no consent or transparency.

Knowledge asymmetries leading to power inequalities are directly related to the access to information individuals have. In the online context, these power inequalities can be automatically created. The practice of structurally excluding individuals from access to information or options limits the opportunities for the individual to get a full picture of the available options and interests at stake. Reconfirming the position of the individual can be compared to the reconfirming of the interests, which results in a filter bubble.[467] The individual is caught in his social position (as profiled by the service provider) and opportunities to escape from this position are reduced.

Wrong decisions as result of false positives and false negatives can lead to unfair inclusion or exclusion. The data on which a decision is based are incorrect. However, in online contexts, the individual often does not have the opportunity to correct the data. In particular, in the case where distributive profiles are applied to a group of individuals, for instance, with weblining based on IP addresses, the individual can receive offers for credit cards with lower limits, while he may financially be perfectly able to

---

[466] See Chapter 5, section 4.3.
[467] Pariser 2011.

have a higher limit. Applying for a higher credit wil, however, be difficult online. It is the decision as such with which the individual is confronted. It may even be the case that the individual does not even notice the decision being taken, because he is simply not receiving information or an offer. In case the individual becomes aware of the decision, there may be an option to fight this decision. Nevertheless, the data on which the decision was based may remain incorrect. Moreover, being subjected to decisions "based on false assumptions derived from infringements of privacy is self-evidently damaging and potentially unfair."[468] In relation to profiling, Bernal even argues that privacy and autonomy are threatened by the use of true data as well as false data. Even if things are true, privacy includes the right to keep things secret and private.

Threats to due process are in particular relevant in relation to law enforcement or national security practices and not in the commercial context. However, as was shown, the cooperation between commercial companies and law enforcement agencies is increasing and includes processes where certain decisions on what kind of behavior is deemed suspicious are taken by commercial companies. These decisions can even be based on automated analyses and filtering technologies that constitute profiles of 'suspicious' individuals. Moreover, the activities undertaken by commercial companies to find 'suspicious behavior' are less embedded in legal requirements than when these activities are performed by law enforcement authorities.

The risk of unfair decisions based on correct profiles that allow for unwarranted and invisible discrimination is directly relevant in the context of the democratic state as well. When data controllers do not operate responsibly and fairly, the categorization of individuals will lead to increased social exclusion and marginalization of individuals that were already vulnerable.[469] Social classes will be reconfirmed and articulated. Society as a whole becomes probably less democratic, while at the individual level the impact of social exclusion is increased, as is the case with weblining.[470] Internet access will further reduce options instead of increasing them by facilitating access to information.

The taking of unmotivated and unilateral decisions about individuals has a strong relation with activities such as weblining, which were described above. Opportunities of individuals are denied based on their digital personae. Credit cards may be offered with a lower limit, not because of the individual credit history, but because of more general attributes, such as

---

[468] Bernal 2011, p. 286.
[469] Lyon 2007, p. 177.
[470] Stepanek 2000.

race, sex or postal code or the types of web sites the individual visits.[471] In the context of advertising, there is the paradox of the mass-personalization: in order to make information relevant to the individual, the individual has to be categorized. The individual's view of the online world is unique, but similarly unique as for others.[472]

The current use of digital personae and profiles can, thus, severely affect the individual. The reasons can be related to the increasing technological possibilities, including data mining, combining data bases, (re-)identifiability, and connecting to individuals without identification. Also the types of data that become available are emerging and can be used in other contexts than in which they were initially disclosed when they are 'publicly' available.[473] The possible level of impact for the individual is related to whether the data set used as a basis for decisions is a profile or a digital persona. The use of a digital persona can have a higher impact than the use of a profile, in particular in relation to legal effects, where it is often necessary that the individual is identified. However, a profile can often easily become a digital persona and the two are on a sliding scale. All actions taken based on profiles can, thus, also move into the direction of taking decisions based on digital personae.

6. Conflicts with the main values and rights to be respected

The conflicts with data protection principles imply that privacy can be harmed by the use of digital personae and, to a certain extent, profiles. It was also shown that the DPD in its current form is inadequate to deal with these threats to privacy when decisions are taken on the basis of digital personae. Next to privacy, the other main values and rights presented in Chapter 4 are at stake. In this section, conflicts with the main values and rights, resulting from the use of digital personae, will be discussed.

The scenarios and practices described above bring considerable challenges to contextual integrity and informational self-determination. To start with the latter, it is obvious that an individual cannot control with whom to share data when he is not aware of the data being collected on another party's initiative. If there is no clear notification of the collection of personal data and the entire process is part of a technical mechanism which is not directly visible, the individual cannot be aware of his data being processed. Data subjects have to be informed about their data being processed and by whom. In many cases this information is absent or has to be found by searching

---

[471] Andrews 2012.
[472] Van 't Hof, Van Est & Timmer 2012, p. 232.
[473] For instance, the use of Facebook data by credit rating agencies: <http://gigaom.com/europe/credit-agency-mines-facebook-data/> (last accessed June 20, 2012).

for a privacy policy on a website. In the case that a contract for a service is closed, however, this information may be disclosed properly. At least, the contracting parties are known and the data processing can be indicated by the data controller. Whether the individual understands the purposes and impact of the processing is questionable, as was seen above.

The storage of information on an external memory, instead of only disclosing in a one on one interaction, makes that telling and listening become two "distinct events separated in time,"[474] implying that one cannot directly see one's audience. Here, two particular reasons can be identified for the loss of control over information. First, each sharing of data is a loss of control in itself, and, second, each online interaction reveals information to the other party, even when no files are shared.[475] The nature of online interactions, thus, makes that there is always more data disclosure than only explicitly communicated data. In particular, the additional data, such as web browsing behavior or click trails within a website that can be automatically collected and analyzed is what commercial companies are looking for.

With regard to contextual integrity, problems also arise due to the multiplicability of data. Data can easily be copied and transferred to other environments than those in which the data (the digital persona) were created or collected. The specific context in which data are disclosed may become blurred because of the covert presence of other parties that may take or transfer the data to a different context immediately. Control over contexts, deciding what data to disclose in what context, and defining the contextual norms in an interaction become, thus, problematic to maintain. However, even without active copying or transferring the data can often be accessed by other parties. Online environments, such as SNS, contain lots of information which is meant for a specific context,[476] but can be accessed by people or organizations from other contexts as well.[477] Moreover, each time information is retrieved it becomes de- and recontextualized because pieces of information are retrieved without their accompanying contexts and presented in a new context of search results.[478] In particular, when data is disclosed in a specific context and not in general, the data may be assumed to be interesting for other contexts. For instance, consider the case where

---

[474] Mayer-Schönberger 2009, p. 29.
[475] Mayer-Schönberger 2009, pp. 85-87.
[476] Leenes 2010.
[477] Information is often sold by entities to other entities: Solove 2003, p. 7. SNS sell advertising opportunities to companies who can have their advertisements targeted at specific groups of SNS users. The SNS functions as an intermediary in this case and sells access to their advertising space and not directly to the profiles.
[478] Mayer-Schönberger 2009, p. 90.

credit reporting agencies[479] sell information to insurance companies who can set their rates based on this information. The "very fact that people are willing to provide their data for one, distinct purpose makes those data especially attractive as bases for action for quite different purposes."[480] Data in electronic form cannot only be easily spread to multiple points, but is also accessible from multiple points. "The grapevine is thorough, scientific, and precise; records of whom we are and what we have done follow us around and even sometimes precede us."[481] Next to information being publicly accessible or being decontextualized, the digitization of data also increased the risk of data leakage. Obviously, when data are leaked, the risk of decontextualization is very high if not directly present.

The risk of decontextualization is increased by the behavior of individuals themselves as well, resulting from technological possibilities. People work from home, make business phone calls in public environments, and send private emails from their offices. Mobile technologies used by businesses, together with the economic landscape which has individuals 24/7 available, make that context and location no longer coincide.[482]

When different partial identities are connected to each other the contexts to which these partial identities relate collapse. This means that information from one context becomes available in another context. People who have access to a context will then also have access to the information, even when they initially were not able to access the other context as well. One can imagine examples of an employer getting access to information, posted, for instance, on Facebook by either the employee or by others, about an employee's drinking party last night and the resulting hangover while the employee was reporting ill because of a fever.[483] Obviously, an employer will confront the employee with the clear facts and the employee then becomes aware of the information being available to the employer. Painful as it may be, the employee at least gets some knowledge about the collapsed contexts. However, in the case of digitally available information things may even be worse, because this knowledge is often lacking. The collection and combination of data takes place behind the scenes. Individuals are not, or only partially, aware of their data being collected. How and by whom these data are combined is even more opaque. It is clear that the individual has no

---

[479] Experian, for instance, can provide information on creditworthiness of individuals based on combinations of online and offline data.
[480] Goold & Neyland 2009, p. 9.
[481] Nissenbaum 2010, p. 40.
[482] Hildebrandt 2011, p. 37.
[483] For this and other examples, see: < http://www.natlawreview.com/article/status-update-fired-social-media-great-way-to-market-company-it-also-great-way-to-get-fired-> (last accessed June 20, 2012).

freedom to disclose what he wants and to decide to whom things are disclosed. Because the individual is not actively involved, there cannot be consent for the disclosure and the lack of knowledge implies that there is no mechanism for control afterwards. Also the purposes for which the data are used remain unclear or may even be undetermined beforehand. With individuals being totally unaware, there can be no informational self-determination, and with collapsing contexts there is no contextual integrity. Thus, privacy is violated on its main aspects.

Another issue concerns the construction of identity free from unreasonable constraints.[484] As an example of an unreasonable constraint the forced disclosure of data irrelevant or unnecessary for the service at stake was given. Obviously, when numerous data are collected and combined this unreasonable constraint is at stake as well. There are no means for individuals to avoid disclosure, because new technologies and ways of circumventing privacy enhancing tools are developed continuously.[485] As a result, the individual is not able to carefully construct several partial identities and to stay in control over the data disclosed in each partial identity. An additional problem is the difficulty to determine whether some constraint is 'unreasonable'. The use of proactive technologies, for instance to serve personalized advertisements or to automatically apply personalized preferences, has a nudging influence,[486] which is invisible to the individual. Potentially, automated decisions are an unreasonable constraint to the freedom of identity construction. Whether the constraint is indeed unreasonable, however, can only be judged when it is clear on what grounds (data) the decision was based and what the effects will be.[487] It is, thus, very difficult to foresee what information is derived from individual behavior and what inferences result in a particular proactive treatment by a service provider, which is also known as the 'inference problem'.[488]

Individual autonomy means that the individual is able to make his own choices and to specify his own desires. When data are collected and analyzed in order to make decisions concerning the individual, autonomy can be affected. The individual is not always involved in the decision making process, but is particularly affected when decisions have a nudging effect and/or when there are no clear options for the individual to challenge the decision. Besides, targeted advertisements and even the relatively simple decision to confront

---

[484] In line with the privacy definition by Agre 1997 (see Chapter 4).
[485] See, for instance, evercookies (<http://samy.pl/evercookie/>) and HTTP cookie respawning (McDonald & Cranor 2011).
[486] See above, section 5.3.
[487] Hildebrandt 2011, p. 43.
[488] Dwyer 2009, as referred to by: Hildebrandt 2011, p. 42.

an individual with a certain advertisement or not can have influences on the freedom of choice. In particular, the options that are not shown to the individual cannot, or only in limited cases, be detected by the individual, therewith limiting the overview of options an individual could have. The phenomenon of limited choices, combined with difficulties to take notice of alternative viewpoints and information, is what Pariser has called the 'Filter Bubble'.[489] Targeted advertising or selectively providing information can create a vicious circle, which continuously reaffirms earlier choices based on limited information. Content providers supply 'tailored' information as a reply to (implicitly or explicitly) provided personal information concerning traits and interests of individuals. Newly provided personal information will be based on the information previously provided by the content provider. This 'vicious circle' will " 'push' individuals towards certain products or services in which they initially were not interested [...]. This is achievable by narrowing down the options they receive and offering persuasive arguments at exactly the right time, thus impeding their autonomy."[490] Taking the idea of the 'database of intentions'[491] a step further makes clear that companies are trying to predict future behavior in a broad sense. Also possible desires or wishes are determined, or companies decide to influence an individual directly in order to steer the development of desires. In that case the individual is no longer sufficiently free to decide for himself which choices to make and which desires to specify. As was shown in Chapter 5, on-the-fly web personalization facilitates the steering of decisions and desires at an individual level by including specific content displayed in specific forms, while making it more difficult for other content to be found. Long term goals are specified by other parties and the individual is at least influenced in his decisions.[492] An individual must be able to retreat from such influence in order to achieve some kind of autonomy.[493]

Strikingly, negative impact on individual autonomy may also occur as a result from general inclusion. For instance, in the US, in the context of underserved classes, internet access has been promoted.[494] At first sight, internet access would bring new chances and benefits. Basically, lack of access to the internet and limited abilities to benefit from this access, for instance concerning job search and retrieving information, can result in social inequalities[495] and providing internet access can help solving these problems. However, it also allowed for data profiling of underserved classes in order to offer

---

[489] Pariser 2011.
[490] Zarsky 2002-2003, p. 38.
[491] Battelle 2005-2006.
[492] Zarsky 2002-2003, p. 38.
[493] Hildebrandt 2008a , p. 310.
[494] Gangadharan 2012.
[495] Witte & Mannon 2009.

subprime mortgages. The "subprime lending boom highlights the harmful consequences of mining, triangulating, and targeting. It highlights the intersection between data profiling and exclusionary practices of the subprime industry to exploit and disempower the underserved."[496] The inclusion in new technologies, thus, can also create more social exclusion instead of only promoting equality and social justice.[497] In this respect, the 'digital divide' acquires a new meaning. There is a shift from a 'digital divide', the distinction *between* haves and have-nots, to digital inequality, which is the inequality *among* persons with formal access to the internet.[498]

Another aspect is lack of transparency. An individual gets confronted with a decision. This can even be in the sense that an individual just notices nothing but is excluded from some service or product, such as an insurance which is not shown on a website, because, based on profiling information, the individual seems not to belong to the target group. What data a digital persona consists of is often difficult to know completely. However, the way the data are processed and which data or indications lead to a certain decision is even more difficult to find out. Besides, it is not always clear where data come from and with whom they are shared. In particular, in cases where it can be argued that there are no personal data, data protection regulations may not be applicable, leading to less protection of the privacy of the individual. Nevertheless, privacy is often indicated as a necessary condition for the fulfillment of the right to autonomy.

Lack of transparency and (informational) self-determination leads to barriers for the proper fulfillment of the right to autonomy. The use of digital personae creates a distance between the service provider and the individual. The individual is no longer necessarily involved in the interaction, or to a lesser extent, to come to a decision. It can be the case that a service provider only asks for some information from the individual, which is then accomplished with data the service provider already has in the digital persona representing this individual. It can, however, also be the case that a service provider asks for all information, but compares the information from the individual with the information in the digital persona and still comes to another decision. In these cases, misinterpretation of data can have huge consequences and relying blindly on the data and ignoring the information from the individual even makes it worse. In the commercial sector this kind of mistake is often made, with great negative impacts. Mainly in the US, employers have commercial companies run background checks on future employees. To perform these checks, several sources are combined, ranging from public

---

[496] Gangadharan 2012.
[497] Gangadharan 2012.
[498] DiMaggio & Hargittai 2001.

records and court records to private records and internet profiles which disclose interests of the individual. Mistakes can occur, for instance when there are more individuals with the same name, and the data are not checked accurately. As a result, individuals can be denied a job or loan.[499]

A relatively new practice is the close cooperation between Facebook and law enforcement authorities.[500] Facebook is automatically scanning postings and chats in order to search for criminal or suspicious behavior.[501] When something suspicious is found, the information is handed over to the police. An example was a man who was arrested because he allegedly solicited a minor.[502] The automated scanning activities now imply that over 1 billion individuals, the amount of monthly active members Facebook now has,[503] are closely monitored. At the moment it is unclear whether 'suspicious' chats or posts are deleted afterwards or whether they are stored permanently.[504] Even though it may be a good thing that Facebook is helping to prevent crime, there is an important problem. It is unclear how the algorithm works and what activities or words are flagged as suspicious. When a series of events (or probably one single event) is registered, the information is handed over to the police. The workings of the algorithm, however, influence what information is presented and how. Because of the automated process, the risk of decontextualization of the information is high. The risk of false positives is, thus, equally high. The individual, however, may be arrested and accused of criminal activities.

In relation to digital personae and inclusion or exclusion of customers based on categorization of these digital personae the lack of choice and the lack of protection against influences external from the individual are important. An individual can be positively affected when, for instance, serendipity is increased by attending him to products he would not have found otherwise.[505]

---

[499] Robertson 2011.
[500] See Facebook's help page on 'Law Enforcement and Third Party Matters': < https://www.facebook.com/help/?page=211462112226850>, last visited 4 October 2012.
[501] Morozov 2012. What 'suspicious behavior' exactly means is unclear. Most likely, it is related to a number of specific criminal acts that often take place via SNS, such as soliciting minors or trafficking.
[502] See < http://www.reuters.com/article/2012/07/12/us-usa-internet-predators-idUSBRE86B05G20120712>, last visited 4 October 2012.
[503] See < http://www.reuters.com/article/2012/10/04/us-facebook-idUSBRE8930N320121004>, last visited 4 October 2012.
[504] See < http://mashable.com/2012/07/12/facebook-scanning-chats/>, last visited 4 October 2012.
[505] This is, for instance, in line with the corporate philosophy of Google, which aims to understand what people mean and to make information accessible and as relevant as possible: <http://www.google.nl/about/company/products/> (last accessed June 27, 2012).

On the other hand, however, there can be a negative effect in the sense that an individual is excluded from certain choices or products.[506] For instance, banks can decide on the basis of carefully collected information how much time and effort to spend on a specific customer. If the customer seems not to have much money, it is not worthwhile to invest much time. But jobs can also be denied based on profiling. While there is a right which allows job applicants not to indicate that they are pregnant, and there is no obligation to share their race or sexual preferences, this information can be derived from online sources and used to discriminate against certain applicants.[507] The limitation of opportunities negatively affects autonomy.

To conclude, when choices are influenced by others or when collected and analyzed information leads to restrictions on identity construction, the individual is affected. So, the creation and use of digital personae and profiles certainly has implications for the real-world individual. Lack of transparency in data collection, data usage, and decision making processes makes the individual vulnerable to restrictions on autonomy and identity construction. Unfortunately, it seems that there is no real escape possible due to technological developments.[508] Also protection measures taken by website providers are often insufficient to prevent privacy leakage.[509] Even in the case of promising initiatives, such as the DoNotTrack (DNT) system, problems arise concerning the interpretation by businesses[510] as well as expectations amongst internet users.[511] A user may clearly indicate that he does not want to be tracked, but a company can decide to do so, but not to use the data for targeted advertising purposes. When an individual wants to have certain aspects of his browsing behavior excluded from tracking, but is fine with other parts, he may switch the DNT feature on and off. A result of the diverging interpretation by a company may be that the part that should be excluded from tracking is still used as inut for targeted advertisements.

Ultimately, when the individual is unable to construct his own individual identity in a manner that is free from unreasonable constraints, and in line with his own wishes and desires, the human dignity of this individual

---

[506] As is the case with weblining, where, comparable to redlining, groups of people are systematically excluded from offers based on where they live (via IP address) or what their expected spending behavior is: Stepanek 2000.

[507] Stefanovic 2012.

[508] See Chapter 5.

[509] Krishnamurthy, Naryshkin & Wills 2011.

[510] Businesses appear to interpret DoNotTrack as DoNotTarget, meaning that they still track individuals over the web, but do not use the collected information for providing targeted advertisements. More on the DNT technology: Tene & Polonetsky 2011; and on the distinction between tracking and targeting: Bilenko, Richardson & Tsai 2011.

[511] McDonald & Peha 2011.

is affected. The uniqueness of the individual as a human being, unique in his own kind, and developing according to his own desires, is affected by others. Moreover, practices of companies making their profit out of the use and sale of personal information may conflict with human dignity, since the individual is seen as an asset. The classifications are based on the interests of the profiling companies and their clients and not on the interests of the individual.[512] The individual is in these cases negatively affected and not able to profit from his economic value, which would better balance the interests of companies and the individuals. The current information society, or data society, is to a large extent based on the monetization of data, which was not yet the case at the introduction of the DPD in 1995. Moreover, the increasing use of monitoring and profiling technologies to analyze and influence individual behavior has an effect on individual autonomy. Autonomy is affected by actual threats as well as by perceived threats,[513] in the form of a chilling effect, where individuals adapt their behavior in order to prevent being classified in a certain manner. Behavior is no longer completely free.

A way to solve the problems described above may be to protect the digital persona, because this is the direct link between the individual and the information concerning the individual which is used to affect the individual. Protecting digital personae may offer legal safeguards and in the end offer better protection for the individual as a human being with an inherent value. Appropriate protection of privacy and individual autonomy facilitates free identity construction. The current legal system is insufficient to offer this protection. In particular, the narrowing down of human dignity to privacy, and of privacy to data protection, are crucial points of attention when addressing this problem. This implies that an alternative approach has to be taken in regulation, which explicitly addresses the individual with human dignity as the ultimate goal of protection.

7. Problem definition: Legal uncertainty for data controllers and inappropriate protection of individuals

In this section, the key problems related to the protection of the rights and values of individuals will be described on the basis of the analysis provided in this and the previous chapters, which leads to a definitive formulation of the main research question of this study.

---

[512] Bernal 2011, p. 150.
[513] Bernal 2011, p. 288.

7.1. Two key problems

In principle, the practical issues described in the previous sections can be summarized as two key issues. First, there are problems related to the applicability of the DPD. Commercial companies often deny the link to the individual, therewith trying to declare the DPD inapplicable to their data processing activities. The fact that data are collected from individuals does not necessarily imply that it concerns personal data. Aggregated sets or sets of data that are not linked to an individual, such as group profiles, are considered anonymous data. However, at some point in time an individual may be recognized as carrying one or more attributes from the data set and the data set can be connected to this identified or identifiable individual. The data set, then, becomes an individual or personal profile, and a digital persona. The problem is that all the data that were processed before the link to an individual could be made were not subjected to the DPD, but the data set can be very rich and include inferred data as well. When the processing was started, however, a ground for legitimizing the processing was lacking, simply because it was not yet needed. Moreover, the profiles as such are also used to affect individuals, so some form of protection of individuals in relation to profiles is needed as well.

The concept of personal data is broadly interpreted by the Article 29 Working Party and, in their opinion, can include IP addresses and cookie identifiers. Nevertheless, this opinion focuses on the option of the data becoming related to an identifiable individual while this may be very uncertain. In fact, the inclusion of too many data sets (and profiles) in the DPD regime leads to legal uncertainty for data controllers and individuals. The EGE indicates that, as a consequence of the broad and flexible concept of personal data, there are "numerous cases where it is not always clear whether individuals enjoy data protection rights and whether data controllers should comply with the obligations imposed by the Directive."[514] Besides, if the DPD is rendered applicable, data controllers can probably not always fulfill their information duties[515] as long as the individual is not identifiable and, thus, not be compliant with the DPD. Adding information in order to identify the individual for this purpose would have a counter-effect on the protection offered by the DPD. Taking account of the fact that any other person might be able to relate data that are anonymous for the controller to an identified or identifiable person is too much of a burden in the current technological

---

[514] European Group on Ethics 2012, p. 46.
[515] It can be argued that based on the cookie or IP address a device can be recognized and the information can be provided. This would, however, in many cases need the cooperation of numerous parties, in particular when third parties provide services to website owners, because the first party would have to provide space on his website for the information.

system of web interactions, which include several parties and possibilities for others to obtain the data.

The second issue is a complex of purpose binding and legitimate ground difficulties. One difficulty relates to the weighing of the economic interests of companies against the privacy interests of the individual. There are several aspects to this, ranging from the way the weighing of interests is performed by the data controller to the practice of covering data processing activities based on contracts. Also enforcement is relevant in this respect. Enforcement takes place ex post and data protection authorities are insufficiently equipped to adequately perform their tasks.[516] As a result, the balance between the free flow of information and the privacy of the data subject, which are the two protection goals of the DPD, is absent. Moreover, data mining practices may reveal information that was never intended to be disclosed by the individual, even though the separate pieces of data may have been gathered with his consent. As it is unknown what information may be revealed, it is impossible to specify the exact purpose for which the data will be used, which may make data mining practices incompatible with the use limitation and purpose specification principles.[517] Besides, it is simply impossible to make a proper weighing of interests if the effects of processing are unpredictable, making it hard to determine how the data subject's interests are affected. The same problem is present in relation to informed consent. The individual cannot properly be informed when purposes are too vague or when possible future implications are unclear and difficult to predict. Technological practice, thus, runs out of step with the protection needed from the DPD.

7.2. Synthesis and research question

Digital personae often contain personal data in a broad sense. They are related to individuals that can be affected by decisions based on the representation. This is also the case for profiles, even though the decisions may be less significant in most cases. There is the possibility to make a connection to the individual. Whether this individual is 'identified' or 'identifiable' in the sense of the Data Protection Directive is not relevant. More importantly, however, the problem is not just related to the processing of personal data. In cases where digital personae indeed contain personal data, the processing of these data can completely take place in conformity with the law. The DPD provides requirements for the lawful processing of personal data. Nevertheless, the processing is the central focus point in data protection legislation and not

---

[516] Robinson, Graux, Botterman & Valeri 2009, p. 35. Whether an infringement of data protection legislation is taken up for investigation by a DPA is dependent on capacity and priorities. A complaint, thus, not always results in enforcement.
[517] European Group on Ethics 2012, p. 57.

the effects this processing may have. The right to data protection has to be seen as a procedural right.[518] In the case of digital personae, real-world individuals are affected by decisions taken based on the processing of the data. Even when the processing is lawful, i.e. in accordance with the DPD, the impact of a decision concerning the individual can have implications for his privacy and autonomy, and ultimately impact human dignity. The right to privacy and identity, and the related concepts, are substantive rights.[519] Because of the procedural nature of data protection rights as opposed to the substantive nature of the rights and concepts it aims to protect, a mismatch occurs. This implies that current data protection legislation only provides limited protection for the individual.

Even when all data of which the processing can affect an individual should be considered personal data, this problem remains. The reason for that is that the digital persona is a potentially extremely fine-grained representation of an individual in the form of a data set. It does not concern separate data parts that can be considered personal data or not. Instead, the concept entails the complete picture that is available as a representation of the real-world individual. The completeness of the representation makes it a valuable source for decision making. Basically, decisions are taken based on characteristics which are the attributes or facets of the personality of the individual, and the right to identity of the individual is infringed,[520] because the individual does not have the option to keep partial identities separated and to decide what his identity looks like autonomously. By using the digital persona as a representation instead of directly interacting with the represented individual, the distance towards the individual is growing.[521] As a result, the impact of the decisions still affects the individual, because he is excluded from certain options or services or is denied a job or a loan, but the means for control by the individual are diminished or simply not available. Even though data protection regulation offers data subject rights, such as the right to access, erasure, or modification of data, these rights cannot help the individual to protect his autonomy. Assuming that the data subject has knowledge of the data set, the rights may only be helpful to have data changed or erased, but the data subject cannot directly influence or challenge the decision based on the data. Next to that, obtaining insight on the algorithms used to process the data may not provide sufficient clarity, since this is often too technical for individuals to understand.

---

[518] Andrade 2012, p. 125.
[519] Andrade 2012, p. 125.
[520] Andrade 2012, p. 125.
[521] Gürses & Berendt 2010, p. 309.

In the DPD, the legitimate ground for the processing of personal data with which the data subject seems to have most control is consent. Basically, in these cases the individual has given his consent for the processing of his personal data. If the data processor abides by the DPD, the processing is even bound to a specific purpose beforehand. Nevertheless, the description of this purpose can be very general. But more importantly, the data subject cannot foresee the impact the processing may have. As a result, the autonomy of the individual may be seriously affected despite the consent for processing personal data.

The DPD stems from 1995 and the technical possibilities for processing personal data at the time were not at the level they are now. Back in 1995, the key activities were mainly related to relatively simple registration purposes, such as digitizing address books and probably some mailing lists, whereas now personal data processing is part of a large variety of activities. From that perspective, it is not that strange that the data subject's rights included in the DPD seemed sufficient safeguards. However, even in the current reform of the DPD the focus is on consent and personal data protection. Taking into account that the current technologies can have many more implications for the autonomy of the individual, it is not likely that the reforms will solve these problems when the regulators stick to the original starting points and try to strengthen them. The processing of personal data as such is just not the main issue, but the effect it may have on the individual is the most important point.

For the same reason, applying a broad interpretation of the concept of personal data and, thus, considering the DPD applicable to most processing activities, does not help. Of course, data such as IP addresses and location data can sometimes be considered personal data and bringing these data within the scope of the DPD can be useful. However, the focus should not be on separate types of data, but on the affected individual. Data protection, as regulated by the DPD, is only a part of privacy and privacy is instrumental to individual autonomy. In the end, individual autonomy is therefore a much broader and higher level concept than personal data protection. Protecting, or regulating, the way personal data can be processed does not necessarily offer sufficient protection of privacy. Nevertheless, in the preamble of the DPD, privacy is mentioned several times as a right of the individual to be protected by the Directive.[522]

---

[522] "[T]he rights and freedoms of individuals, notably the right to privacy, which are contained in this Directive". Preamble (2), (7), (10), (11), and (68). Strikingly, the proposed General Data Protection Regulation (see Chapter 7 below) hardly refers to privacy as a normative background, but mentions a right to data protection instead (Costa & Poullet 2012, p. 255).

Moreover, the problems as described in this study are more related to human dignity, individual autonomy, and identity being affected as a result of insufficient protection of privacy. The DPD has a process-oriented approach towards privacy and data protection, whereas the problem described in this study is result-oriented, looking at the impact on the privacy and autonomy of the individual. Privacy and autonomy are necessary conditions for the achievement of respect for identity and human dignity in the end.

The problem is that there appears to be a lot of legal uncertainty. In the case of profiles, the DPD is not always applicable or the applicability is uncertain. Data controllers have to base their decisions on the applicability on probabilities. Moreover, applying the DPD to profiles concerning non-identifiable individuals is difficult in practice and not logical from a legal perspective. The exact scope of the DPD is unclear and, even though profiles can be anonymous, individuals may be affected by the use of their profiles. Individual autonomy and the construction of identity free from unreasonable constraints may be infringed upon. The focus in the DPD, however, is on the protection of privacy by means of regulating the processing and not the impact of the processing.

In order to better respect human dignity and the related concepts that deserve protection, a starting point may be to protect digital personae. Moreover, the importance of profiles has become clear throughout this study. Therefore, when including profiles as well, the final main research question of this study is:

Can the (legal) protection of digital personae and profiles as coherent data sets, taking into account that they are used by businesses as a basis for making decisions that affect real world individuals, improve the protection of privacy and autonomy of the individuals represented by these digital personae?

Protecting the persona by providing a certain status or by granting rights will set limitations on the use of digital personae. Since the digital persona represents the real-world individual, the limitation of use on the digital persona could in the end help to protect the individual against decisions based on the digital persona. When searching for a solution to improve the protection of individuals, profiles will also be kept in mind, since this study has shown that these are relevant in relation to decision making concerning individuals as well. In the next chapter, several legal approaches from existing legal regimes will be assessed on their applicability to digital personae in order to find out whether these could be helpful for achieving better protection of the individual.

Part III

Protection of Digital Personae

Chapter 7
Protection of Digital Personae

1. Introduction

In this Chapter, existing legal concepts that may be helpful in solving the problem will be explored. The previous chapter showed shortcomings in the DPD. Shortcomings in the data protection system in general were an incentive to revise the data protection framework. In January 2012, a draft proposal became available for a General Data Protection Regulation, which will replace the current Data Protection Directive (DPD). In order to assess whether the shortcomings with regard to the use of digital personae may be solved by the newly proposed Regulation, the relevant changes proposed in this Regulation will first be discussed here. Then, a number of legal concepts that are currently in place will be discussed in order to assess whether these can offer a solution, either directly or by analogy. These concepts will be discussed hypothetically, as if they are applied currently, in order to provide a lively view of the implications if these concepts would be applied to digital personae.

2. Draft proposal for a General Data Protection Regulation

In Chapter 6, it was argued that the current legal framework for privacy and data protection insufficiently protects the privacy and autonomy of the individual in view of digital personae. The main source of protection with regard to data processing is the DPD. This Directive is currently under revision and will be replaced in due time. The revision of the EU data protection framework concerns the complete framework, including data protection in the context of law enforcement.[523] A proposal for the new regulatory framework is already available, so an assessment can be made of the major changes that may have an impact on the creation and use of digital personae and on the privacy and autonomy of the individual. An important change with regard to data protection in commercial contexts is in the instrument: the new proposal is a Regulation[524] instead of a Directive. This Regulation - General Data Protection Regulation (GDPR) - has

---

[523] The entire proposed package is available online at: <http://ec.europa.eu/justice/newsroom/data-protection /news/120125_en.htm> (last accessed June 28, 2012).
[524] Brussels, 25.1.2012, COM (2012) 11 final. Proposal for a regulation of the European Parliament and of the Council on the protection of individuals with regard to the processing of personal data and on the free movement of such data (General Data Protection Regulation).

general applicability in all EU Member States and has direct applicability
without discretionary power for the Member States (as was the case with
the DPD). For the context of Police and Criminal Justice a separate Directive
is proposed. This Directive sets the minimum standards for EU Member
States for the protection of personal data and the free movement of these
data for the purposes of prevention, investigation, detection or prosecution
of criminal offences or the execution of criminal penalties. Since this study
focuses on commercial use of digital personae and not on the use by public
authorities or law enforcement, only the draft Regulation will be discussed
here.

The Preamble of the GDPR contains a number of important recitals in
relation to digital personae. For instance, recital 24 concerns identifiers.
It states that: "When using online services, individuals are associated with
online identifiers provided by their devices, applications, tools and protocols,
such as Internet Protocol addresses or cookie identifiers. Since this leave[s]
traces which, combined with unique identifiers and other information
received by the servers, can be used to create profiles of the individuals and
identify them, this Regulation should be applicable to processing involving
such data." IP addresses and cookie identifiers are explicitly mentioned
here. Furthermore, it is indicated that these identifiers facilitate the creation
of profiles of individuals and identify them. In the context of cookies and
IP addresses, identification is, thus, also considered possible based on
recognition or singling out of an individual web visitor. Cookie identifiers
or IP addresses can function as connectors between online activity and the
offline individual. When combined with, or including a unique identifier, the
data sets become digital personae instead of profiles. For instance, Facebook
can connect online activity of an individual member to this person's account
based on the user ID in the cookie. The name of the individual member is
known[525] and is a direct identifier.

Recital 30 specifies a number of the data protection principles: lawfulness,
fairness, transparency, data quality, and data minimization. The principles
of proportionality and subsidiarity are also highlighted. Proportionality is
underscored in relation with limitation to "the minimum necessary for the
purposes for which the data are processed", and subsidiarity by indicating
that "[p]ersonal data should only be processed if the purpose of the
processing could not be fulfilled by other means."

The GDPR is with 91 Articles significantly more extensive than the DPD (34
Articles). The most important changes concern clarifications and updates of
existing definitions, and the introduction of new concepts. An important

---

[525] Facebook requires users to use their real name and actively checks this.

change as regards the definitions is in the definition of 'consent',[526] where the criterion 'explicit' is added. The reason for this is to avoid confusion with 'unambiguous consent' and to have "one single and consistent definition of consent, ensuring the awareness of the data subject that, and to what, he or she gives consent."[527] Obtaining consent, thus, requires an explicit action by the data subject. Next to that, the burden of proof that consent has been provided lies with the data controller, who, thus, has to store the (actions signifying) consent. The data controller has to include an explicit step for the individual to give consent in his processes and show that this step really shows an explicit action of the individual. With regard to digital personae, this means that meeting the condition for legitimate processing based on consent is made more severe.

A new right introduced in the GDPR is the 'Right to be forgotten' (Article 17). It is an extension to the right to erasure of data in the DPD. It provides "the conditions of the right to be forgotten, including the obligation of the controller which has made the personal data public to inform third parties on the data subject's request to erase any links to, or copy or replication of that personal data. It also integrates the right to have the processing restricted in certain cases, avoiding the ambiguous terminology 'blocking'."[528] These conditions are somewhat limited compared to an earlier draft[529] of the proposal, in which the obligation to inform third parties was still an obligation for the data controller to erase any public internet link, copy of, or replication of the personal data relating to the data subject contained in any publicly available communication service. In the earlier draft proposal it was provided that the data controller "shall in particular ensure the erasure of any public Internet link to, copy of, or replication of the personal data relating to the data subject contained in any publicly available communication service which allows or facilitates the search of or access to this personal data."[530] The final proposal asks for the data controller to "take all reasonable steps, including technical measures, in relation to data for the publication of which the controller is responsible, to inform third parties which are processing such data, that a data subject requests them to erase any links to, or copy or replication of that personal data. Where the controller has authorised a third party publication of personal data, the controller shall be considered responsible for that publication."[531] In particular the right to have all publicly available copies of data erased was a big step taken in the draft proposal. It

---

[526] Article 4(8) GDPR.
[527] Explanatory Memorandum of the GDPR, p. 8.
[528] Explanatory Memorandum of the GDPR, p. 9.
[529] Version 56, 29.11.2011. Online available at <http://statewatch.org/news/2011/dec/eu-com-draft-dp-reg-inter-service-consultation.pdf> (last accessed July 29, 2012).
[530] Article 15(2) of draft Version 56.
[531] Article 17(2) GDPR.

includes all public Internet links, so it seems that the aim is on links to pages on which the content is publicly available, i.e. without the need for a login. However, it would be inefficient not to include data on, for instance, social networking sites on non-public profile pages that are only accessible for Friends of the profile owner after logging in. Parts may be erased by the data subject himself, but there may also be information, such as tags on photos, which were placed by others and cannot always directly be erased by the profile owner. The extensive approach taken in the draft proposal might have been unrealistic, since the data controller will not always have the means to achieve deletion of all copies made by others. In the final proposal, are more reasonable approach is taken, which is based on a duty of effort of the data controller.

As opposed to the draft proposal, the relatively limited provision regarding the right to be forgotten in the GDPR proposal avoids an obligation for data controllers to police the entire internet,[532] while at the same time there is an emphasis on the responsibility of the data controller. Next to this practical approach, there is discussion on the scope and meaning of the right to be forgotten. Koops[533] indicates that there are several opinions on what the right should entail, mostly related to the envisioned aim of the right. He distinguishes between three guises: A right to have data deleted in due time, a claim on society to have a clean slate, and an individual interest in unrestrained expression in the here and now.[534] The latter seems to be of a different kind than the others, namely more related to forgetting as such, than to a legal right.[535] For the first two options, have data deleted in due time and the claim to have a clean slate, Koops sees (potential) 'harm' as main characteristic leading to a plea for a right to be forgotten.[536] Looking at the reasonable effort to be expected on a case-by-case basis seems the most appropriate way to go forward in distilling the exact, and feasible, meaning of a 'right to be forgotten'. With respect to digital personae, the right to be forgotten would be mostly relevant in the interpretation of the right to have data deleted in due time or the right to have a clean slate. Digital personae consisting of (outdated) data should be deleted and not be used as a basis for taking decisions. Next to that, a clean slate would imply that an old digital persona should not be compared to a more recent one. The most recent version should be leading or even the only one available. Some of the obligations for controllers, such as accuracy and transparency, support this idea: data have to be updated regularly and have to be checked on their

---

[532] Kuner 2012.
[533] Koops 2011.
[534] Koops 2011, p. 236.
[535] Koops 2011, p. 254.
[536] Koops 2011, p. 240 and 250.

accuracy in the current situation. The right to be forgotten can, thus, also support the principle of data quality.

Another new proposed right for the data subject is the right to data portability.[537] The data subject should be able to transfer data concerning him "from one automated processing system to and into another, without being prevented from doing so by the controller. As a precondition, it provides the right to obtain from the controller those data in a commonly used electronic format."[538] A digital persona, then, can be used in different systems on the initiative of the represented individual. This is even the case when the digital persona is not (solely) created by the individual. The individual can ask the controller to provide the digital persona in an electronic format and share it with other parties.

The DPD contains a prohibition against automated individual decisions in Article 15. In the GDPR, Article 20 builds on this article with some modifications and additional safeguards. It gives every natural person "the right not to be subject to a measure which produces legal effects concerning this natural person or significantly affects this natural person," based on automated processing for profiling purposes. By the formulation of this provision, digital personae and profiles are both covered, since the profiling has to concern a 'natural person'. This person does not necessarily have to be identified or identifiable yet, but as soon as identification is possible, rights of data subjects as provided for by the GDPR apply.[539] The exact reason for the changed terminology is unclear, but in any case it opens ways for including profiles as well. In the DPD, the term 'data subject' was used, which implies being identified or identifiable. Profiles could, thus, not be covered by the provision. According to Article 20, the profiling has to be meant to "analyse or predict in particular the natural person's performance at work, creditworthiness, economic situation, location, health, personal preferences, reliability or behaviour." Obviously, the question rises what 'significantly affects' means. The fact that the effect for the individual is not restricted to legal effects only is important. Moreover, the explicit mentioning of analyzing or predicting personal preferences or behavior is directly in line with the problems that arise from contemporary profiling practices. Being included or excluded for certain offers seems not to be a legal effect per se, but it certainly affects the individual. In addition, for drafting the new

---

[537] Article 18 GDPR.

[538] Explanatory Memorandum of the GDPR, p. 9.

[539] Strictly spoken, the GDPR only applies in cases where the data concern data subjects (identified or identifiable natural persons). As long as the data concern anonymous individuals, the individuals cannot exercise data subject rights either, or at least this may be very difficult.

Article account was taken of the Council of Europe's Recommendation on Profiling,[540] in which it was considered that "profiling an individual may result in unjustifiably depriving her or him from accessing certain goods or services and thereby violate the principle of non-discrimination."[541] Mere inclusion or exclusion can, thus, be indicated as a legal effect when it results in violation of non-discrimination principles. These principles form the starting point for legal provisions in which specific forms of discrimination as such are prohibited and are a specification of the fact that each individual has human dignity, regardless of personal characteristics or circumstances. Besides, the Recommendation indicates that different contexts should be kept separated when data are collected and analyzed for profiling purposes, since the right to privacy and protection of personal data "entails the existence of different and independent spheres of life where each individual can control the use she or he makes of her or his identity."[542] This is interesting in relation to digital personae. These are, as indicated earlier, created within a specific context. The transfer of digital personae to other contexts, or the use of digital personae for other purposes than originally intended, that is to say other than intended at the time of creation, is prohibited. In line with this, the combination of different digital personae that represent the same individual for different purposes or contexts is not allowed,[543] since this almost inevitably collapses the boundaries between different spheres of life. The link between profiling and potential limits on individual control in relation to the use of an individual's identity indicates that disrespecting contextual integrity can be considered a significant effect.

Section 4 of Article 20 GDPR provides some specific safeguards. The controller has to provide information as to the existence of processing for a measure and the envisaged effects of such processing on the data subject. These safeguards are very welcome in light of the protection of the data subject. Moreover, attention is paid to the effects of the processing and not only to the processing itself. However, there are some limitations. The safeguards only apply in a few cases, which are mentioned in section 2 of the Article, namely the entering into or the performance of a contract, lodged by the data subject; processing based on authorization by law, or; based on the consent of the data subject. In these cases, reference is made to the data subject, which means that the safeguards do not apply to profiles. In some cases, the safeguards may apply to digital personae, but only if the processing

---

[540] CM/Rec (2010)13.
[541] Preamble to the Council of Europe recommendation on Profiling.
[542] Preamble to the Council of Europe recommendation on Profiling.
[543] See also the proposed Article 5(b) on purpose binding: "Personal data must be collected for specified, explicit and legitimate purposes and not further processed in a way incompatible with those purposes."

is based on a contract (which is often not that straightforward) or for the performance of a contract. However, in particular in cases where profiling techniques are applied to target advertisements or to make other types of automated decisions on the fly, according to Article 20(2)(a) the safeguard would also require the opportunity for human intervention. This may be lacking in practice. The safeguards as presented are thus very ambitious and relate directly to the core problems of restrictions on autonomy and contextual integrity. Nevertheless, the wordings used as well as the limitation to cases where there is a data subject result in less protection than may be desirable.

The attention paid to profiling activities in the proposal is not surprising in light of a broader debate that is taking place with regard to online tracking and monitoring practices performed by several companies. The European Commission is closely collaborating with the American Federal Trade Commission (FTC) in order to come to a standard approach towards profiling. As can be derived from the preamble of the GDPR concerning (cookie) identifiers and the provision on automated decisions, the aim is to give users more control over the use of their browsing data. In particular, online behavioral advertising (OBA) is focused upon.[544] This was also reflected in Directive 2009/136/EC,[545] in which it is required that a user gives his consent[546] for being monitored and tracked. How this consent has to be expressed is still debated, but Recital 66 of the Directive states that such consent can be expressed by using the appropriate settings of a browser or another application.

Next to the regulatory initiatives concerning OBA, there are technical means being developed to provide the user with control. The most successful example thus far is the DoNotTrack (DNT) initiative. This initiative started back in 2007, when several interest groups asked the FTC to create a Do Not Track list for online advertising, comparable to the Do Not Call lists that already existed.[547] The idea was to have internet users being able to opt-out for tracking in one single step, instead of having to delete cookies on a

---

[544] Including a right to object to processing for direct marketing purposes in Article 19(2) GDPR.

[545] Directive 2009/136/EC of the European Parliament and of the Council of 25 November 2009 amending Directive 2002/22/EC on universal service and users' rights relating to electronic communications networks and services, Directive 2002/58/EC concerning the processing of personal data and the protection of privacy in the electronic communications sector and Regulation (EC) No 2006/2004 on cooperation between national authorities responsible for the enforcement of consumer protection laws, OJL 337/11.

[546] Article 5(3).

[547] Soghoian 2011.

regular basis. Several mechanisms have been experimented with, leading to the conclusion that the best option was to include a browser header that is being sent to advertising networks automatically when they provide content for a website a user is visiting.

The FTC took the lead towards a broad implementation of the system by publishing a staff report[548] on consumer privacy in relation to technological developments in 2010. The report was also aiming at receiving additional input on feasible technological systems for the implementation of a Do Not Track mechanism.[549] The internet standardization body, the W3C, is now taking care of the standards that have to be applied for implementations of the technology.[550] Nevertheless, the W3C seems to be hindered in this by lobbyists from the advertising industry (who have to cooperate towards a standard) and lots of issues are still heavily debated. For instance, the combination of online and offline data is part of the controversy. It is not clear whether a data controller is allowed to buy offline data on specific individuals if these individuals have DNT enabled. The combination of online and offline sources, however, is an emerging practice in marketing.[551] Besides, user expectations differ a lot as well.[552] Users may believe that DNT will stop all data collection, while in fact data collection often continues in aggregated form. Other users expect data collection with DNT to take place only for law enforcement or demographic purposes, or to measure interactions with ads, while none of these purposes is related to DNT. The currently available implementations (e.g. in IE9, Safari) in different browsers are not consistent with each other either. This indicates that a clear choice has to be made in the standardization process of the technology.

Altogether, the GDPR has some important improvements in comparison to the DPD. The introduction of a right to data portability and a right to be forgotten are welcome additions that can be of help in providing the individual with more control over his data and preventing the individual from being confronted with information that is outdated or irrelevant for the context in which it is used. Also the specification of the prohibition on profiling as including analyzing personal preferences and individual behavior as a basis for making decisions is highlighting an important practice. This addresses one of the main problems discussed in this study and gears attention to

---

[548] Federal Trade Commission 2010b.
[549] This input was, for instance, delivered by Stanford scholars, who participated in the development of DoNotTrack: Mayer & Narayanan 2011.
[550] Schwartz 2011.
[551] See, for instance, Mindshare's CORE which offers this service: <http://www.mindshareworld.com/who-we-are/news/@Mindshare_Launches_Core> last accessed July 29, 2012.
[552] McDonald & Peha 2011.

the effects of data processing activities instead of the requirements of the processing alone. Influencing personal preferences, which relates to individual autonomy, is indicated as an effect of profiling and targeting activities. Nevertheless, it is still uncertain whether the GDPR will offer the required level of protection. The main focus is still on the processing of the data and not on the effects. Besides, even though the aim of the instrument of a Regulation is total harmonization amongst all EU Member States, there is still room for a number of aspects to be explicated in additional legislation, sometimes even at the national level of the Member States.[553] The Articles where Member States have discretionary powers concern, for instance, Art. 9 (processing of sensitive personal data), 17 (exception on the right to be forgotten), 20 (exception on the provision on profiling), 21 (limitation of the scope of several Articles of the Regulation), 27 (mandatory processing of data), 44 (diversions from the rules on transfer of personal data), 78 (determination of sanctions), 81 (processing of health data), and 82 (processing of data in the context of an employment relationship).[554] A number of the improvements of protection offered by the GDPR are, thus, not necessarily always applicable and at a national level there may be exceptions on the rights.

To conclude, the GDPR reaffirms the current principles behind data protection legislation and provides a number of new rights for data subjects and requirements and accountabilities for data controllers. There are, however, still exceptions and open ends that have to be specified in lower regulation forms or at national levels. Moreover, the Regulation indirectly pays more attention to individuals affected by data processing, for instance in the form of data breach notification duties and the right to be forgotten, but does not directly add strong new tools for individuals to have their rights to autonomy and identity better protected. So, even though the Regulation proposal seems to be able to take data protection a significant step forward, the impact of the Regulation beyond the mere processing requirements will be limited. Individuals remain very dependent on the willingness of data controllers to comply with the Regulation.[555]

---

[553] Cuijpers, van Eecke, Kindt & de Vries 2012, p. 199.
[554] Cuijpers, van Eecke, Kindt & de Vries 2012, p. 186.
[555] Even though the Data Protection Authorities will receive more enforcement powers.

3. Legal personality[556] and legal status

The GDPR is still a proposal, and is expected to be adopted not earlier than the end of 2013 and enter into force in 2014 at the earliest. Nevertheless, as indicated above, it is not to be expected that the GDPR will provide better protection of the privacy and autonomy of individuals in relation to the use of digital personae and profiles. There are, however, a number of legal concepts that are already in place that may be helpful in achieving better protection for the individual with regard to the rights and values discussed in Chapter 5. A first approach is to look at granting certain rights or forms of protection to the digital persona itself.[557] This is possible by analogously applying the concepts of legal personality and legal status.

3.1. Legal personality and legal status in general

Digital personae can be seen as persons, albeit in a digital form. Therefore, a first step when considering existing legal concepts is to look at legal personality. Legal personality is a concept incorporated in law in order to have entities acquire the capacity to be the bearer in their own name of rights and obligations (legal capacity), to enter in other legal transactions (acting capacity), and to participate in a law suit (litigation capacity). Legal personality is the capacity of an entity to perform legally significant acts, such as concluding a contract. To be a legal person, thus, means to be the subject of rights and duties.[558] Adult natural persons essentially have legal personality, because they have to be able to perform legal acts, such as concluding contracts. Without legal personality for (adult) natural persons, no transactions would be possible and daily life would be obstructed. Associations of natural persons until relatively recently did not have legal personality. The lack of legal personality made that these associations as such had no rights and duties and were not covered by a state's jurisdiction. The associations are not natural persons with rights and duties, but entities formed by a group of natural persons. Legal personality is a legal fiction that was conceded to an entity in order to gain jurisdiction over natural persons behind it.[559] Moreover, these natural persons were enabled to perform legal acts on behalf of the association and, thus, to represent the association in transactions. By analogy, digital personae can be considered to be entities

---

[556] 'Legal personality' and 'legal personhood' are used as synonyms in this section. The choice for which of the two to use depends on the term used by the discussed or cited author.

[557] Profiles can become digital personae and are closely related, so, in order to avoid repetition, I will not discuss these as a separate category throughout this Chapter.

[558] Zimmer 2005, p. 270.

[559] Zimmer 2005, p. 269-270.

related to the natural persons they represent. In order to protect individuals, it is, thus, worthwhile to consider whether a digital persona can be attributed legal personality in order to give it rights and duties. A corporation cannot act on itself, since it is not autonomous, but individuals have to act in the name of the corporation. The same holds for digital personae. Because it might be possible that the digital persona as a legal entity can be connected to the natural person behind it, i.e. the represented individual, granting certain rights to digital personae may offer protection against undesired use.

In continental law systems, there are several theories concerning corporate bodies and legal personality. The most important approaches concerning legal personality include legal personality as a legal fiction, corporate realism, theory of the Zweckvermögen, and the aggregation theory.[560] According to the first concept legal personality of entities is, other than that of human beings, artificial, i.e. the result of a fiction. The legal capacity is based on positive law, so the state grants legal personality to certain types of entities. In corporate realism, legal personality is based on the real existence of a corporate body. The mere fact that a corporate body exists (as recognized by registration) or the presence of warrants concerning this existence is enough to grant a corporate body a certain legal status. The theory of the Zweckvermögen exists in legal systems where certain institutions are legal persons, characterized by an object and a purpose. These are seen as entities on their own and not as representing individual members. Finally, the aggregation theory conceptually relates to the fictionist theory. Here, human beings are considered the only subjects of rights and duties. The corporate body, thus, is not a legal person, but merely a collective name, a symbol for the members of the cooperation.

In modern national laws, legal personality is often treated as a combination of the realist and the fictionist view. On the one hand, the social reality behind legal personality is recognized, whereas on the other hand the legal person is in some respects treated as a legal fiction.[561] The theories are usually applied to corporations or other institutions formed by a group of people with a shared interest, but with different rights and liabilities than individual human beings.[562] Legal personality, however, is also relevant in relation to non-human entities that are not corporations, such as electronic agents. The debate on electronic agents and the possible attribution of legal personality may provide more tools for assessing legal personality in relation to digital personae.

---

[560] Cp. Zimmer 2005, pp. 267-269.
[561] Zimmer 2005, p. 269.
[562] Karnow 1994, p. 3.

There is a tendency to personify non-human entities, which makes it relevant to look at when these non-human entities can be seen as legal persons. To a large extent, this is related to the participation in legal transactions. The corporation or institution is a legal entity that itself is not a natural person, but that acts (legally and factually) similar to a natural person. With regard to non-human entities and legal personality, much of the debate has taken place with regard to electronic agents. A major contribution was delivered in 1992 by Lawrence Solum,[563] who discussed whether artificial intelligences could have legal personhood. At the time, this question was only theoretical, but he brings some important insights to the fore. Legal personality is related to the capacity to perform legal acts. The performance of these acts has to be autonomous. What autonomous means is often debated and there are different approaches towards autonomy or intelligence. To avoid this debate, Solum took a rather pragmatic approach for a legal discussion, comparable to the consequence-based approach described above, by discussing concrete scenarios[564] and looked at what the objections might be for legal personhood being attributed to artificial intelligences in these scenarios. He looked at the advantages and possible drawbacks of attributing legal personhood and related this to the level of consciousness of the entity. The conditions for legal personhood given by Solum can be described as the capacity to perform complex actions and to act in a deliberate way (personhood as consciousness). The level of consciousness determines whether an entity can be made the subject of legal rights and duties The "particular bundle of rights and duties that accompanies legal personhood varies with the nature of the entity."[565] Next to (adult) human beings, however, this legal personhood "is often attributed to entities that do *not* qualify for such personhood. Legal theory refers to this as a legal fiction: the law attributes personhood though in 'normal' life we would not think of the relevant entity as a person."[566] This opens the way for attributing legal personhood to artificial intelligences.

Allgrove presents three ways to approach the question of legal personality for artificial intellects.[567] The characteristics of legal personality are similar in al three approaches, but depending on the approach taken, other categories of entities may be eligible for legal personality. First, it is possible to look at the entity itself, an entity-centric approach, which is comparable to corporate realism. In this approach, the characteristics and capacities of the entity it concerns are central in order to decide whether the entity

---

[563] Solum 1992.
[564] Whether an artificial intelligence could serve as a trustee, and whether an artificial intelligence could invoke constitutional rights.
[565] Solum 1992, p. 1239.
[566] Koops, Hildebrandt & Jaquet-Chiffelle 2010, pp. 519-520.
[567] Cp. Allgrove 2004.

has or should have legal personality. When looking at the characteristics, a general approach should be taken, including capacities such as a certain degree of consciousness or an intrinsic value of the entity. Depending on the characteristics, different levels of legal personality can be distinguished. For instance, legal effects related to liability differ according to legal contexts, such as criminal liability or civil liability. Liability in criminal law requires a higher level of consciousness than in civil law.[568] If the only relevant characteristic would be a certain intrinsic value, there is no legal personality, but probably a legal status (see below).

A second approach is consequence-based and looks at the consequences of attributing legal personality to a certain entity. In this approach there is an incentive for regulators to investigate whether an entity should be granted legal personality, because the entity is relevant in a legal transaction, for instance, the closing of a contract. Without legal personality, the contract would not be legally valid. The main focus is on a legal consequence related to something the entity does or does not and the legal consequences of the act of an entity plea for a legal status. Legal personality can, then, validate the acts as legally relevant and also instigate legal protection mechanisms towards others, such as liability. This approach seems appropriate, since it is practical and allows for attributing legal personality when the acts an entity performs have legal significance.

A third approach is conditions-based. In this approach, the central question is under what conditions an entity is treated as a legal person. So, "[i]t looks at the circumstances, and not the identities, involved."[569] The conditions as well as the scope of legal personality may differ per situation. The legal construct sought for determines the outcome. This is a very practical approach, strongly related to what is needed from a legal point of view in a specific situation. Without the legal construct, there is no legal consequence. For instance, the legal construct for entering a contract can form a condition for granting legal personality to companies, so that representatives of the company (agents) can close a contract on behalf of the company, but only when they are in the capacity of their function within the company. The condition is, thus, not necessarily present continuously and legal effects (validity) only occur when the legal act is performed under the specific condition.

All the approaches discussed above take as a starting point that the entity is able to perform certain acts with some degree of autonomy, so it concerns active agents. Digital personae, however, are passive entities, so legal

---

[568] Compare Jaquet-Chiffele, Anrig, Benoist, Haenni, Hildebrandt, Kosta & Lefever 2008, p. 18.
[569] Allgrove 2004, p. 38.

personality as described here does not seem relevant or necessary. A form of protection for passive entities that cannot perform legal acts, but deserve to be protected because of their intrinsic value may be more appropriate and can be found in legal status.

A legal status provides legal protection to an entity which cannot perform acts or invoke rights autonomously. Legal status is related to legal personality, but "legal status can both be relational and absolute, whereas legal personality can only be absolute."[570] Nevertheless, legal personality is a form of a legal status.

If legal personality is not a necessary requirement for recognizing an entity as having legal status, the possibilities for attributing legal status increase significantly, because autonomous capacities become less relevant. An entity does not need to be capable of acting on itself, or to perform a legal duty. It can, however, enjoy certain rights and, therewith, gain some legal protection. In order to receive this protection, a legal status is necessary. For instance, Allgrove states that "[t]hough not legal persons at Common Law, some jurisdictions treat the killing of a foetus as murder pursuant to statute, implicitly, if not expressly, recognizing its legal personality [...]."[571] The reasons for legal recognition, however, "have nothing to do with *its* legal rights, but are designed to secure the rights of others."[572] And "[o]f course, an entity can have extra-legal significance and differential legal treatment as a result, without necessarily warranting recognition as a legal person."[573] In the context of a foetus, its independent legal status is designed to nail down the *parents'* legal rights, so they can file a malpractice case against the doctors.[574]

The specific form of the legal status is related to the function of granting the protection. These functions can be "distributive, determining who is to have ownership or access to the resources; conservatory, preserving the resources as such, or at least doing so at levels that can sustain exploitation; or proscriptive, prohibiting, for conservatory, ethical, or moral reasons, exploitation of the resource or particular forms and methods of exploitation."[575] For instance, animals have been granted legal status in order to protect them. This status is usually referred to as 'animal rights'. The background of these rights is based on two different perspectives; the

---

[570] Allgrove 2004, p. 49.
[571] Allgrove 2004, p. 39.
[572] Stone 1985, p. 23.
[573] Allgrove 2004, p. 39.
[574] Stone 1985, p. 23.
[575] Birnie, Boyle & Redgwell 2009, p. 593-594.

perspective of welfare advocates, considering that "all species should be protected for ethical and humanitarian reasons", and the perspective of environmentalists, who state that "particular species should be protected for ecological reasons, that is, as part of an ecosystem."[576] Next to the practical application of legal status to animals, there have been discussions and thought experiments in academic debate on legal status for non-human entities with the aim of protecting a specific interest. For instance, in order to protect the environment, it has been debated whether trees should have legal status. If trees have a legal status, they may also have standing in litigation. The question of whether trees should have standing is not aiming at trees itself, but seeks for a way of litigating environmental issues.[577] To have standing, a tree should be considered a legal actor, even though a tree is a passive entity. The tree itself cannot go to court, so others do so on behalf of the trees. It can be argued that the fact that organizations or individuals take action on behalf of trees does not turn these trees into legal actors. Teubner, however, argues that "it is attribution of communicative events to an entity as 'its' acts and the attribution of rights to an entity that transforms this entity into an actor. And if an agent acts on behalf of this entity then the 'actor' is not the agent but the entity itself."[578] Thus, according to Teubner, trees have a legal status and can perform legal acts (have standing) when being represented by another entity.

3.2. Legal personality and legal status for digital personae?

Having discussed legal personality and legal status, it is now time to see whether these concepts can be of help in order to protect the rights and values of the individual when represented by a digital persona. Legal personality may not be the most appropriate concept to offer protection for the individual who is represented in the form of a digital persona. In practice it would only bring some value in the case of active digital personae (Agents), since closing a contract requires acting[579] to express the declaration of the will of the contracting parties. A passive digital persona cannot close contracts or express a will, because it does not act. Nevertheless, the debate on legal personality for digital agents brought some insights on the conditions and reasons for protection. The discussed forms of protection or legal responsibilities are welcome as a backdrop for assessing digital personae as non-human entities.

---

[576] Birnie, Boyle & Redgwell 2009, p. 597.
[577] Stone 1985, p. 2-3.
[578] Teubner 2006, 497-521, p.1, fn. 1.
[579] This 'acting' can be performed actively or passively.

Passive entities, unable to close or perform a contract, cannot be granted legal personality[580], but can be valuable to protect. For instance, animals, which were briefly mentioned already, cannot perform legal acts, but they are recognized as entities that need protection. In order to grant such protection, animals have a legal status. The concept of a legal status offers some benefits. As indicated, it can be argued that the attribution of rights to an entity may fictively turn this entity into an actor which 'acts' by means of an agent – there is a principal-agent relationship. Acting on behalf of this entity (representation/agency) can then be interpreted as if the entity acts itself. The entity is unable to perform acts, but his 'rights' can be invoked by others. When applying this line of thinking to digital personae, the digital personae might be worthwhile protecting with the aim of protecting the individual which is represented. If someone takes action on behalf of a digital persona, for instance to object against unlawful processing by a third party, it can be said that the digital persona itself is seeking protection. The represented individual data subject, or someone else, instantiates a communicative action between the digital persona and the third party, because the digital persona is unable to object autonomously.

In the case that an individual takes action on behalf of its digital persona, he controls the processing and affects the way the data can be used to take decisions concerning the individual. This form of control, either immediately, or *post-hoc*, if something went wrong, retro-actively via standing in court, is a desirable characteristic of a legal status for digital personae. An action by an individual is essentially similar to an action based on the data subject's access rights as they are formulated in the DPD. However, in the case of the DPD protection mechanism it is the individual himself who has a right as a data subject, whereas in the case of a digital personae with a legal status, the digital persona has a right on itself, which has to be effectuated by an agent.

Attributing a legal status to digital personae may bring some protection for the personae. That means that they may, for instance, not be harmed. The primary focus is then on the digital persona, and the represented individual seems out of scope, even though the individual might enjoy better protection, just like the environment enjoys protection via the protection of trees. Nevertheless, the link between the digital persona and the individual that needs protection remains an indirect link, while, in the end, the data that form the digital persona are data concerning the individual. Direct control over the data might be a more appropriate approach, in particular from the viewpoint of aiming to protect the autonomy of the individual. It is thus worthwhile to look at whether some form of ownership to the data can be helpful.

---

[580] Apart from the fact that there is no specific need for granting them legal personality, since they do not participate in legal transactions.

4. Property

Property law gives rules defining who has rights concerning a thing and what these rights are. Property law distinguishes a number of categories of things that can be the subject of a property right. Absolute property rights can concern things (movable as well as immovable), proprietary rights or entitlements (shares, securities, etc.), and intellectual productions of the human mind. First, property rights with regard to things will be discussed, followed by a discussion on intellectual property rights.[581]

4.1. Ownership of things

"To put it at its simplest, property law is about the legally recognized relationships we have with each other in respect of things."[582] So, a thing itself is not property, but can be the subject of property, while property itself is the right one has in relation to this thing.[583] [584] So, when talking about property the rights that someone has are discussed.

Property laws define what can be the object of a property right. Only things that are mentioned as such in law can be potential objects of property rights. The objects are, thus, limited and defined in categories, such as goods, real estate and proprietary rights. Property rights give the holder of these rights forms of control over the object on which the property rights see, because the holder has certain entitlements. Usually, the holder of a property right is called the owner of the object. The owner, for instance, has the right to sell the object, to give it away, or to change or destroy it. The only limitations are given by public order and rights of others that may not be infringed upon. The rights of the owner have an *erga omnes* effect. That means that the rights can be enforced against everyone. This is an important difference with a personal right in relation to a particular thing, which can only be claimed against the person who is obliged to the holder of the personal right,[585] such as the right to *usufruct* where the right holder (e.g. someone who may reap the fruits of a tree) has a claim against the owner of the thing (the owner of the tree).

---

[581] The proprietary rights will not be discussed separately, since their legal construction is basically the same as for property rights to things.

[582] Clarke & Kohler 2005, p. 3.

[583] Cp. Clarke & Kohler 2005, p. 17.

[584] It is important to distinguish layman's speech from legal speech. The term property is often used by laymen to indicate a thing which is claimed to be a property.

[585] Mattei 2000, p. 78.

Because property are the rights itself and not the object of these rights, property from a legal perspective is neither tangible nor intangible.[586] This implies that the object of the property rights can in principle be anything and that lawmakers have some space in facilitating the applicability of property law on new (categories of) things. "Consequently, a noticeable characteristic of the concept of property is its fluidity,"[587] and actual property rights are meant to address practical needs that have emerged in society. It is, thus, possible to make digital personae the object of property rights.

Property law is a rigid field of law, with fine-grained provisions on what rights someone can have, how these rights can be obtained and transferred, and what the limits of property rights are. What can be the object of property rights is also defined by the main categories mentioned earlier. Something can be the object of property when it is recognized as such by law. The requirement is that the rights have to be listed in law as property rights, which is also known as the *numerus clausus* principle. The approach taken is often very practical: can subjecting something to property law provide benefits, for instance with regard to regulating behavior or for economic purposes?[588] As Purtova states: "provided that it serves the current needs of a jurisdiction and there is political will to transform it, there is nothing in the nature of the legal phenomenon of property to prevent it from changing to include personal data as one of its objects."[589] The same conclusion would apply to digital personae as possible new objects.

Once there is property, one can also enjoy ownership rights. "[T]he relationship between property rights and ownership is that of genus to species."[590] Ownership "refers to the legal right that a legal system grants to an individual in order to allow him [...] to exercise the maximum degree of formalized control over a scarce resource"[591] (the object of the property right). In Continental law systems, ownership rights are basically distinguished in three prerogatives: *usus*, *usufruct*, and *abusus*. Ownership is a bundle of rights and these separate rights can be held by different people.[592] In that case, there is a fragmented ownership of an object. Someone can have the right to *usus* (absolute right) and grant a right of *usufruct* to another person (restricted absolute right). The absolute property rights have an *erga omnes* effect; they apply against everyone. As a result, the central question of

---

[586]   Purtova 2011, p. 54.
[587]   Purtova 2011, p. 59.
[588]   Compare Purtova 2011, p. 59, referring to the practical needs that have emerged in a particular society.
[589]   Purtova 2011, p. 62.
[590]   Mattei 2000, p. 78.
[591]   Mattei 2000, p. 77.
[592]   Purtova 2011, p. 70.

whether something should be considered for protection with property rights is whether an interest should deserve *erga omnes* protection.[593]

Property and property law are concepts with a variety of interpretations in different jurisdictions. A major distinction can be made between the Common Law and the Civil Law approaches towards property. The aim of this study, however, is not to elaborately discuss property law. In the context of this study, it is sufficient to take a more general perspective, and discuss some of the main characteristics of property and property law. I will clarify the exact rights related to property based on the Dutch law, but the concepts are applicable in most European (Civil Law) countries.

A property right is a right a person has in relation to a 'thing'.[594] In the Netherlands, property rights are laid down in the *Burgerlijk Wetboek*, (Dutch Civil Code (DCC)).[595] According to Article 3:2 DCC, 'Things' are tangible objects that can be controlled by humans. Things comprise of movable and immovable things. Article 5:1(1) DCC states that "[o]wnership is the most comprehensive property right that a person, the 'owner', can have to (in) a thing." Next to ownership, there is 'possession', which is defined as "the legal status in which a person holds an asset for himself."[596] The person who has the possession over an asset does not have to be the person who has ownership of the thing. The requirement is that the person holds the asset for himself, regardless of whether he has reasonable grounds to think that he is the owner or whether he knows not to be the owner (for instance a thief). In case someone holds an asset for another person he is the keeper, and this is called 'keepership'.[597]

Possession assures a certain power over the thing. Possessing something means that you also have access to it. At the same time, the owner is not always necessarily the possessor of the thing, since it can be stolen or lent to

---

593   Purtova 2011, p. 79.
594   At a European level there is an initiative for a European Civil Code. This project, however, has a limited scope concerning property, implying that is does not sufficiently cover the issues raised in this study, and has not led to an applicable framework, yet. For that reason, in this study reference is made to the provisions on property at a (Dutch) national level. The concepts are applicable in most civil law jurisdictions. Nevertheless, there is a Common Frame of Reference: Study Group on a European Civil Code, Research Group on EC Private Law (Acquis Group): Principles, Definitions and Model Rules of European Private Law: Draft Common Frame of Reference (DCFR). Sellier European Law Publishers, Munich (2009).
595   For the English translation of the Burgerlijk Wetboek, I made use of Brecht's Dutch Civil Law, the Civil Code. Online available at: <http://www.dutchcivillaw.com/civilcodegeneral.htm>.
596   Art. 3:107(1) DCC.
597   Artt. 3:107(4) jo. 3:108 DCC.

someone else. The owner of the thing is free to "use the thing to the exclusion of everyone else, provided that he respects the rights and entitlements of others to the thing and observes the restrictions based on rules of written and unwritten law."[598] Someone who merely possesses a thing- without being the owner - does not have this right. However, in the case of keepership, holding an asset for someone else, it may be that the keeper has certain rights concerning the thing. Think, for instance, of a borrowed bike, which the keeper may use to go to his work, but has to return to the owner at one point. The same goes for hired things, such as cars or tools. Whether someone is a possessor is to be determined based on the factual circumstances. These factual circumstances have to indicate that the thing belongs to the possessor. In other words, the factual relation between a person and a thing has to reflect the power position that is provided by law to the person.[599]

Whether someone is the owner, the possessor, or the keeper of a thing determines what rights this person has with regard to the thing. The limitations of the rights are relatively clear, and so are the distinctions in power with regard to the thing. Nevertheless, it may sometimes be difficult to determine whether someone is the owner, possessor, or keeper. In order to assess this, it is helpful to look at how someone can acquire ownership to a thing. The ways of obtaining ownership are usually divided into two categories: original and derivative obtainment of ownership. Original obtainment of ownership takes place when a new right originates with the recipient. Derivative ownership is the obtainment of a right to ownership that previously belonged to someone else.

Original obtainment of a movable thing can take place by occupation (taking possession),[600] finding,[601] accession,[602] and the creation of a new thing.[603] [604] Derivative obtainment of ownership takes place in, for instance, cases of heritage[605] or marriage,[606] and in cases where a property right is transferred.[607] [608] Once there is ownership, the owner can use the thing to the exclusion of all others. This means that he can do whatever he wants with the thing, but also that, in case someone else is keeping the thing for him, decide

---

[598] Art. 5:1(2) DCC.
[599] Asser 2006, nr. 118.
[600] Art. 5:4 DCC.
[601] Art. 5:6 DCC.
[602] Artt. 5:3 and 5:14 DCC.
[603] Art. 5:16 DCC.
[604] Compare Asser 2006, nr. 192.
[605] Art. 4:189 DCC.
[606] Art. 1:93 DCC.
[607] Art. 3:83 DCC.
[608] Compare Asser 2006, nr. 193.

what the keeper is allowed to do with it as long as it is in his possession. In the end, ownership implies a huge amount of control (claims of right), provided by the law,[609] and is therefore a strong concept to protect things against unauthorized use.

An important point of attention is that ownership rights are related to things and that these things are described as tangibles. There are also ownership rights related to intangibles, namely shares and proprietary rights. These can better be described as entitlements instead of the standard property concept. Digital personae, as intangible data sets, are not considered things to which ownership applies.[610] Next to that, if ownership would be applied, it might turn out in many cases that the data subject is not the owner, because he is not the (sole) creator of the digital persona. Nevertheless, the owner is the one who would obtain the strongest rights with respect to the digital persona, implying that in most cases another person than the represented individual has most control over the digital persona. Ownership is, then, counter-effective as a means to protect the privacy of the individual. A form of an entitlement might solve this issue.

It is possible to create a *sui generis* property right for digital personae. In that case, the rules of property law can be applied by analogy. This approach was taken by Purtova[611] with respect to personal data. She recognized the problem of personal data being processed outside the control of the data subject. This lack of control was brought to the fore as a major problem with regard to the protection of the privacy of the data subject. To solve this problem, propertisation was proposed as a solution. The data subject gains control as being the owner of his personal data. He has the right to sell the data for specific purposes. What purposes and uses are allowed can be defined in licenses. A second important advantage of granting data subjects property rights to their data is the *erga omnes* effect of these rights. Property rights work against everyone who has access to the personal data. Current data protection legislation is aimed at 'controllers' of the data, which has a more limited scope, so, an *erga omnes* effect can have a positive impact when it concerns protection of the individual against unwanted processing of his personal data.

---

[609]   Coyle & Morrow 2004, p. 10.
[610]   Even though there are discussions on whether certain intangible goods, such as electricity, have to be considered as things subjected to property. However, a criterion in the discussion seems to be the uniqueness of possession: only one person can 'own' or 'use' the electricity, which would not necessarily be the case with digital personae, since these can be copied.
[611]   Purtova 2011.

Furthermore, Purtova indicates that property rights are better than contracts. There is less opacity, since property is a relatively clear right, and it is less burdensome. A contract has to be concluded and determines what rights and duties the contracting parties have. This means that these rights and duties do not always have to be the same. This may facilitate flexibility, but also means that it is not always evident what the contract entails. The property right exists by law, which means that no extra action has to be undertaken to establish the right. When there is property, licenses can be granted with respect to the propertised object. There can be standard licenses which are easy to grant, instead of the necessity of drafting a specific contract every time. A license is a form of a contract, but with standardized licenses it is possible to let people use the object under the attached license. It is not necessary to draft the contract including identifying information concerning the parties involved. For instance, Creative Commons[612] licenses are standardized formats attached to contents. The contents may be used by anyone as long as they accord to the license. An individual agreement between the rights holder and the entity who wants to use the content is not necessary. Finally, property rights in personal data improve top-down implementation, since there just is a license or not. This makes it easy to implement the system on a general overarching level.

The idea of property rights in digital personae seems promising. In particular, the *erga omnes* effect is relevant because it sets discussions about controllership aside. This is absolutely contributing to a solution for the current problems. However, some points of attention remain, such as the question who obtains ownership rights and the issue of the intangibility of digital personae.
.

Suppose that a *sui generis* right is established which grants property rights to the individual whom the digital persona concerns, so this individual can exercise ownership rights. These rights are exclusive and have an *erga omnes* effect. The individual can decide to grant some rights to others, such as *usufruct*, allowing for using the digital persona and reap the fruits of it. The 'fruits' could be considered to be the commercial value resulting from the use of the digital persona. The individual can grant similar rights to multiple people, since the digital persona can be copied without losing the original. This can make it difficult to decide upon the value of a digital persona when granting a license. It is very well possible that the value of a right of *usufruct* is heavily influenced by the number of parties that have this right. The more parties that are allowed to use the digital persona, the less the value for each individual party may be, due to competition and, in the end, probably even

---

[612] Used for licensing intellectual property, mainly copyright protected works. See: <www.creativecommons.org>.

general availability of the digital persona as an asset. Most likely, this issue will in practice be solved by market functioning. The value of the digital persona depends on how many parties show an interest in the data set related to the scarcity of the digital persona. If only one party obtains a license to use the digital persona, this may bring stronger commercial opportunities, due to the exclusivity. The value of this position will be relatively high, which will be reflected in the price of the license.

To summarize, ownership to things is a valuable concept which functions as a means to provide extensive control over things. When merely applying the concept to digital personae, problems occur: digital personae are not tangibles and differ from the intangible objects or property rights that are in fact entitlements, and there are many instances in which the data subject would not obtain ownership rights. This may be solved by law when implementing provisions that would recognize digital personae as objects of property rights. However, it is worthwhile to look whether there are other existing concepts that may also cover these issues. To start with intangibility, a look will now be taken at intellectual property rights.

4.2. Intellectual property

Under the heading of intellectual property, there are also ownership rights related to intangibles, namely products of the human mind. Intellectual property rights relate to, for instance, music, videos, images, databases, and books. There are several types or categories of intellectual property rights, of which copyright is the most prominent one. The rationale behind intellectual property rights is to stimulate innovation and cultural expression.[613] Developing an idea takes time and often other investments as well, such as pen and paper (book), recording materials (music or video), or prototypes (patentable invention). Inventive minds, however, were not able to gain back their investments, which might hamper innovation. For instance, until about two centuries ago, publishers had rights concerning books, but the authors did not. This meant that publishers were able to gain back their investments in the printing of the books. Once an author had sold a text to a publisher, there was no opportunity left to generate income from the text or to have some form of control over how the text was used.

This position of the authors was considered unfair and, as a result, copyright protection at an international level started in the middle of the nineteenth century, based on bilateral treaties.[614] Separate treaties were not convincing in appropriateness, however, and a standard way of dealing with copyright at

---

[613] WIPO 2004, p. 3.
[614] WIPO 2004, p. 262.

an international level was welcome. "The need for a uniform system led to the formulation and adoption on September 9, 1886, of the Berne Convention for the Protection of Literary and Artistic Works."[615] The aim of the Berne Convention is 'to protect, in as effective and uniform a manner as possible, the rights of authors in their literary and artistic works."[616] In 1996, the World Intellectual Property Organization (WIPO) adopted the WIPO Copyright Treaty. This Treaty is meant to reinforce the protection as provided by the Berne Convention, but also to provide "adequate solutions to the questions raised by new economic, social, cultural and technological developments."[617] It was recognized that technological developments and the convergence of information and communication technologies had a profound impact on the creation and use of literary and artistic works.[618] This becomes particularly clear when looking at the provisions that offer protection for computer programs as literary works (Art. 4) and for compilations of data (databases) that constitute intellectual creations (Art. 5). Databases were also granted protection at an EU level earlier in 1996, by means of the Database Directive (see below).

Images are protected by copyright. Digital personae are, in fact, 'images' of the individual in the form of data sets. When digital personae are recognized as images, copyright can, thus, provide legal rights concerning digital personae. However, digital personae are also essentially data sets and data sets as such can be protected by database rights. So, protection along the lines of database rights may be another option with regard to digital personae. In the following subsections, copyright and database rights will be discussed in order to examine whether digital personae can be considered images or databases and, if so, what this would imply in terms of rights related to digital personae. I will start with copyright, since this provides the basic terminology in the context of intellectual property rights.

4.2.1. Copyright

Copyright law governs the rights concerning 'works of literature, science or arts'.[619] The holder of a copyright has the right to reproducing the work and/ or making it public. These are exclusive rights for the holder of the copyright or his assignees.[620] An important characteristic is that a copyright exists by

---

[615] WIPO 2004, p. 262.
[616] Preamble of the Berne Convention for the Protection of Literary and Artistic Works.
[617] Preamble of the WIPO Copyright Treaty, adopted in Geneva on December 20, 1996.
[618] Preamble of the WIPO Copyright Treaty, adopted in Geneva on December 20, 1996.
[619] Spoor, Verkade & Visser 2005, p. 1.
[620] Art. 1 Dutch Copyright Law (*Auteurswet*).

law.[621] At the moment the object is created the author automatically has the copyright.[622] No formalities need to be undertaken before the rights can be exercised. A form of expression of the work is needed, however, because the work as such has to be recognizable: others have to be able to take notice of the work. A mere idea of something is not protected, but first has to be expressed, for instance by putting it on paper, by speaking out a text, or by playing a song.

Copyright is an exclusive right. This means that the holder of the copyright is the only person entitled to make the work public or to reproduce it. The copyright holder can grant licenses to others to do so. This is an important aspect of copyright as opposed to ownership, where, for instance, selling or *usufruct* implies that the owner distances himself from certain rights and, in general, cannot enjoy these rights at the same time himself. The ownership rights to the thing can usually only be exercised by one person at a time. However, intangibles often have the characteristic of multiplicity. Copies can be made without the original work being affected. The copies can be copied again and again. As a result, numerous instances of the same work can exist. In the same way, when talking about a digital persona as a work in terms of copyright law, the digital persona could be copied without the original being affected, and the reproduction could be regulated by licenses.

As stated, the copyright exists by right with the author of the work. Copyright consists of so-called exploitation rights that can be transferred to others, and moral rights, that cannot be transferred. These moral rights belong to the author of the work and are meant to avoid that others make derivative works that are so distinctive in meaning from the original work that it cannot have been the intention of the author. The personality of the author is protected, which means that he can object to these works, so he is not associated with the derivative work. The author can, thus, object to derogatory treatment of the work.[623] A second part of moral rights is the right to be recognized as the author of a work and to be mentioned correctly as the author.[624] Moral rights, thus, provide the author of a work with the means to limit the use of his work by others.

The central aspect of copyright is the 'work'. There is no straightforward definition of a 'work', but it is described as a work of literature, science or art. In this respect, books, magazines and all other writings, pictures, music,

---

[621] Art. 5(2) Berne Convention.
[622] Other forms of intellectual property, such as patents, require registration of the object to obtain the right.
[623] Spoor, Verkade & Visser 2005, p.4.
[624] See also: Bainbridge 2007, p. 28.

films, oral presentations, and computer programs are, among other things, recognized as works that can be protected by copyright. The protection applies regardless of the way or form in which the work is expressed.[625]

Copyright is not as encompassing as ownership. Copyright only applies to the subjective form of the work, not to objective content, which means that facts and data as such are not protected; these may be reproduced.[626] The focus of copyright on the subjective form of the work also indicates that the work itself is leading. In order to obtain copyright protection, the work has to be original. What original exactly means is usually determined at a national level, with some jurisdictions using a stricter test than others. In the Netherlands, the work has to have an individual, original character and has to carry the personal mark of the author.[627] From this description, three requirements can be derived: own character, personal mark, and originality. If these requirements are fulfilled, the work is protected by copyright and the copyright is held by the author of the work.

The individual character requirement means that the author, when creating a work, uses existing elements, such as facts, theories, style figures, or an idiom, but connects these in his own way in the work.[628] The author has "expended skill and judgment in its creation, in a conceptual way rather than just in the manufacture of the physical embodiment of the work."[629]

The personal mark of the author as a requirement for a work to be protected by copyright implies that there needs to be a human being involved in the creation of the work. The work reflects the personal vision of the author.[630] The required involvement in the creation does not mean that the use of technical means is not allowed. It might only become different when the creation is completely automatically performed, without the author (who is then merely an operator) exercising any influence. This may, for instance, be the case when a computer translates source code to object code.[631] There is discussion on whether copyright protected works can also be created by computers. The central aspect in this discussion is whether creativity can be performed by artificial intelligences. It is often argued that computational creativity is inherently algorithmic, so works produced autonomously by computers are not comparable to creative works as created by humans,[632]

---

[625] Article 10 Dutch Copyright Act (*Auteurswet*).
[626] Spoor, Verkade & Visser 2005, p. 4-5.
[627] Spoor, Verkade & Visser 2005, p. 65.
[628] Spoor, Verkade & Visser 2005, p. 65.
[629] Bainbridge 2007, p. 40.
[630] Spoor, Verkade & Visser 2005, p. 72.
[631] Spoor, Verkade & Visser 2005, p. 74.
[632] Bridy 2011.

which implies that these computer generated works are not protected by copyright. Nevertheless, increasingly digital content used in everyday life has little or no human intervention in its creation, while it is still delivered with copyright claims attached.[633] Approaches towards this issue can be based on the question who should be rewarded; the program maker, the program user, the program, or nobody.[634] Current copyright law may also offer a solution via the "work made for hire doctrine, which is a mechanism for vesting copyright directly in a legal person who is acknowledged *not* to be the author-in-fact of the work in question."[635] In that case, the entity that initiated the creation of a digital persona by a computer will receive the copyright, while not being the creator.

The requirement of originality does not necessarily mean that the work has to be innovative or new in an absolute sense. It does not have to be unique. "Rather, originality is more concerned with the manner in which the work was created and is usually taken to require that the work in question originated from the author, its creator, and that it was not copied from another work."[636]

The question that arises is whether a digital persona can be a 'work' and whether a digital persona can be protected by copyright law. The data that together constitute a digital persona are stored in a digital format. The choice of what to store exactly and in which form determines what the digital persona will look like. A digital persona can, thus, be considered 'a form of writing' as far as it concerns text, and images or films as far as it concerns photos or videos. As a result, a digital persona can very well be recognized as a 'work' (of literature or art).

In order to assess whether a digital persona can also be protected by copyright, the three additional requirements mentioned above need to be discussed.

The individual character requires a conceptual way of combining elements. The data that form the digital persona are the elements. The way the data are combined, the selection of data used, and the way in which the data are captured may result in an individual character of the work. A series of digital personae with similar characteristics with regard to the conceptual combination is very well possible. Obviously, the paintings of Mondriaan in which elementary colours are used in square forms all have their own character, even though they are created in the same conceptual way. The

---

[633] Perry & Margoni 2010.
[634] Perry & Margoni 2010.
[635] Bridy 2011.
[636] Bainbridge 2007, p. 37.

individual character can, thus, also be a specific (personal) style. A digital persona can, thus, fulfil the requirement as to 'individual character'.

The personal mark requirement implies that there has to be human involvement in the creation of the digital persona. If a digital persona is only created by a computer collecting and storing, for instance, internet browsing data, there is no personal mark of the author.[637] Simply, there is no author. It is not the case that creating the software and programming the computer to perform its tasks is fulfilling this requirement, either. This, probably, results in a copyright in the software, but not in the output of the software when used. The output as such has to be assessed on the fulfilment of the requirements for copyright protection. However, with regard to computer generated works there is no 'work' in the meaning of copyright law, since the computer does exactly what the software programmer wants. Nevertheless, there are numerous cases where there is indeed human involvement in the creation or composition of a digital persona. For instance, if a party collects data and manually adds these to a data set, there is human involvement already. The amount of human involvement as opposed to automated processing is irrelevant as long as a personal mark of the author can be recognized. This personal mark, however, may not be easily present, in particular in cases of massive creation of digital personae along a structured line, without any creativity added to each digital persona.

Originality requires that the work is not copied from an existing work, but created by the author. The creation of the work, then, has to involve a certain amount of labour investment. However, it may occur that two persons create a similar work independently from each other. In that case, both authors obtain a copyright in their work. For all new digital personae being created, the requirement of originality as not having been copied is easily met.[638] The requirement does imply that digital personae that are essentially copies, but which have the data stored in a different order may not meet the requirement of originality. They consist of the same elements, but may be combined in another way. This may lead to an 'own character' with a 'personal mark' of the author, but not to 'originality' which would make it a new work that is protected by copyright. Moreover, originality requires that the work is not something obvious, without creativity. A list of mere facts is, thus, not protected by copyright, unless they are written down in an original, creative manner. In the case of digital personae created automatically or with limited human intervention, this original, creative presentation of factual data will often be lacking.

---

[637] This can be challenged, however, when a lighter test is applied to prove the 'originality' of the work. See the discussion above on works created by artificial intelligences.

[638] Unless a digital persona is considered to be a copy of the represented individual. This is not likely, however, due to its different presentation form.

To conclude, there may be occasions in which a digital persona can be recognized as a work that can be protected by copyright, but the majority of digital personae will most likely not meet the requirements of a personal mark and originality. Copyright law could, thus, only to a limited extent be an applicable concept in the context of digital personae. Another concept that may be applicable is database law. Digital personae are essentially data sets and so are databases. It is, thus, worthwhile to consider what protection database rights can bring and how this relates to copyright protection.

4.2.2. Database rights

Databases are protected as intellectual property, based on the implementations of the EU Database Directive.[639] The Directive created a *sui generis* right, parallel to copyright, because a proper protection regime for valuable databases was lacking.[640] In the Directive, a database is defined as "a collection of independent works, data or other materials arranged in a systematic or methodical way and individually accessible by electronic or other means."[641] The core provision of the Directive is Article 7. "Art. 7(1) requires a substantial investment, paralleling 'originality' in copyright as threshold for the right to come into existence."[642] The exact meaning of this 'substantial investment' is the most discussed issue concerning the Database Directive. Recital 40 of the Database Directive states that the aim of the Directive is to protect "any investment in obtaining, verifying or presenting the contents of a database" and that "such investment may consist in the deployment of financial resources and/or the expending of time, effort and energy." The substantial investment concerns the entire database. It seems that the Database Directive offers a broader protection than the WIPO Copyright Treaty, since the latter requires that the selection or arrangement of the contents constitutes an intellectual creation.[643] This 'intellectual creation' seems to be related to the requirements of own character and personal mark of the author as these exist in copyright,[644] whereas the substantial investment mainly relates to originality. Art. 7(2) of the Database Directive sets forth the exclusive rights enjoyed by the maker."[645] These exclusive rights are practically similar to the rights provided by 'normal'

---

[639] Directive 96/9/EC of the European Parliament and of the Council of 11 March 1996 on the legal protection of databases, OJ L 77, 27.3.1996, p. 20–28.

[640] This was also recognized by the WIPO, which introduced database protection later in 1996 in the WIPO Copyright Treaty.

[641] Article 1(2) of Directive 96/9/EC.

[642] Westkamp 2003, p.2.

[643] Art. 5 WIPO Copyright Treaty.

[644] See above.

[645] Westkamp 2003, p.2.

copyright. They are described as the right to prevent others from 'extraction' and 're-utilization' of the database. Extraction means the transfer of the whole or a substantial part of the database, temporarily or permanently, to another medium by any means or in any form, and can be compared with reproduction in copyright. Re-utilization is any form of making available to the public. With these rights, reproduction or making public is allowed by the creator of the database exclusively. Nevertheless, similarly as in copyright law, the rights are transferable.[646]

The substantial investment concerns the creation and maintenance of the database as such. In the cases on the British Horseracing Board (BHB) and Fixtures Marketing[647] the database owners had generated the data during the course of their businesses. A key question was whether the investment in generating these data amounted to an investment in obtaining the data for the purposes of the Directive. The ECJ "ruled that the investment made in creating and verifying the data at the point of its creation in these circumstances should not be taken into account. As a result, neither the BHB's nor Fixtures Marketing's databases qualified for protection despite the large amounts of investments involved."[648] Taking this into account, it may be questionable whether a database with data concerning, for instance, individual browsing behaviour is protected by a database right. The data are collected during, and as part of, the business of advertising and analytics companies. Putting these data in a database as such does not protect the database; a(nother) substantial investment is necessary.

In the context of digital personae, usually someone has created a database with a number of data sets, each constituting a digital persona. This database is covered under the Directive. This does not offer any protection for the individual's persona (records) constituting the database, but only for the database as a whole. The Directive, however, may also offer protection for individual records if the database is modular; a database is divided into different parts (modules) which can be used independently, but can also be combined in the entire system. If the digital personae can be used independently, these can be considered modules, while the combined set of digital personae forms a database as well. A database with digital personae can, thus, be seen as a whole, but also as a modular database. In the Apis

[646] Article 7(3) Database Directive.
[647] The *British Horseracing Board and Others v. William Hill Organisation Limited*, Judgment of the European Court of Justice (Grand Chamber), 9 November 2004, Case C-203/02, and the associated cases involving *Fixtures Marketing*, C-46/02, C-444/02 and C-338/02, 9 November 2004.
[648] Nettleton & Llewellyn 2009, p. 478. These authors also indicate that the BHB database costs four million pounds per year to maintain and requires extensive hardware and software and approximately 80 employees to run it.

case,[649] the European Court of Justice decided that, for the applicability of the protection regime to a modular database, it first had to be established whether each separate module constituted a database on itself. The modules would then be protected as separate databases. For instance, a database with demographic data of the entire world is one big database. The database can, however, be split up in a number of modules, each containing the demographic data of a continent. The separate modules are independent databases that can be protected, because they can be used independently from the rest of the set.

Depending on the contents, it can be argued that one digital persona should be considered a database. Based on the definition of a database, then, there has to be a systematic or methodological arrangement that would facilitate, for instance, the comparison or selection of data, which would add value to the mere collection of data. Basically, all data concern one individual, so there is not that much to compare. But if the digital persona consists of, for instance, browsing data, it is very well possible to make selections of data based on a day of the week or a certain time on a day, or to look for categories of browsing interests of the individual. The possibility of a modular database, with each digital persona being a separate module, will then be related to the type of data and the amount of data collected that belong to a specific category (such as the browsing data). Putting modules (digital personae) together facilitates comparison or selection of individuals based on browsing behaviour. In the case of smaller data sets or ordinary data such as name and address, comparison or selection only has added value when it concerns a number of individuals that share or not share certain characteristics or information. In that case, the digital personae will not be recognizable as separate modules.

Database rights will, thus, not be applicable to a large part of personal data collections. This is due to the lack of a substantial investment and digital personae as records are not likely to make the database a modular database. Besides, if the mere collection of data would constitute a protected database, numerous databases with similar or at least comparable digital personae would be protected with database rights, because several companies collect information on, for instance, browsing behaviour and, thus, create comparable contents. The rights would be held by the owners of the databases.

---

[649] *Apis-Hristovich EOOD v. Lakorda AD*; Judgment of the Fourth Chamber of the European Court of Justice dated 5 March 2009 (C-545/07). The case was about the extraction or re-utilization of a *substantial* part of a database.

From the perspective of this study, it seems that database rights cannot offer the appropriate protection. If a database right would apply, there is protection against extracting and/or re-utilizing substantial parts of the database, so it is not allowed to copy a large amount of individual profiles. This means that there is legal protection possible against transfer of data to other contexts. Nevertheless, the rights are obtained by the owner of a database, not by the individuals represented in the database. When the database contains data about a number of individuals, these individuals do not own the database. A database concerning one single individual, held by the individual himself is, as indicated, not likely.

4.2.3. Limitations of copyright and database rights as protecting concepts

A specific issue, relevant in the context of digital personae, is the mentioned requirement of human performance in the creation of the work in order to recognize the work as protectable by copyright. Something solely created by (the processing of) a computer does not meet this requirement. As a result, there are cases where the digital persona cannot be the object of a copyright. Besides, digital personae consisting of data entered into predefined forms may lack the creative element necessary for originality or the personal mark of the author.

In the cases where the requirements to qualify as a work are met, copyright protection may be applicable to a digital persona. The problem of the intangibility, which made that ownership could not directly be applied, is solved by seeking protection under copyright. Similarly as with ownership, the right can come into existence by creating an object. The creation of a digital persona is by law protected under copyright law. The fact that copyright exists by law is also a drawback, because it means that in the case someone else creates the digital persona (imposed persona) he, as being the author, obtains the copyright, and not the represented individual. In the case of projected personae the individual himself does have the copyright, but for hybrid digital personae it may be problematic to determine who the author is.

Database rights cannot offer a complete solution either. Single digital personae can sometimes be considered as a database, but the more common situation will be a database with numerous digital personae in it as entries. The database as such is protected, then, against extraction and re-utilization of the entire database or at least a substantial part. A few entries may not be considered a substantial part, but can still be a number of digital personae, or contain specific elements of a selection. Next to that, the contents as such are not protected, but the database and its functionality are. This means that the use by others of the digital personae as contents of the database is allowed.

Database rights can, thus, overcome the issue of intangibility, but protect the wrong object, i.e. the database instead of its contents.

Moreover, the second problem that was identified in relation to ownership, namely that the wrong party obtains the right, is not resolved yet, neither by copyright nor by database rights. Even in the case that digital personae autonomously created by machines would be recognized as copyright protected works, the represented individual will usually not be the one who obtains the right. The fact that the rights will not always be applicable to digital personae is not contributing to legal certainty either.

The challenge is to find a solution for intangibles where protection is focused on the image of an individual and not on the creator of the image. This protection may be found in a specific part of copyright law: portrait law.

4.2.4. Portrait law

Portrait law[650] is a form of intellectual property law regarding images of individuals. A portrait has value. This idea was first recognized in the context of famous people whose image was used for commercial purposes. The idea that the printing press could spread photographs and images at a large scale and that this could conflict with legitimate interests of portrayed individuals was already developed by Warren and Brandeis, back in 1890.[651] They stated that "[i]nstantaneous photographs and newspaper enterprise have invaded the sacred precincts of private and domestic life; and numerous mechanical devices threaten to make good the prediction that what is whispered in the closet shall be proclaimed from the house-tops."[652] In order to avoid the unauthorized use of portraits or the commercial gain based on portraits without the permission of, or without any gain for the portrayed person, portrait law was introduced. Portrait law offers the individual the opportunity to object to unauthorized use of their portrait by the creator of the portrait and all other third persons.[653] The objectives are twofold; the protection of the privacy (reasonable interest) of the individual, and the protection against unauthorized use of a portrait where the individual could be able to capitalize his popularity. Because it is often in the context of commerce, the portrayed people are usually famous people with a specific personal 'image' that can be used to add a certain status or image to a product. Even though portrait law is an element of copyright law, it is actually not about copyright itself; one does not create one's own appearance. Instead, it is about protection of

---

650 In the Netherlands regulated in Articles 19-22 of the Copyright Act.
651 Warren & Brandeis 1890.
652 Warren & Brandeis 1890.
653 Spoor, Verkade & Visser 2005, p. 310.

privacy of the portrayed person.[654] The personality rights of the portrayed individual are protected. In this respect, portrait law is a *lex specialis* where *leges generali*, such as Article 6:162 of the Dutch Civil Code on unlawful acts can be used as secondary means to compensate damages. That means that an individual who is harmed by or suffers damages because of the use of his portrait can base a claim on portrait law. In the case that portrait law offers insufficient protection, Article 6:162 of the Dutch Civil Code can be applied, because such an act infringes on a personality right of the portrayed individual, which constitutes a tort.[655] Insufficient protection by portrait law can, for instance, occur when the use of the portrait is accepted because of the public character of a famous person. Being famous means that a person has to accept that people take pictures (make portraits) in public that can be used in magazines or books.

A case in point concerned a famous Dutch soccer player, Johan Cruijff, who objected to publication of a book with pictures of him.[656] The pictures were taken during his career as a soccer player and, in fact, gave a historical overview of his career. A claim on privacy was dismissed: the pictures were taken in public, were not defamatory, and were taken in relation to the free gathering of news. A situation in which the right to protection of private life (Article 8 ECHR) was infringed upon or should prevail over the freedom of expression (Article 10 ECHR) was not at stake.[657] Next to that, in the decision of the Court of Appeal it was stressed that there is no requirement of consent from the portrayed person to make a portrait public, because this would hinder the freedom to send or receive information or views via pictures too much.[658] It is not the case that portrait law provides an exclusive right of exploitation as is the case with (normal) intellectual property rights. That would deny the rights of the author of the portrait, without whose creative performance the pictures would not even exist. To the contrary, portrait law should be seen as a limitation on the exploitation rights of the author, provided for by copyright, with an eye on the reasonable interests of

---

[654] Spoor, Verkade & Visser 2005, p. 303.

[655] The provisions on unlawful acts can, in principle, always be invoked due to their general applicability. However, when there is a specific provision for a situation this often is more favourable to use, since it matches a specific case, which leads to a lower burden of proof. The general provisions on tort require proof of damage and causation, which may be relatively difficult in practice. For instance, the unauthorized use of a digital persona may not always result in directly specified damages. Even if it is possible to prove damages, it has to be shown that these damages are the result of the unauthorized use of the digital persona (causation).

[656] Court of Appeal Amsterdam, 03-01-2012, 200.070.228/01, LJN: BU9938.

[657] Court of Appeal Amsterdam, 03-01-2012, 200.070.228/01, LJN: BU9938, at 3.4.

[658] Court of Appeal Amsterdam, 03-01-2012, 200.070.228/01, LJN: BU9938, at 3.5.

the portrayed.[659] Portrait law is, thus, an exception or limitation on copyright and not a right in itself.

The general aim of portrait law is to protect the privacy of the individual and to prevent illicit use and unlawful publication of the individual's portrait. In order to qualify as a portrait, the individual needs to be identifiable from the picture. Similar to data protection law, when the individual can be identified, the regime is applicable. To assess whether the individual can be identified, the 'test of identification' can be applied, which tests whether someone can recognize the portrayed person from the image. For identification, courts use a broad interpretation, which means that direct identification is not necessary. Closer investigation and comparison of the portrait with the portrayed person himself is sufficient. Other circumstances can help to identify the portrayed person. The portrait right usually protects the portrait of the face of a person with or without further parts of the body visible. But also an image of a part of a body which identifies the individual, even without seeing the face, can be considered a portrait. For instance, a tattoo on someone's back or arm may identify the individual. The scope of protection of the portrait right is very broad. The court applies a test of identification, in which the face can be inspected more closely and can be identified with the help of other characterizing circumstances, such as a typical posture of the body.[660] So, even when only a limited (or no) part of the face is visible, the total picture may lead to identifiability of the portrayed person. In case of identifiability, a portrait right is applicable.

Portrait law is about one's image and offers protection against unauthorized use. That is why this is potentially relevant for the protection of digital personae.

4.2.5. Protection of digital personae by portrait law?

The digital persona is also an image of an individual, albeit in the form of an entire data set and not a picture or video (even though these may be part of the data set). In the same way, protection is sought. The portrayed person has the portrait rights and obtains these rights by being portrayed. This implies that the rights also come into existence at the moment of creation. The creation of a digital persona would then, by analogy, mean that the represented individual automatically obtains portrait rights with regard to his digital persona. To obtain the rights, identification of the individual has to be possible, which, by definition, is the case for a digital persona. The broad interpretation of the identification test can be applied to digital personae by

---

[659]   Court of Appeal Amsterdam, 03-01-2012, 200.070.228/01, LJN: BU9938, at 3.7.
[660]   Pinckaers 1996, p. 132-133.

analogy as well. It is not necessary to identify the individual immediately. A closer look at the digital persona and comparing the digital persona with the individual can be sufficient for fulfilling the identification requirement. This is very important, since this opens the way for considering data sets that have no name included but still form a clear image of the individual as portraits. Even though the data set does not directly identify the individual, the identification test, based on recognition, may still be passed successfully. Digital personae with specific characteristics can, thus, be protected by portrait law in the same manner. In terms of data protection law, this can be considered a form of indirect identification, which is also sufficient to consider data personal data and, therewith, make data protection law applicable to the processing of the data.

The aim of this study is to find protection for the data subject who is represented by a digital persona. When approaching the digital persona as a portrait, the concept of portrait law may offer the desired protection. By means of portrait law, protection is provided against unauthorized use of the portrait and the individual data subject has the right to object to publication of the portrait or to receive a reasonable (financial) compensation. With this right, the portrayed individual can limit the rights of exploitation the author of the portrait has. The intangible form as well as the object of protection is in conformity with the needs.

A limitation of portrait law in its current form is the focus on either commercial use of the portrait, which also means that most protection is given to famous people or celebrities, or the protection of reasonable interests of the portrayed that would limit the rights of others to publish the portrait. Famous people often gain money with their image, for instance, in advertisements. The use of digital personae central in this study is not on displaying the digital personae in advertisements, but on making money by using the digital personae to select advertisements to be displayed to the individual, or to take other decisions that may affect the individual. It is, thus, about monetizing the image of the individual, since many applications are related to financial gain for a company. The use of the image is aimed at maximizing this gain by increasing the chance of an advertisement being clicked on or by selectively presenting offers to individuals. The use of digital personae, however, also affects the autonomy of the individual in taking decisions and setting goals. Using portrait law as a solution would, thus, not only require application by analogy, because digital personae are not strictly portraits, but also broadening the scope of portrait rights, since monetization is not based on displaying/publishing the portrait.

Another limitation of portrait law is that it is not providing rights in itself, but merely providing an instrument to limit copyrights of the author of an image. The application of portrait law, however, not necessarily requires that the portrait has to be protected by copyright.[661] Nevertheless, in cases where copyright is applicable, this is the primary line of defense. The portrayed person can object to publication of the portrait or ask for a reasonable compensation. In the case of digital personae, the creator would, thus, have copyrights, including the right to make the digital persona public and to multiply it. The digital persona can be commercially exploited by the creator of the digital persona. In most cases, not the individual data subject but another person will have this right. The individual can only object to the publishing (making public) of the digital persona. Internal use by a company for the selection of targeted advertisements or any other purpose may be allowed and cannot be prevented based on portrait law.[662]

Even though portrait law, applied by analogy, does not offer a complete solution for the problem discussed in this study, it offers valuable insights that may be helpful in working towards a solution. In any case, the approach of offering rights or protection mechanisms to the portrayed individual, next to, or instead of, the rights the author receives, seems promising. Besides, portrait law is applicable when the individual is identifiable, regardless of whether the portrait as such is protected by copyright. The identification of the individual is approached broadly and includes recognition when comparing the portrait and the individual.

5. Conclusion

Regulating the creation and use of digital personae may be helpful to improve the protection of privacy and autonomy of individuals. In this Chapter, a number of existing legal concepts have been discussed in order to assess to what extent these can be helpful in offering regulatory means that can be applied to digital personae.

The legal concepts described above offer certain characteristics that can be of help. It has become clear that attributing legal personality or a legal status to the digital persona is not a good solution. The focus is, in these cases, on the digital persona itself. Legal personality implies that the digital persona is an active entity, which by definition is not the case. Legal status could be attributed to digital personae. This would bring some level of protection, but still recognize the digital persona as an entity in itself, without capabilities to enforce this protection on itself. Claims in name of the digital persona

---

[661] Dutch Supreme Court, November 22, 1966, NJ 1967, 101.
[662] Note that this internal use may be prohibited by copyright when it implies reproduction of the digital persona, but only if the digital persona is recognized as a copyright protected work.

appear to be comparable to the exercise of currently existing data subject access rights. However, the concepts and practice are too diverging to apply the concepts as a solution to the problem.

This observation led to the idea of looking at positions of control over the digital persona. A strong form of control is provided by the legal concept of property or, more specifically, ownership. In particular, the *erga omnes* effect is useful, because it makes the property right an absolute right. With regard to digital personae, however, ownership has two important drawbacks that make it not applicable directly. Firstly, ownership concerns tangibles. The main requirement for ownership, however, is legal recognition, so this problem could be solved by recognizing digital personae as objects of property in the law. Secondly, however, ownership rights can be obtained by the creator of a thing because he creates it, which implies that digital personae often would become owned by others than the data subject. The control is, therewith, still not in the hands of the data subject.

The issue of tangibility can also be solved by following the regime of intellectual property rights. For digital personae, copyright seemed to be appropriate. Copyright is applicable to intangibles and gives the right holder exclusive rights to make the digital persona public or to make copies. The copyright holder can also give licenses to others to do so. Another important aspect of copyright are the moral rights, which cannot be transferred, and are meant to protect the digital persona against derogation. The rights holder can object to these derogatory works and also has the right to be mentioned as the author of a work. Depending on the exact way the digital persona is created, i.e. not completely automatically, a digital persona can be considered to be a 'work' in the sense of copyright law if the requirements of own character, personal mark of the author, and originality are met. In most cases of digital persona creation it is not likely that the latter two requirements will be fulfilled, so copyright will not be applicable to all digital personae. Moreover, the issue of who obtains the rights remains also in copyright. The creator of a work obtains the copyright. As was the case with ownership, the right is, thus, often obtained by others than the data subject. Next to that, copyright exists automatically by law, which implies that transfer of the rights is necessary to give these to the data subject. With property this was also the case. In copyright law, however, the moral rights always remain with the author, so complete transfer of the copyright would not even be possible.

Since digital personae are essentially data sets, a closer look was also taken at database rights. The problem of who would obtain the rights also exists in this legal concept. Besides, the rights obtained concern the database (infrastructure) as such, and not the contents of the database. Copying of parts of a database would, thus, not be prohibited so that a part of the records could be extracted. One record might be a complete digital persona, so database rights certainly do not offer appropriate protection. After this observation, it seemed necessary to focus on the data subject as being represented, and not on the work itself as the central focus. This focus is provided by a specific category within copyright law, namely portrait law.

The most promising approach appears to be the analogous application of portrait law. Nevertheless, two important issues remain. Firstly, portrait law is, in cases where the digital persona is also protected by copyright, only a limitation on the rights of the copyright holder, but it does not provide independent protection right away. Nevertheless, the opportunity to limit the rights of the user of the digital persona could provide the individual with a good instrument to exercise control. Secondly, internal use of a digital persona is not covered by portrait law, since it focuses on the making public of a portrait. However, in relation to individual autonomy, the most problematic uses of digital personae are the internal uses for taking decisions which affect the individual. The scope of protection of portrait law would need to be broadened up to cover this important part as well.

Although the existing legal concepts thus turn out not to offer a complete solution directly, an important conclusion is that the digital persona as a concept is promising. In this chapter, it has been assessed to what extent digital personae as an existing fact are legally protected. The digital persona can be related to several legal constructs and an analysis demonstrates why legal constructs can or cannot be applied and what the problems with application of the legal constructs are. This means that the digital persona could be introduced as a legal concept since it is well-defined enough to work with. Even though the digital persona can change in its exact form and appearance over time, the key characteristics indicate whether a data set is a digital persona or not. An interpretation of the concept from a teleological viewpoint is helpful in this respect. When using the concept, the focus should be on the protection of privacy and autonomy of the individual. The implementation of the digital persona as a legal concept is a means to achieve such protection.

The digital persona as a new legal concept could offer opportunities to achieve better protection of privacy and autonomy of the individual. What this would look like will be described in the subsequent chapter. A specific challenge that will be taken into account is related to profiles. The use of these can also impact the rights and values of the individual. Nevertheless, protection may be even more complicated. As was seen in this Chapter, an important part of the discussion in relation to existing legal constructs concerned the obtainment of rights. Either the data controller or the individual could obtain these and, therewith, some level of control. Profiles, however, are related to individuals that are not identified or identifiable. The paradoxical issue here is that, in order to achieve some control, the individual needs to be identified as being the represented individual, while remaining anonymous seems to provide better protection of privacy. To conclude, even though profiles and digital personae are closely related, the link to an identified individual appears to be a crucial point when trying to regulate the use of digital representations with a view on the rights and values of the individual that need better protection.

Chapter 8
The Digital Persona as a New Legal Concept

1. Introduction

Over the past years, there has been much EC funded research related to the ontology of privacy and identity, such as FIDIS,[663] Prime,[664] and PrimeLife.[665] Combinations of legal, sociological, and technical research have proven successful in these projects. A large part of contemporary issues in the field of privacy and identity concerns the collection of personal data. In relation to this, these projects show, amongst others, analyses of data collection, problems surrounding linkability of data to individuals, and issues arising from the persistence of data as lifelong digital representations. The collection of data related to individuals leads to digital personae and profiles. The sources of data are numerous, but, at least from the perspective of the individual, not all data are considered publicly available. For this reason, these data should not always be accessible by others to include them in a digital persona or a profile, which is important from a privacy perspective. Moreover, the interpretation of the data may diverge from the individual's own ideas, which leads to tensions with their sense of identity, in particular when data are accessed and used unexpectedly. "In cyberspace, there is no real wall between private and public. And the version of you being constructed out there – from bits and pieces of stray data – is probably not who you think you are."[666] Nevertheless, even when the representation is very accurate, privacy and autonomy of the individual may be affected by the creation and use of the digital persona or profile. In this study, the relation between privacy and autonomy was emphasized, in particular in relation to other rights and values that aim to ultimately protect human dignity. The creation of identity free from unreasonable constraints is what makes individuals unique. Privacy and autonomy are necessary conditions to achieve free identity construction. The more practical principles of informational self-determination and contextual integrity support this, and these are the principles that are most clearly supported by current data protection legislation.

In this study, the concept of the digital personae has been described from different disciplinary viewpoints, leading to an integrated definition. The

---

[663] See: <http://www.fidis.net/> (last accessed June 27, 2012).
[664] See: <https://www.prime-project.eu/> (last accessed June 27, 2012).
[665] See: <http://www.primelife.eu/> (last accessed June 27, 2012).
[666] Rosen 2000.

differences between digital personae and profiles have been discussed, which also made clear that the two concepts are closely related and on a sliding scale. It has been analyzed how the use of digital personae and profiles relates to the values and rights of human dignity, autonomy, identity, informational self-determination, contextual integrity, and privacy. Existing legal instruments fall short in properly protecting individuals when they become represented by digital personae or profiles, as we have seen in Chapters 6 and 7. In order to find proper ways of protecting digital personae and profiles, their legal status in light of current data protection legislation was assessed. Subsequently, relevant other legal constructs were analyzed in order to test whether they could be of help in providing protection for digital personae. Two important conclusions can be drawn from that analysis. First, the digital persona has proven useful as a concept to be used in law, because it defines a relevant category of data, a set of data relating to an individual, which can be used to improve legal certainty for individuals as well as for companies who want to use the digital persona. Second, even though valuable insights and starting points could be derived from existing legal constructs, none of the current legal constructs offers an adequate and satisfactory system for protecting digital personae. This means that this study has a theoretical value in defining relevant concepts and the related problems that occur in light of data processing activities. A remaining challenge is to find a proper way of implementing or embedding digital personae in law that improves the protection of the individual's interests online in practice. The exact manner in which digital personae and profiles can be implemented goes beyond the scope of this study. However, while in a late stage of writing this study, the proposal for the GDPR has been presented by the European Commission as part of the Data Protection Reforms. Part of the problems seems to be covered by the GDPR, which makes the GDPR a good starting point for further development of the protection of the individual's interests. The need for radical changes in the legal framework has become less prevalent with the GDPR, but still, the findings of this study can be used as input for the further negotiations and drafting of the GDPR towards its final form.

Since it seems that the concept of the digital persona is useful, but cannot be directly applied based on existing legal constructs, this Chapter will look into alternative ways of embedding the digital persona in law. First, an analysis will be made of the effect of incorporating digital personae in portrait law, because this field of law has proven to show the most promising starting points for the digital persona as a representation of an individual (2.1). Second, a proposal will be presented for embedding the concept in data protection law, because this field of law is the most directly related to digital personae as data sets related to individuals (2.2). In section 2.3, a combined approach will be presented, which combines the benefits of both approaches. Subsequently, in section 3, there will be an analysis of the extent to which the issues are already taken up in the proposed GDPR. In section 4, remaining points of attention will be discussed and some suggestions will be made for directions in how to practically embed digital personae and profiles in law. Finally, in section 5, a final conclusion to this study will be drawn, including an answer to the main research question.

2. Proposal for implementing the concept of the digital persona in law

In this section, two alternative ways of embedding the concept of the digital persona in law will be analysed. These two ways, embedding in portrait law and data protection law respectively, result from the findings on the applicability of existing legal constructs from Chapter 7. The aim of assessing the embedding of digital personae in these regimes is to find the main advantages and limitations which can function as preliminary input for a legal solution to the problem described in this study. First, however, some of the main aspects relating to the use of digital personae that have to be taken into account will be described.

2.1. Main points of attention related to the use of digital personae

The most important aspect is that the digital persona is recognized as a set of data that belong together and form a digital representation of an individual. The approach as a set of data is crucial to avoid discussions about pieces of data and whether these data qualify as personal data or really can identify the individual. In many cases, especially those central to this study, the data are consciously collected to create a representation of individual internet users. It is those representations that cause specific concerns. Ongoing technological developments have to be taken into account as well. While currently technologies can help alter judgments with obvious economic and social consequences, in the near future technologies may make "information about individuals seep into interactions where it is presently unavailable."[667] With the emerging trend of ubiquitous computing, the availability of information will become independent of time and location and may enter everyday interactions in offline environments as well. For instance, smart phones can be used to show real-time advertisements for an offer in the neighborhood where the individual at a specific time is or provide additional information to support (or steer) decisions the individual is taking.

A second point of attention is that identification can be based on a direct identifier or an L-identifier or quasi-identifier in the data set. It is not

---

[667] Strahilevitz 2007.

necessary to have a real name included in the data set. The data set just has to contain enough relevant data to make it easy to single out an individual. This can be based on, for instance, a unique identification number, which also implies that the data set does not necessarily have to contain much further data. This became particularly clear in relation to profiles, which may contain an R-identifier and therewith enable decisions being made at an individual level. Another possibility is that the data are so specific or characteristic that it is relatively easy to know whom the data concern. This can also be the case when entries in a database are unique sets and where identifiability is possible due to a low k-value in k-anonymity.[668] Finally, a data set can be very extensive and based on the accumulated data facilitate identification of the individual to whom the data relate.

A third relevant aspect is the direct relation between the use of digital personae and its potential impact on human dignity, autonomy, identity, informational self-determination, contextual integrity, and privacy. As was shown in Chapter 6, the use of a digital persona can affect the represented individual and, therewith, infringe upon their autonomy or privacy, or restrict the construction of an identity and ultimately impact upon human dignity. The possibility to influence an individual based on the available data is what makes the data set a digital persona. The protection of digital personae by embedding the concept in law ultimately aims at offering better protection of individuals in light of the mentioned rights and values. This has to increase awareness of data controllers concerning their data processing activities and to limit legal uncertainty concerning the applicability of data protection regulations.

Digital personae can be considered to reflect partial identities of an individual. When a digital persona, and in specific cases even a profile, is used to effectively steer the individual in his behavior or development, this affects the creation of the (partial) identity of the individual. Structurally limiting or predefining options to choose from, can unreasonably limit the development of the individual's self. The individual, then, is not respected in the construction of his own unique identity. Limitation of options and steering or even forcing specific choices to be made also impacts on individual autonomy. The individual cannot freely define his own short term and long term desires and goals to achieve, because of a lack of possibilities available. Ultimately, because of these restrictions human dignity is not respected.

Another important consideration is the relation between a digital persona and specific contexts. The context in which the digital persona is created and used should be very clear to the individual as well as the entity using

---

[668] See Chapter 6, section 3.2.

the digital persona. The data that belong to this context as well as the norms and rules applicable to that context should be leading in the way the digital persona is used or treated. On the one hand, data stemming from another context should, in principle, only be collected and added on the individual's initiative or with the individual's consent. A digital persona is usually related to a partial identity. This partial identity may be the outcome of conscious choices made by the individual to disclose certain data or to keep data secret for the specific context. Bringing in these data from other contexts would have implications for the free construction of identity, in particular as supported by informational self-determination. On the other hand, the digital persona should in principle not be transferred to or otherwise used in another context, since this would also conflict with contextual integrity. There may be circumstances where specific interests should prevail, such as in cases where the availability of information is of vital interest for the individual or for public security. These cases are listed in the DPD in Article 7(c), (d), and (e) as legitimate grounds for processing. Contextual integrity requires considering specific protection of the data in relation to the norms and rules applicable to the context from which the digital persona originates.

The creation and use of digital personae by others than the individual himself may also constitute an infringement of the right to privacy of the individual. In particular, when data are analyzed or when data sets are enriched with data resulting from profiling practices, this may reveal information concerning the individual which the individual himself may not have been aware of. Also monitoring activities on the internet to create profiles can lead to an infringement of the right to privacy, since the behavior of the individual is observed in detail while they stay unaware of the monitoring taking place. The websites an individual is visiting, or the information he is looking for, however, belong to the private sphere of the individual and is not publicly shared information or information that is consciously shared. When this information is collected and used to create a profile or enrich a digital persona, the privacy of the individual is affected, because informational self-determination and contextual integrity are affected. At least, in line with legal information obligations of data controllers, individuals have to be made aware of their data being processed and for what purposes the data are processed. The duty to inform lies with the data controller. Currently, companies can fulfill their information obligations by providing terms of service or privacy policies to their users. In these privacy policies, the way the company processes data is described and an indication is given of the purposes for which the processing takes place. However, the privacy policies are usually very extensive (and unattractive to read) and do not always offer clear information. In fact, privacy policies will not solve the information asymmetries between individuals and companies with regard to the data processing.[669] Moreover, information duties may be difficult to fulfill in the case of profiling, since the data processor cannot (yet) identify the individual.

Finally, individual autonomy is at stake when behavior is steered and, more particularly, when the individual is forced to take certain decisions. For instance, individuals can sometimes be obliged to create a digital persona in the form of a user account, which can also be used and enriched by the service provider for which the account is needed. For many services, a user account is necessary. This is comparable to leaving certain personal details, such as a delivery address, to enter into a contract in the offline world.[670] Online, however, as was shown in the example of Spotify,[671] an individual can be forced to use the same account for several different services. In order to sign up to Spotify as a new user, a Facebook account is required,[672] requiring non-Facebook users to create a Facebook account first. Moreover, it is possible that an individual has a Facebook account, but does not want to use this for other purposes outside the Facebook platform. Facebook, however, does not allow creating a (different) profile under a pseudonym, so creating a separate account would be a violation of the general terms of Facebook. As can be seen, access to a service depends on the presence of a specific type of digital persona. The creation and use of this persona is not always a free choice. At least, the choice is not whether the individual wants to create or use such a digital persona or not, but whether the individual wants to access a certain service. Combining services and means of access limits the individual autonomy of users, because the used digital persona will contain data originating from different services, while the individual has no option to prevent this. Not only autonomous choice is limited, but there is also a conflict with contextual integrity as different contexts are combined in one digital persona.

It has been shown that the use of digital personae and profiles can have an impact on the privacy and autonomy, and related rights and values, of individuals. Embedding digital personae, and as a subcategory profiles as well, in law, may be helpful to improve the protection of the individual. The following subsections will preliminarily analyse what embedding of the concepts in portrait law and in data protection law would mean respectively, in order to extract advantages and limitations that have to be taken into account in the search for a legal solution. The main points resulting from this

---

[669] Vila, Greenstadt & Molnar 2003.

[670] In many offline cases this is not even required, because the individual directly buys a product in a store and takes it home himself.

[671] Chapter 5, section 4.1.

[672] For the Netherlands, this has been changed back in September 2012. Scrolling to the bottom of the sign-up page now shows the option to register with an email account.

exercise will be assessed in relation to the GDPR subsequently. The concept of the 'digital persona' is proposed to be incorporated under the following definition:

A digital persona is a digital representation of a real-world individual, which can be connected to this real-world individual and includes a sufficient amount of (relevant) data to serve, within the context and for the purpose of its use, as a proxy for the individual.

2.2. The digital persona in portrait law

When looking at the existing legal regimes it turns out that portrait law and data protection law seem to be the most promising to embed digital personae and profiles in order to achieve better protection of the rights and respect for values of the individual. Nevertheless, both have drawbacks which limit reaching the desired result. The two regimes will briefly be discussed to summarize advantages and drawbacks, which will serve as input for working towards a legal solution for the problems identified in this study.

Portrait law offers some specific advantages. A first important advantage is the right for the portrayed individual to object to the publication of the portrait. In case the person using the portrait still wants to publish it, he has to prove that the interest of the portrayed individual to object to the publication is unjustified. So, there is a right to object for the individual and the burden of proof that the objection is unwarranted lies with the publisher. When applying this by analogy to the use of digital personae, it would provide the data subject with a right to object to the processing of his digital persona. Moreover, the burden of proof concerning the legitimacy of the objection would be with the data controller. In terms of control, this would be an achievement for the individual. Another important advantage of portrait law as a legal frame is that the emphasis lies on the relation to the individual. This may have a psychological effect, paying attention to the interests of the individual, instead of to the processing of data. The focus on the legitimate interests of the individual, in particular privacy rights, is emphasized as the background of data protection law.

An important drawback of this approach is that copyright law, of which portrait law is part, does not include notification duties. As a result, the individual cannot always be aware of his digital persona being created and used, in particular when this use is taking place internally, such as copying and internal use within a company.[673] Without this awareness, the individual

---

[673] This may often involve copying as well, but can also be 'consulting' the digital persona to make a decision.

cannot exercise his right to object to the use. Obviously, the same argument holds for 'traditional' portraits, but in the case of digital persona the issue of awareness is much more pressing due to the invisibility of the portrait being used. Moreover, the test of identification as a basis to decide whether something is a portrait or not implies that identification has to be possible for the application of the portrait law regime. Profiles can, thus, not be included in this form of regulation.

2.3. The digital persona in data protection law

A second option to implement the digital persona in law and to offer it protection is by making it part of (current) data protection law. A prerequisite for making the digital persona part of the data protection regime is that the relation to personal data has to be clear. As was shown in this study, the digital persona can be connected to an individual and can be used to identify this individual, so, the digital persona fits in the data protection regime. The category of profiles consists of data concerning an unknown individual and does not fit in the data protection regime. However, they have to be taken into account as well, because they can become a digital persona and, at least, can be used to affect an individual, even without identification.

When protecting the digital persona in data protection law, it should be explicated that the digital persona is a set of data and that the data are to be protected as a set. The data are used as a set as well and derive their value from being a data set. Separating them could have the effect of no longer being able to connect single data to an individual. The digital persona then becomes an anonymous profile and the DPD would not be applicable.

With regard to the applicability of the DPD it becomes clear that this is not always evident, in particular when it becomes unclear whether a data set is a digital persona or a profile. When the digital persona contains an L-identifier, the DPD is applicable and when the data set cannot be connected to an individual in any manner the DPD is not applicable. There are, however, a number of categories in between. Removing the L-identifier from a digital persona does not always imply that the individual is not identifiable. There is a sliding scale from direct identifiability, via identifiability with some effort, to (group) profiles. The significance of the effects of the use of the digital persona or profile is parallel to the sliding scale, from very significant to hardly relevant.[674] Whether the DPD is applicable depends on the specific case, which means that there is a lot of legal uncertainty. The thin line between the categories and the ease of transforming a profile into a digital

---

[674] Although it should be noted that even in the case of group profiles, the use of profiles for structural exclusion may in the end have discriminatory effects.

persona by adding an L-identifier, make that profiles also deserve attention when aiming to improve the rights of the individual. For instance, in the context of consumers, Pridmore talks about the combination of information files: "some information gathered on consumers through more personalized interactions may be attached to a personal information file – the digital space within databases from which a data-image is drawn."[675] And, "[r]egardless of whether additional personalized information is added, the consumer is routinely seen as the digitized collection of various segments or categories (deemed significant by the corporation) that he or she is perceived to belong to."[676] The use of digital personae and profiles can, thus, be identical and both can be used as a basis for decisions concerning the individual. The main difference is that a digital persona clearly concerns a specific individual, while for profiles this may be more difficult to see.

The fact that digital personae and profiles are both used to affect the individual indicates that an improvement of the protection of the rights of the individual must also be related to legitimate use of these data sets. It can be assumed that the best protection is offered when the legitimate use is directly related to an action of the concerned individual which explicitly indicates consent. While this ground for legitimate use is the most closely related to individual autonomy, proper protection based on this ground can only be achieved when consent is indeed well-informed. Even though this has appeared to be problematic, consent should still be used as the most appropriate ground for legitimate processing and specific attention should be paid to informing individuals of the purposes and possible implications of the use of profiles and digital personae.

Embedding the digital persona in data protection law directly will clearly define this category of data sets as data concerning identified or identifiable individuals. For data controllers, it will be clear that the DPD is applicable to the processing activities. Nevertheless, the burden of proof with regard to consent, as well as legitimate grounds for processing may be difficult to distinguish from the general provisions when the digital persona is merely defined as a set of data concerning an individual. It is still the case that data controllers process data and are not fully aware of the fact that they are affecting individuals. The weighing of interests may still be unbalanced, and when the processing is based on consent of the data subject, the data subject may have difficulties to withdraw this consent and stop the processing of his digital persona. A stronger emphasis on the digital persona as a holistic image of the individual, combined with the specific effects the processing of digital personae has on the individual would be welcome. Besides, a

---

[675] Pridmore 2008, section 4.1.
[676] Pridmore 2008, section 4.1.

legal opportunity to object to processing may provide the individual with a stronger position against data processors.

2.4. The digital persona as a portrait in data protection law?

It appeared that both forms have their drawbacks or limitations, but a combination may achieve better protection of the privacy and autonomy of the individual. The positive elements from portrait law that are absent in data protection law can be used as a source for inspiration to improve the protection of the individual. This would mean that the individual, next to the familiar rights provided by the DPD, also has the right to object to the (non-)commercial use of his digital persona based on his privacy rights or to claim financial compensation.[677] A right to object also exists in the DPD, but there are some important differences. One difference concerns the burden of proof. In portrait law the right to object is the starting point and the party who wants to use the portrait (the data controller) has to prove that the objection is unjustified, while under the DPD the data subject has to prove that he has "compelling legitimate grounds relating to his particular situation" to object against the processing.[678] On the basis of portrait rights, the individual has a stronger position, because the burden of proof concerning the legitimacy of the processing and the prevailing interest lies with the data controller.

Moreover, portrait rights are related to the identifiability of the individual, so the direct link between the digital persona and the individual is emphasized as well. With regard to the making public of a digital persona, rights to object based on portrait law may also be of help in solving problems stemming from changes of settings by service providers. Such problems, for instance, occurred in relation to the introduction of Facebook Timeline, where profile data of users became available to a larger audience, because Facebook changed the settings without prior notice to its users.[679] There are more options for users to manage the data available in their timeline with regard to visibility, but the example clearly shows the power position of the provider who can make major decisions concerning the public availability of lots of data of millions of users by simply introducing a new feature or switching a setting. In particular, the legal backdrop of such an initiative as implying

---

[677] Financial compensation for the use would be most appropriate in relation to commercial usage, where the data controller wants to make money by the use of the digital persona of the individual.

[678] Article 14(a) DPD.

[679] With the introduction of Facebook Timeline, Facebook made all previous posts of a member visual in a virtual CV: S. Choney, Facebook Timeline: There's no escaping it now, Technolog MSNBC: <http://www.technolog.msnbc.msn.com/technology/technolog/facebook-timeline-theres-no-escaping-it-now-84762> (last accessed July 31, 2012).

the making public of the portraits of all users will make clear that this kind of processing differs from the processing necessary to provide the service.

An important remaining issue concerns profiles. These do not directly fit under the portrait law regime or under the DPD regime, since the individual to whom the profile relates is unknown. A profile will, thus, not pass the test of identification at first glance. However, as became clear in Chapter 7 of this study, the test of identification can also be passed when the portrait is compared to an individual and the individual is recognized as being the portrayed person. With regard to individual profiles, which contain some form of an R-identifier, such as a cookie ID or an IP address, this means that they can be covered by the legal regime combining portrait law and the DPD, because the individual is identifiable. The profile data have to be combined with or related to other data to come to the identification and to establish the link between the profile and the individual. This is in line with the idea of the L-identifier, where the data can be compared with other data to identify the individual whom the data concern. Once the link is made, the profile becomes a digital persona.

Group profiles cannot be covered in this manner, since these are not individualized. The implication is that it cannot be argued that the profiles concern individual natural persons. However, as was shown in this study, the impact of the use of group profiles is usually less severe, unless they are used for structural inclusion or exclusion. This practice tends towards weblining. The most appropriate solution in this respect might be to prohibit weblining in a similar way as the prohibition of the offline equivalent redlining. In the context of the DPD, it would be useful to indicate the possibility of affecting individuals based on profiles as a point of attention, in order to emphasize the link to individual profiles. As soon as an R-identifier is added and the profile can be applied to an individual, the profile becomes an individual profile and can be covered by the regime as described above.

The shift in the burden of proof and the recognition of the digital persona as a portrait will bring advantages for the individual. The required efforts to object to information processing will be limited to some extent. Moreover, the digital persona as a portrait will emphasize that the data concern an individual and that decisions based on the data will affect an individual. This might be an incentive for data controllers to be accountable. Moreover, in line with portrait rights, options may be opened for individuals to monetize the usage of their digital personae. Finally, options are opened to include individual profiles in the DPD regime as well.

3. Issues covered by the GDPR

A number of the issues discussed above are taken up in the proposal for the GDPR. For instance, a shift in the burden of proof is covered by Article 19(1) of the GDPR.[680] In my opinion, this right should also be applicable to the use of profiles, since these can be used to affect individuals as well. In the context of direct marketing, this is facilitated by section 2 of Article 19 GDPR. Moreover, Article 20 GDPR provides a prohibition on measures based on profiling without the consent of the individual. The scope of the GDPR is, therewith, much broader than the DPD. The fact that anonymous profiling is not really an opportunity is addressed in this manner, because the formulation of the provision makes no differentiation between types or purposes of profiling. The topic of tracking of browsing behavior, which was discussed elaborately in this study, is, thus, covered as well. The lack of differentiation, however, is also a drawback, because it emphasizes the use of a type of technology instead of the interests of the individual that need to be protected by the provision.

A positive effect of the lack of differentiation is that it can also contribute to legal certainty for data controllers. In cases of uncertainty in practice as to which information collected by a service provider or internet company is personal data, the Article 29 Working Party indicates that all data have to be treated as personal data, including the applicability of the DPD to the processing of these data. The approach taken in the GDPR seems to be in line with this opinion. Nevertheless, this stringent approach clearly may conflict with the interests of commercial companies who wish to process anonymous data or who have developed innovative privacy-friendly approaches towards profiling.[681] The European Data Protection Supervisor (EDPS) seems to be more lenient and indicates that this approach is "reasonable except where it becomes clear that the existence of personal data in a system is negligible."[682] This is more in line with a purpose-based approach towards identifiability and limits the influence of 'any other person' who may be able to identify an individual based on the data set. According to the EDPS, in cases where it is not reasonably likely that the data controller will (try to) identify the individual the profile is anonymous and not subjected to the DPD. This approach may offer an 'escape' for data controllers when they argue not to have the intention to identify individuals. Based on the foregoing

---

[680] "The data subject shall have the right to object, on grounds relating to their particular situation, at any time to the processing of personal data which is based on points (d), (e) and (f) of Article 6(1), unless the controller demonstrates compelling legitimate grounds for the processing which override the interests or fundamental rights and freedoms of the data subject."

[681] Cave et al. 2012, p. 74.

[682] Hustinx 2009, p. 7.

observations, such an escape should only be available in relation to group profiles. Digital personae and individual profiles are always subjected to the DPD, since they relate to identified or (potentially) identifiable individuals. The approach taken in the GDPR is, thus, the most effective approach from the perspective of protecting the interests of individuals. Obviously, balancing these interests with the interests of commercial data controllers is a challenge.

One of the opportunities to tackle this challenge is by providing the individual with a choice (control) that is applicable to numerous profilers. The individual gains control, but can make a choice concerning a number of profiling activities at once, which makes the control less burdensome and is positive for the commercial companies as well. After all, they benefit from providing a user with a nice web user experience, because this leads to convenience and a positive attitude towards the companies. Providing the user with more control is something on which much work is done currently, at a European level, by requiring consent for the use of cookies via a Directive,[683] even though this concerns separate profilers. Thus far, the initiative is not very effective, however, because it appears difficult to have clear distinctions between types of cookies for which consent is required[684] and how to implement the obtainment of consent in websites. Moreover, the Directive is circumvented, for instance, by giving visitors of a web shop a free item, which is added to the shopping cart immediately. Keeping track of the items in the shopping cart by the use of cookies is allowed. As a result, web shop owners can track their visitors when browsing through the store. Obtaining consent for or objecting to profiling at a more general level seems more efficient, in particular when supported by technical means. A user-friendly way for obtaining this consent or objection is sought for by regulators and advertisers[685] and a valuable initiative in this respect is the DoNotTrack

---

[683] Directive 2009/136/EC of the European Parliament and of the Council of 25 November 2009 amending Directive 2002/22/EC on universal service and users' rights relating to electronic communications networks and services, Directive 2002/58/EC concerning the processing of personal data and the protection of privacy in the electronic communications sector and Regulation (EC) No 2006/2004 on cooperation between national authorities responsible for the enforcement of consumer protection laws, which changed Article 5(3) of Directive 2002/58/EC and includes this requirement of consent.

[684] For tracking cookies, consent is required, but not for functional cookies, which are, for instance, use to 'remember' language preferences or items in a shopping cart. The exact scope of functional cookies is unclear, however.

[685] In the EU, Commissioner Kroes first gave the advertising branch the opportunity to come up with a proper solution before imposing rules from the EC. Initiatives from the branch, however, were not present in time or did not meet the requirements from the Directive. See: Neelie Kroes, Vice-President of the European Commission responsible for the Digital Agenda Online Privacy, speech at Online Tracking and

system of the W3C mandated by the FTC,[686] which is incorporated in several browsers already. Nevertheless, the fact that profiles are on a sliding scale and can become digital personae at some point in time always has to be taken into account.

At least at the practical level, the GDPR brings an improvement in the protection of individuals as opposed to the current DPD. The improvements are to a large extent in line with the protection sought for in relation to the problems described in this study. The GDPR is, thus, a welcome instrument, even though some room for improvement is still present. From the perspective of the use of digital personae and profiles and the related interests of individuals that need to be protected, the following section will provide some indications for improvement. At least the theoretical value which can be achieved by embedding the concepts of digital personae and profiles in law is a worthwhile exercise and can be a source of inspiration for further development of the practical embedding of the concepts.

4. Further points of attention and suggestions

Having discussed the issues that are covered by the GDPR, some specific points of attention remain that need to be taken into account when further developing legal protection of the interests of individuals in an online environment. Besides, some suggestions towards a practical approach of some of the issues will be presented.

The individual has data protection rights which are also applicable to digital personae. The identifiability of the individual is assumed to be present when the digital persona can be connected to a specific individual. Since the individual can be reached, he should also be provided with information to contact the commercial data controller who uses the digital persona. For instance, based on cookie identification, information can be displayed on the website where the cookie is used.[687] The individual, then, can choose either

---

Browsers Workshop, Brussels 22 June 2011, speech/11/461. Online available at: < http://europa.eu/rapid/press-release_SPEECH-11-461_en.htm>, last accessed 6 December 2012.

[686] See Chapter 7. A drawback of the system is its dependence on the data controllers who have to respect the wish of the individual not to be tracked.

[687] In the case of third party cookies, the third party has to negotiate for this displaying space with the website owner, at least when the third party does not display visible content on the website. This can be part of the contracts between the parties. A positive side-effect will be that website owners become (more) aware of the amount of cookies they have on their websites and to which parties those cookies belong. A difficulty is the possibility that a website owner does not know which party will display an advertisement on his website beforehand, for instance, because this depends on

to accept the use of the digital persona or to object to it. When the individual chooses to object, this has to result in termination of the use and even deletion of the digital persona,[688] unless the data controller can show that the objection is unjustified.[689] The argument of the data controller has to provide convincing evidence of his prevailing legitimate interests that cannot be overruled by the objection of the individual. An objection of the data subject can also be conditioned, meaning that the use of the digital persona may be allowed in case a financial compensation is provided by the data controller. In that case, an agreement can be reached and the processing is based on consent. This is comparable to the right for the individual to monetize his image based on portrait law.

As indicated in this study, profiles are often used for targeted advertising. These advertisements appear not always to be in line with the interests of the personally targeted individual. Choices of advertisers to include or exclude individuals may have negative effects for the individual. However, direct negative effects which cannot be circumvented[690] or direct legal effects[691] can usually only be based on a digital persona and not on a profile. Legal effects which take place directly will normally only be possible to achieve when the individual is identifiable, because such an effect is directed to a specific person. A data set which can be used for direct legal effects is, thus, a digital persona and

---

the outcome of a bidding process. This should be taken up via intermediaries that connect advertisers to web site owners.

[688] If the persona has to be deleted, but separate data remain available, the normal regime of the DPD applies to these data.

[689] In cases where the use of the digital persona is related to a service the user wants, a distinction should be made between processing of data that are necessary for providing the service and the processing of additional data for other purposes. Processing of the latter category should be stopped then, but might not imply that the service cannot be used anymore. Moreover, if no identification is necessary for a service, such as is the case with publicly available services which can be accessed without an account, using the service should be possible without a digital persona being created. In this respect, the current practice of the Dutch public broadcasting (*Nederlandse Publieke Omroep, NPO*) of not allowing access to their website and services without accepting cookies is an example of an unnecessary creation of a digital persona in relation to a public service.

[690] Circumvention for example is possible with an advertisement by simply ignoring it. Moreover, advertising to influence behavior of individuals takes place continuously in the offline world as well and does not directly have legal effects either. The only analogy might be that weblining is comparable to redlining and might be prohibited.

[691] Direct legal effects are effects that take place directly because of a specific action, such as granting or refusing a contract. Indirect legal effects take place as a result of an action, but are not the initial aim of the action. For instance, making a selection of individuals who receive a loan based on a number of characteristics can have an indirect effect of discrimination if the characteristics appear to structurally exclude certain people.

not a profile. The use of a profile, however, can have significant effects as well. Structural exclusion, for instance, can be a form of indirect discrimination. Even though group profiles are hard to cover under data protection legislation, simply because they do not relate to an identified or identifiable individual, they have to be kept in mind when searching for further improvement of the protection of the interests of the individual. The solution may, perhaps, not be in a specific embedding in law in the form of a provision, but more in changing the general mindset. The focus should be on the interests of the individual, mainly privacy, but in relation to individual autonomy and identity and ultimately human dignity, that need to be protected by the legal regime. Currently, the focus is much more tended towards processing requirements and not on the effects the processing may have on the individual.

Slight differences with regard to the requirements for the use of digital personae, individual profiles, and group profiles are justified. The justification for this differentiation relates to the possible impact the use of the different categories of data sets may have. In the case of group profiles, companies may earn money by exploitation of data, while these data cannot simply be related to an identified or identifiable offline individual. In cases where this is possible, such as advertising via Facebook where the account is a digital persona and contains a direct identifier (the name of the individual as required by the real-name policy of Facebook), advertisers deliver their content and their target group, after which Facebook displays the advertisement on the profile pages of the members who belong to that target group. Identification is not possible by the advertiser, because he does not receive data about the members. Facebook can identify the individuals to whom an advertisement is targeted and has to be compliant with the GDPR. Moreover, Facebook ultimately decides to whom an advertisement is actually shown. This justifies a relatively lenient approach towards profilers and advertisers, who are using profiles, as opposed to data controllers using digital personae.

Next to the more general points of attention, more concrete issues remain for which some direction can be given as a starting point for implementation. First, the option to monetize the use of a digital persona in the form of a financial compensation, inspired by portrait law, is not included in the GDPR.[692] When taking the proposed Articles 19 and 20 as a starting point, this aspect can be facilitated by adding an option to provide conditioned consent, in which case the condition is a financial compensation. In line with

---

[692] It can be argued that providing a service for free, because it is funded by targeted advertising, is a financial compensation as well. Nevertheless, not all services have such a business model and, moreover, it is not always necessary to create digital personae to display advertisements. In a lot of cases, contextual advertising, for instance, can help in displaying advertisements that relate to the interests of the individual as well.

Article 19, this could mean that there is a right to object to the use of a digital persona, unless financial compensation is provided. In line with Article 20, the consent to be obtained can be conditioned beforehand. Due to the diversity of situations and aims of the processing activities, it may be the most appropriate option to use delegated acts to make the compensations more concrete, or to adopt a Commission Guideline or ruling on this aspect. A similar approach is taken in Article 20(5)[693] concerning suitable measures to safeguard the data subject's legitimate interests. Moreover, the instrument of delegated acts allows for more flexibility when circumstances change as opposed to making it part of the Regulation itself.

The opportunity offered to individuals to monetize their digital persona can be criticized from the perspective of behavioral economics. Research in this area has shown that people do not highly value their privacy (in terms of money).[694] The impact of implementing the digital persona in the way proposed above will be limited by this. However, the findings of behavioral economics research are based on an important condition, namely that the individual is aware of his data being used for commercial purposes.[695] This awareness is an important achievement in relation to autonomy. If the individual is unaware of his data being used, he cannot make an economic decision to adjust his behavior or to take specific action. So, regardless of whether individuals value their privacy high or low, the choices made on this by the individual are more conscious and at least include a choice on whether to accept the use of a digital persona or not. This certainly improves individual autonomy and the free construction of identity, which implies that, in the end, human dignity is better respected.

---

[693] "The Commission shall be empowered to adopt delegated acts in accordance with Article 86 for the purpose of further specifying the criteria and conditions for suitable measures to safeguard the data subject's legitimate interests referred to in paragraph 2."

[694] See e.g. Acquisti, John & Loewenstein 2009; Beresford, Kübler & Preibusch 2012 and; Presentation by Sarah Spiekermann at PI Lab launch event, April 3rd 2012, Tilburg: Privacy as Property. Online available at: <http://www.pilab.nl/presentations/Spiekermann%20-%20Privacy%20As%20Property%20-%20PI.lab%20launch%20-%20Tilburg%203%20April%202012.pdf> (last accessed June 23, 2012).

[695] For instance, in one experiment, there was a clear choice between two shops where in one shop DVDs are cheaper, but the individual has to provide much more personal information than in the other shop. The difference in this data sharing was clearly indicated, but still, individuals choose for the shop with the cheapest DVDs (Beresford, Kübler & Preibusch 2012). In another experiment, a choice was offered between an anonymous loyalty card worth 10 US $ and a non-anonymous card worth 12 US $. Individuals who received the non-anonymous card were not willing to switch to the anonymous card ('paying' 2 Dollars for more privacy) (Acquisti, John & Loewenstein 2009). Depending on the initial situation in the experiment (the priming of the research subjects), the differences in disclosure of personal information are, thus, clearly related to the financial benefit the customer receives.

In order to balance interests, the data controller can, in principle, use a similar kind of analogy based on copyright law by posing himself as the author of the digital persona. The processing of the digital persona may then be allowed based on the legitimate interests of the author, supported by Article 7(f) of the DPD. This interest has to be weighed against the privacy interests of the individual, which is exactly what is provided for by the portrait rights. The privacy of the individual is a central issue, whereas in current data protection law the focus is more on requirements for processing. The weighing of interests that has to take place may also include a negotiation on financial compensation for the use of the digital persona.

A problem that remains here is that the data controller can weigh the interests without involving the individual.[696] Moreover, the data controller can still argue that the privacy interests of the individual do not outweigh their interest, or data controllers may try to apply general rules on financial compensation, therewith buying processing rights on a large scale. Since there is only an obligation to notify data protection authorities of the processing activities and no check is performed on the weighing of interests made by the data controller,[697] this ground hardly offers an appropriate safeguard for the individual. This problem can very well be taken up by a prohibition to make the weighing without consulting the individual. This does not mean that the individual can always successfully object to the processing, but that the individual has to be informed about the weighing of interests. Moreover, the introduction of the concept in combination with this information duty related to weighing of interests improves awareness amongst data controllers of the fact that they are taking decisions that affect individuals, and therewith support accountability. The direct link to the individual becomes clearer, which may result in a different approach when making decisions as compared to taking the idea of a data set as a starting point. This is a more psychological effect, which cannot be fully substantiated here without psychological research. Nevertheless, a change of mindset will emphasize the protection of the individual, which is at the core of privacy rights, instead of emphasizing procedural aspects of data processing practices. Still, the weighing of interests may remain casuistic to a certain extent, in particular when company secrets are at stake. A situation without a weighing, however, is an illusion. The clearer the interests at stake

---

[696] Involving the individual and obtaining consent is still the most desirable ground for processing, but may not always be reasonable in practice, since it cannot always outweigh the legitimate interests of commercial data controllers.

[697] The Dutch Data Protection Authority (College Bescherming Persoonsgegevens, CBP) only performs a formal check on the completeness of a notification. The notification as such does not imply a justification of the data processing or offer any legal rights. See: <http://www.cbpweb.nl/Pages/inf_va_melden_vrijstellen.aspx> (last accessed June 21, 2012).

are, the better the weighing can take place. Moreover, the result may never be that the individual data subject is refused all information, which is already indicated in Recital 51 of the GDPR.

Second, the concept of the digital persona is not included. Including the concept in a specific provision may be an additional complicating factor. Moreover, Article 20 GDPR seems to cover digital personae as well as profiles, so there is already a major achievement in the proposal in this sense. However, more work should be done to achieve a different mindset concerning the impact processing of digital personae and profiles may have on the interests of the individual. Possibly, a start can be made by including the concept in the Preamble, in combination with a mind setting Recital emphasizing the link to individual persons that are affected by the use of digital representations. The relation between privacy, autonomy, and identity is essential to be stressed in this respect. The normative background is supported by a fundamental rights approach, which should be the starting point for the entire GDPR. This requires some rephrasing in the current proposal, because the proposed GDPR even increases the distance with privacy as a fundamental right, by explicating data protection rights instead of privacy rights as the normative background.

If embedding digital personae and profiles in the GDPR seems a valuable improvement, a first step may be to add the following Recital to the Preamble:

Whereas:
(1)The creation of data sets concerning individuals leads to digital personae and profiles.
A digital persona is a digital representation of an individual, which can be connected to this real-world individual and includes a sufficient amount of (relevant) data to serve, within the context and for the purpose of its use, as a proxy for the individual.

A profile is a digital representation of a non-identifiable real-world individual, which can be used to affect this individual by means of unidirectional communications.

(2) The use of digital personae and profiles as a basis for making decisions affects individuals and may impact upon their individual autonomy and privacy. This can restrict the free construction of identity and may ultimately impact upon human dignity. The protection of the fundamental rights of the individual has to be seen in light of the relation between the processing of data and the implications thereof for individuals. Individuals may also be affected by decisions taken based on digital personae and profiles when this is not the primary aim of the data processing entity. The effect a decision may have on the fundamental rights and

related interests of the individual should be taken into account when making a decision.

The proposed addition to the Preamble emphasizes the mindset that has to be the basis for data processing activities that may affect individuals, regardless of whether the data sets are digital personae or profiles. The focus is not that much on the processing activities as such, but on the effects the processing may have for the fundamental rights and related interests of the individual. Obviously, more concrete implementations in the form of provisions would be needed to achieve a more serious effect, for instance, in line of the amendments related to Articles 19 and 20 as discussed above. The exact formulation of these provisions goes beyond the scope of this study and would need a specific effort, taking into account the interests of all actors involved. Nevertheless, this study has shown the importance of the topic and provides a theoretic value in describing and analyzing the concepts of digital personae and profiles and their protection.

5. Conclusion and reflection

Embedding the concepts of the digital persona and profile in order to provide better protection of privacy and autonomy of individuals, with the final aim to better respect human dignity, seems to be well-placed for success in achieving this aim. Practical work on the embedding needs to be done, but the theoretical analysis provided in this study has proven the concept of the digital persona as such to be valuable as a legal concept. The way of implementing the concept as described above does not broaden up the interpretation of the definition of personal data, but takes a holistic approach towards complete data sets, instead of separate pieces of data. The embedding of the concept, starting from a mindset in the Preamble of the GDPR, can bring a better protection of fundamental rights and values for the individual. Moreover, the relation between digital personae and profiles and their use is emphasized.

The main research question of this study was the following: Can the protection of digital personae and profiles as coherent data sets, taking into account that they are used by businesses as a basis for making decisions that affect real world individuals, improve the protection of privacy and autonomy of the individuals represented by these digital personae? It can be concluded that this question can be answered positively. Even though the practical embedding requires more work and some other issues remain that could be taken up in further research, the embedding of the digital persona as a concept in law can improve the privacy and autonomy of individuals, in particular because it will provide for more awareness of individuals about their digital personae being created and used for commercial purposes, as well as a better balance between the interests of commercial parties and those of individuals. Commercial companies will be more aware of the fact that they are making decisions based on digital personae that affect real-world individuals. This is important, since personalized treatment of individuals based on digital personae or profiles is common practice. However, "[i]n the area of automated personalization, we have come to realize that individualization is not a sufficient condition of dignified treatment."[698] Individualised approaches of companies towards individuals do not automatically mean that these individuals are not affected in their privacy and autonomy.

To conclude, digital personae and profiles are valuable concepts to use as a mindset when legally improving the protection of privacy and autonomy of individuals. Connecting the implementation of the concepts to the GDPR will emphasize the approach of the persona as a complete set of data concerning an individual, shifts the burden of proof concerning consent to the data controller, and will probably pay more attention to the effects of the processing of digital personae, instead of on the processing as such.

Even though the proposed embedding can bring improvements for the protection of individuals, a critical reflection brings two points of attention to the fore. The first is a privacy paradox. One of the important points of the proposed approach is to provide the data subject with a right to object, also when the data set is a profile. The individual, then, has to indicate that the profile concerns him. In order to exercise this right, the individual, thus, has to provide more information to identify himself. Better privacy protection, thus, implies less privacy. The same problem arises in relation to financial compensation. If an individual wants to receive a payment for the use of his profile, the data controller has to be able to provide the individual with the financial compensation. This will usually require identifying details from the individual. Nevertheless, the data subject may in many cases be able to object to the profiling without identifying himself. For instance, providing cookie information or an IP address may not directly identify the individual, but enables the data controller to recognize which profile it concerns. With regard to financial compensation, innovative solutions to trade browsing data with content providers may be helpful.[699]

The second point is of a more general nature and concerns the enforcement of data protection legislation. Once the GDPR is in its final form and enters

---

[698] Cohen 2012, p. 251.
[699] An example is the New York City based start-up Enliken: < http://allthingsd.com/20121212/enliken-wants-to-help-you-sell-your-browsing-data-to-your-favorite-content-provider/>, last visited 12 December 2012.

into force, this is the main challenge to be picked up. Enforcement will largely depend on the developments relating to the powers of data protection authorities. This empowerment is one of the important aspects taken up in the GDPR. The enforcement problems can best be combined with a plea for accountability of data controllers, which is also emphasized in the GDPR. In this respect, valuable work that can be used as a starting point has been done by Nissenbaum,[700] who, already back in 1997, discussed accountability in relation to four specific problems related to the complexity of computer systems that fall under the responsibility of the data controller: (1) the problem of many hands, referring to the involvement of high numbers of people and parties in the development and use of data processing technologies; (2) the problem of bugs, which relates to inadvertent mistakes in software resulting from complexity; (3) blaming the computer, which comes across when a company has lost control over its systems, and; (4) software ownership without liability, which may occur in cases of non-proprietary software use or when processes are outsourced.

Another difficulty related to enforcement is due to the involvement of many, often international, parties. This can make it difficult to determine where jurisdiction lies in case of a conflict. In any case, the domestic EU legislation of the DPD has a transnational footprint.[701] However, even if jurisdiction is found, it may still be difficult to enforce a court ruling when the service provider is located elsewhere. A number of issues related to globalization have been discussed by the Article 29 Working Party.[702] Next to identifying problems concerning the applicability of data protection law, several directions for solutions are discussed, such as international standards, international agreements, and Binding Corporate Rules.[703]

In conclusion, the use of digital personae and profiles can have a serious impact on the privacy and autonomy of individuals. This study discussed the concepts of digital personae and profiles from different disciplinary perspectives. Protecting digital personae and profiles to ultimately improve the protection of the individual's interests online has, at least theoretically, proven to be a useful approach. Further research is needed on some specific issues as well as on the way the concept can be embedded in data protection law.

A number of the issues raised in this study are already being addressed in the GDPR proposal. Nevertheless, concrete legal recognition of digital personae

---

[700] Nissenbaum 1997.
[701] Kobrin 2002, p. 4.
[702] Article 29 Working Party 2009b, pp. 9-12.
[703] On Binding Corporate Rules, see also: Moerel 2012.

and profiles is not taking place in the GDPR. Moreover, the normative background for the GDPR is mainly focused on data protection and not on overarching rights, such as privacy and individual autonomy. The proposal of embedding digital personae and profiles in data protection regulation as indicated in this study does emphasize the important link between the use of data sets as representations and privacy and autonomy. In relation to privacy and autonomy, a number of other rights and values were discussed and it has been shown that identity construction and, in some cases, even human dignity is at stake. The mindset of data sets as digital representations in the form of personae or profiles stresses the link to an identity and to an individual human being. Even though several of the problems described in this study can also be addressed based on the current GDPR proposal, the specific approach towards digital representations and the emphasized aspects in relation to individuals and their rights and values which are at stake when digital personae or profiles are used, provides better insight in the interests of individuals and may provide better protection of these interests.

Bibliography

Acquisti, A., & Gross, R. (2006). *Imagined Communities: Awareness, Information Sharing, and Privacy on the Facebook.* Paper presented at the Privacy Enhancing Technologies Workshop (PET).

Acquisti, A., John, L., & Loewenstein, G. (2009). *What is Privacy Worth?* Carnegie Mellon University Working Paper: Carnegie Mellon University.

Agre, P. E., & Rotenberg, M. (1997). *Technology and Privacy : The New Landscape.* Cambridge, MA [etc.]: MIT Press.

Akandji-Kombe, J.-F. (2007). *Positive Obligations under the European Convention on Human Rights.* Strasbourg: Council of Europe.

Allen, T., & Widdison, R. (1996). Can Computers Make Contracts? *Harvard Journal of Law & Technology,* 9(26).

Allgrove, B. D. (2004). *Legal Personality for Artificial Intellects: Pragmatic Solution or Science Fiction.* (Master of Philosophy), University of Oxford, Oxford.

Andrade, N. G. d. (2012). Oblivion: The Right to Be Different... From Oneself: Reproposing the Right to Be Forgotten. *Revista d'Internet, Dret I Politica* (13), 122-137.

Andrews, L. (2012). Facebook is Using You, *The New York Times,* 27 September 2012.

Angwin, J. (2012). Google Faces New Privacy Probes, *Wall Street Journal,* 16 March 2012.

Article 29 Working Party. (2007). *Opinion 4/2007 on the Concept of Personal Data.* 01248/07/EN (WP136). Adopted on June 20, 2007.

Article 29 Working Party. (2008a). *Opinion 1/2008 on data protection issues related to search engines,* 00737/EN (WP 148). Adopted on April 4, 2008.

Article 29 Working Party. (2008b). *Opinion 2/2008 on the review of the Directive 2002/58/EC on privacy and electronic communications (ePrivacy Directive).* 00989/08/EN (WP150). Adopted on May 15, 2008.

Article 29 Working Party. (2009a). *Opinion 5/2009 on online social networking.* 01189/09/EN (WP 163). Adopted on June 12, 2009.

Article 29 Working Party. (2009b). *The Future of Privacy: Joint contribution to the Consultation of the European Commission on the legal framework for the fundamental right to protection of personal data.* 02356/09/EN (WP 168). Adopted on December 01, 2009.

Article 29 Working Party. (2010). *Opinion 2/2010 on online behavioural advertising.* 00909/10/EN (WP 171). Adopted on June 22, 2010.

Article 29 Working Party. (2011a). *Opinion 15/2011 on the definition of consent.* 01197/11/EN (WP138). Adopted on July 13, 2011.

Article 29 Working Party. (2011b). *Opinion 16/2011 on EASA/IAB Best Practice Recommendation on Online Behavioral Advertising.* 02005/11/EN (WP 188). Adopted on December 8, 2011.

Asser. (2006). *Algemeen Goederenrecht Asser* 3-1.

Ayenson, M., Wambach, D. J., Soltani, A., Good, N., & Hoofnagle, C. J. (2011). *Flash Cookies and Privacy II: Now with HTML5 and ETag Respawning.*

Bainbridge, D. I. (2007). *Intellectual Property* (6th ed.). London: Pearson Longman.

Barney, D. (2004). *The Network Society.* Cambridge [etc.]: Polity.

Barrigar, J., Burkell, J., & Kerr, I. (2006). Let's Not Get Psyched Out Of Privacy: Reflections on withdrawing consent to the collection, use and disclosure of personal information. *Canadian Business Law Journal,* 44(54).

Battelle, J. (2005-2006). *The Search; How Google and Its Rivals Rewrote the Rules of Business and Transformed Our Culture.* London/Boston: Nicholas Brealey Publishing.

Baumeister, R. F., & Muraven, M. (1996). Identity as adaptation to social, cultural, and historical context. *Journal of adolescence,* 19(5), 405-405-416.

Bennett, C. J. (1997). Convergence Revisited: Toward a Global Policy for the Protection of Personal Data? In P. E. Agre & M. Rotenberg (Eds.), *Technology and Privacy: The New Landscape* (pp. 99-123). Cambridge: The MIT Press.

Berg, B. van den (2009). *The Situated Self; identity in a world of Ambient Intelligence.* (PhD Dissertation), Erasmus University, Rotterdam.

Bernal, P. (2011). *Do deficiencies in data privacy threaten our autonomy and if so, can informational privacy rights meet this threat?* PhD thesis London School of Economics and Political Science.

Bilenko, M., Richardson, M., & Tsai, J. Y. (2011). *Targeted, Not Tracked: Client-Side Solutions for Privacy-Friendly Behavioral Advertising.* Paper presented at the TPRC, Waterloo, Canada.

Birnie, P., Boyle, A., & Redgwell, C. (2009). *International Law and the Environment* (3rd ed.). Oxford: Oxford University Press.

boyd, D. (2008a). Why youth (heart) social network sites: The role of networked publics in teenage social life. In D. Buckingham (Ed.), *Youth, identity, and digital media* (pp. 119-142). Cambridge: MIT Press.

boyd, D. (2008b). None of this is Real (Identity and Participation in Friendster). In J. Karaganis (Ed.), *Structures of Participation* (pp. 132-157).

boyd, D., & Ellison, N. B. (2007). Social Network Sites: Definition, History, and Scholarship. *Journal of Computer-Mediated Communication*, 13(1), Article 11.

boyd, d., & Hargittai, E. (2010). Facebook Privacy Settings: Who Cares? *First Monday*, 15(8).

Bridy, A. (2011). *Coding Creativity: Copyright and the Artificially Intelligent Author.* Legal Studies Research Paper Series, (Working Paper No. 2011-25). Online available at: <http://ssrn.com/abstract=1888622>.

Brin, S., & Page, L. (1998). *The Anatomy of a Large-Scale Hypertextual Web Search Engine.* Paper presented at the Seventh International World-Wide Web Conference (WWW 1998), Brisbane, Australia.

Brouwer, E. R. (2008). *Digital Borders and Real Rights: Effective Remedies for Third-Country Nationals in the Schengen Information System.* Leiden: Koninklijke Brill N.V.

Brown, G. (1990). *The Information Game; Ethical Issues in a Microchip World.* London: Humanities Press International, Inc.

Bruns, A. (2009). From Prosumer to Produser: Understanding User-Led Content Creation. Conference proceedings: *Transforming Audiences 2009*, 3-4 Sep, 2009, London.

Bygrave, L. A. (2001). Automated Profiling; Minding the Machine: Article 15 of the EC Data Protection Directive and Automated Profiling. *Computer Law & Security Report*, 17(1), 17-24.

Canhoto, A., & Backhouse, J. (2008). General Description of the Process of Behavioral Profiling. In M. Hildebrandt & S. Gutwirth (Eds.), *Profiling the European Citizen: Cross-disciplinary Perspectives* (pp. 47-63): Springer.

Cannataci, J.A. (2008). Lex Personalitatis & Technology-driven Law, *Script-Ed* Volume 5(1), April 2008.

Cave, J., Schindler, H.R., Robinson, N., Horvath, V., Castle-Clarke, S., Roosendaal, A. & Kotterink, B. (2012). Data Protection Review: Impact on EU Innovation and Competitiveness. Study for the European Parliament, ITRE Committee.

Chin, A., & Klinefelter, A. (2012). Differential Privacy as a Response to the Reidentification Threat: The Facebook Advertiser Case Study. *North Carolina Law Review*, 90(5), 1417-1456.

Choudhary, V., Ghose, A., Mukhopadhyay, T., & Rajan, U. (2005). *Personalized Pricing and Quality Differentiation*. Carnegie Mellon University.

Christman, J. (1989). Introduction. In J. Christman (Ed.), *The Inner Citadel; Essays on individual autonomy* (pp. 3-23). Oxford: Oxford University Press.

Ciriani, V., S. De Capitani Di Vimercati, Foresti, S., Samarati, P. (2007). k-Anonymity. In: Yu, T., Jajodia, S. (Eds.), *Secure Data Management in Decentralized Systems*. Heidelberg: Springer-Verlag.

Claes, M. L. H. K. (2009). 64 Het Verdrag van Lissabon en de Europese grondrechtenmozaiek . *Sociaal-economische wetgeving*, 57(4), 162-168.

Clarke, A., & Kohler, P. (2005). *Property Law: Commentary and Materials*. Cambridge: Cambridge University Press.

Clarke, R. (1994). The Digital Persona and its Application to Data Surveillance. *The Information Society*, 10(2). Retrieved from <http://www.anu.edu.au/people/Roger.Clarke/DV/DigPersona.html>.

Clarke, R. (2003). *Authentication Re-visited: How Public Key Infrastructure Could Yet Prosper*. Paper presented at the 16th Bled eCommerce Conference eTransformation, Bled, Slovenia.

Clarke, R. (2008). Dissidentity. *Identity in the Information Society (IDIS)*, 1, 221-228. doi: DOI 10.1007/s12394-009-0013-7.

Clauß, S., Hansen, M., Pfitzmann, A., Raguse, M., & Steinbrecher, S. (2009). *Tackling the challenge of lifelong privacy.* Paper presented at the eChallenges Conference 2009.

Cohen, J. E. (1999-2000). Examined Lives: Informational Privacy and the Subject as Object. *Stanford Law Review*, 52, 1373-1438.

Cohen, J.E. (2012). *Configuring the Networked Self.* New Haven: Yale University Press.

Conti, G. (2009). *Googling Security; How much does Google know about you?* Boston: Addison-Wesley.
Costa, L. & Poullet, Y. (2012). Privacy and the Regulation of 2012. *Computer Law & Security Review*, 28, pp. 254-262.

Côté, J. E. (1996). Sociological perspectives on identity formation: the culture-identity link and identity capital. *Journal of adolescence*, 19(5), 417-417-428.

Coyle, S., & Morrow, K. (2004). *The Philosophical Foundations of Environmental Law; Property, Rights and Nature.* Oxford: Hart Publishing.

Craig, P., & Búrca, G. d. (2008). *EU law: text, cases, and materials.* Oxford [etc.]: Oxford University Press.

Cranor, L. F. (2003). *'I Didn't Buy it for Myself'; Privacy and Ecommerce Personalization.* Paper presented at the WPES 2003, Washington.

Cuijpers, C., Roosendaal, A., & Koops, B.-J. (2007). D11.5: *The legal framework for location-based services in Europe.* FIDIS : Brussels.

Cuijpers, C. M. K. C. (2007). A Private Law Approach to Privacy; Mandatory Law Obliged? *ScriptEd*, 4(4), 304-318.

Custers, B. (2004). *The Power of Knowledge; Ethical, Legal, and Technological Aspects of Data Mining and Group Profiling in Epidemiology.* Nijmegen: Wolf Legal Publishers.

Custers, B., Calders, T., Schermer, B., & Zarsky, T. (Eds.) (2013). Discrimination and Privacy in the Information Society: Data Mining and Profiling in Large Databases. Heidelberg: Springer.

Davenport, T. H., & Harris, J. G. (2005). Automated Decision Making Comes of Age. *MIT Sloan Management Review* (Summer 2005), 83-89.

Dijk, P. van, & Hoof, G. J. H. v. (1998). *Theory and Practice of the European Convention on Human Rights* (3rd ed.). The Hague: Kluwer Law International.

DiMaggio, P., & Hargittai, E. (2001). *From the 'Digital Divide' to 'Digital Inequality': Studying Internet Use as Penetration Increases.* Center for Arts and Cultural Policy Studies, Princeton University.

Dobias, J., Hansen, M., Köpsell, S., Raguse, M., Roosendaal, A., Pfitzmann, A., . . . Zwingelberg, H. (2011). Identity and privacy Issues Throughout Life. In J. Camenish, S. Fisher-Hübner & K. Rannenberg (Eds.), *Privacy and Identity Management for Life* (pp. 87-114). Heidelberg: Springer.

Donath, J., & boyd, D. (2004). Public displays of connection. *BT Technology Journal*, 22(4), 71-82.

Driel, H. v. (1991). *Het semiotisch pragmatisme van Charles S. Peirce.* Amsterdam: Benjamins.

Durkheim, E. (1973). The Division of Labor in Society. In R. Bellah (Ed.), *Emile Durkheim on Morality and Society.* Chicago: University of Chicago Press.

Dworkin, G. (1989). The Concept of Autonomy. In J. Christman (Ed.), *The Inner Citadel; Essays on individual autonomy* (pp. 54-62). Oxford: Oxford University Press.

Dwyer, C. A. (2009). *Behavioral Targeting: A Case Study of Consumer Tracking on Levis.com.* Paper presented at the 15th American Conference on Information Systems, San Francisco, California.

Dwyer, C. (2009). The Inference Problem and Pervasive Computing. In: *Proceedings of internet research 10.0.* Milwaukee, WI, 2009.

Eckersley, P. (2010). *How Unique Is Your Web Browser?* Electronic Frontier Foundation (EFF).

Eco, U. (1984). *Semiotics and the Philosophy of Language.* Bloomington: Indiana University Press.

EDPS (2007), *Opinion of the European Data Protection Supervisor on the Communication from the Commission to the European Parliament and the*

Council on the follow-up of the Work Programme for better implementation of the Data Protection Directive (2007/C 255/01).

Elliott, A. (2001). *Concepts of the Self*. Cambridge: Polity Press/Blackwell Publishing Ltd.

Esch, R. E. v. (2004). Elektronische Handel. In H. Franken, H. E. W. Kaspersen & A. H. d. Wild (Eds.), *Recht en Computer* (pp. 151-192). Deventer: Kluwer.

European Commission. (2010). *Communication from the Commission to the European Parliament, the Council, the Economic and Social Committee and the Committee of the Regions on a comprehensive approach on personal data protection in the European Union*, COM(2010) 609 final, 04.11.2010.

European Group on Ethics in Science and New Technologies. (2012). *Ethics of Information and Communication Technologies*. Brussels: European Commission.

European Social Networks (2011). *Response to the Commission's Public Consultation on the Comprehensive Approach on Personal Data Protection in the European Union*.

Federal Trade Commission. (2010a). *Google Letter October 27 2010*. Federal Trade Commission. Washington D.C.

Federal Trade Commission. (2010b). *Protecting Consumer Privacy in an Era of Rapid Change: A Proposed Framework for Businesses and Policymakers*. Federal Trade Commission. Washington D.C..

Feinberg, J. (1989). Autonomy. In J. Christman (Ed.), *The Inner Citadel; Essays on individual autonomy* (pp. 27-53). Oxford: Oxford University Press.

Fischer-Hübner S. & Hedbom, H. (eds) (2007). *A Holistic Privacy Framework for RFID Applications*, FIDIS deliverable D12.3, available at <www.fidis.net>.

Fogg, B. J., & Iizawa, D. (2008). Online persuasion in Facebook and Mixi: A cross-cultural comparison. In H. Oinas-Kukkonen, P. Hasle, M. Harjumaa, K. Segerstahl & P. Ohrstrom (Eds.), *Persuasive 2008*, LNCS 5033 (pp. 35-46). Heidelberg: Springer-Verlag.

Foley, S. (2011). Database boasts it will track web behaviour of everyone in UK, *The Independent*. June 28, 2011.

Gangadharan, S. P. (2012). Digital Inclusion and Data Profiling. *First Monday*, 17(5).

Garfinkel, S. L. (2001). *Database Nation; The death of privacy in the 21st century*. Sebastopol: O'Reilly.

Gecas, V., & Burke, P. J. (1995). Self and Identity. In K. S. Cook, G. A. Fine & J. S. House (Eds.), *Sociological Perspectives on Social Psychology* (pp. 41-67). Boston: Allyn & Bacon.

Geurts, R. (2002). Legal Aspects of Software Agents. In J. E. J. Prins. et al. (Eds.), *Trust in Electronic Commerce* (pp. 223-265): Kluwer Law International.

Giddens, A. (1991). *Modernity and Self-Identity: Self and society in the late modern age*. Cambridge: Polity Press.

Goffman, E. (1959). *The presentation of self in everyday life*. Garden City, N.Y.: Doubleday & Company.

Gomez, J., Pinnick, T., & Soltani, A. (2009). *KnowPrivacy*. UC Berkeley, School of Information.

Goody, J. (1997). *Representations and contradictions : ambivalence towards images, theatre, fiction, relics and sexuality*. Oxford: Blackwell.

Goold, B. J., & Neyland, D. (2009). *New Directions in Surveillance and Privacy*. Devon: Willan Publishing.

Greer, S. (2008). What's Wrong with the European Convention on Human Rights. *Human Rights Quarterly*, 30, 680-702.

Grimmelmann, J. (2009). Saving Facebook. *Iowa Law Review*, 94, 1137-1206.

Groothuis, M. M. (2004). *Beschikken en digitaliseren: Over normering van de elektronische overheid*. (PhD), Universiteit Leiden, Leiden.

Gürses, S., & Berendt, B. (2010). PETs in the Surveillance Society: A Critical Review of the Potentials and Limitations of the Privacy as Confidentiality Paradigm. In S. Gutwirth et al (Ed.), *Data Protection in a Profiled World* (pp. 301-321). Heidelberg: Springer.

Gutwirth, S., & Hildebrandt, M. (2010). Some Caveats on Profiling. In S. Gutwirth, Y. Poullet & P. d. Hert (Eds.), *Data Protection in a Profiled World* (pp. 31-41). Heidelberg: Springer.

Hansen, M. (2008). Linkage Control – Integrating the Essence of Privacy Protection into IMS, *Proc. eChallenges 2008*, pp. 1585-1592.

Hart, H. L. A. (1961). *The Concept of Law* (2nd ed.). Oxford: Clarendon Press.

Hekman, S. J. (2004). *Private Selves, Public Identities: Reconsidering identity politics.* Pennsylvania: The Pennsylvania State University Press.

Helmond, A. & Gerlitz, C. (2012) The Like economy – Social buttons and the data-intensive web, *New Media and Society,* (forthcoming).

Hert, P. d. (2008). *A Right to Identity to Face the Internet of Things.* Retrieved from http://portal.unesco.org/ci/fr/files/25857/12021328273de_Hert-Paul.pdf/de%2BHert-Paul.pdf. Also on the CD included in the study of Commission Nationale française pour l'UNESCO, Ethique et droits de l'homme dans la société de l'information. Actes, synthèse et recommandations, Strasbourg, Unesco & Council of Europe publishing, 13–14 septembre 2007, Strasbourg. 2008, 63p.

Hildebrandt, M. (2006). Profiling: From Data to Knowledge. *Datenschutz und Datensicherheit,* 30(9), 548-552.

Hildebrandt, M. (2008a). Profiling and the Identity of the European Citizen. In M. Hildebrandt & S. Gutwirth (Eds.), *Profiling the European Citizen: Cross-Disciplinary Perspectives* (pp. 303-343). Heidelberg: Springer.

Hildebrandt, M. (2008b). Profiling and the Rule of Law. *IDIS,* 1(1), 55-70.

Hildebrandt, M., Koops, B.-J., & Vries, K. d. (2008). D7.14a: *Where Idem-Identity meets Ipse-Identity. Conceptual Explorations.* FIDIS Deliverable. Brussels: FIDIS.

Hildebrandt, M. (2011). Privacy na de 'computationele wending'? In V. Frissen, L. Kool & M. v. Lieshout (Eds.), *De Transparante Samenleving; Jaarboek ICT en Samenleving 2011* (pp. 29-48). Gorredijk: Media Update Vakpublicaties.

Hildebrandt, M., & Dijk, N. van (2010). Klantenprofielen: de onzichtbare hand van internet. In G. Munnichs, M. Schuijff & M. Besters (Eds.),

Databases: over ICT-beloftes, informatiehonger en digitale autonomie (pp. 65-73). Den Haag: Rathenau Instituut.

Hildebrandt, M., & Gutwirth, S. (Eds.). (2008). *Profiling the European Citizen; Cross-Disciplinary Perspectives.* Heidelberg: Springer.

Hof, C. van 't., Est, R. van, & Timmer, J. (2012). Slotbeschouwing: Hoe het internet jouw leven leidt. In C. van 't. Hof, R. van Est & J. Timmer (Eds.), *Voorgeprogrammeerd: Hoe internet ons leven leidt* (pp. 221-240). The Hague: Boom Lemma.

Hof, S. v. d., Leenes, R., & Fennell, S. (2009). *Framing Citizen's Identities; The construction of personal identities in new modes of government in the Netherlands.* Tilburg: Tilburg Institute for Law, Technology, and Society (TILT).

Hoofnagle, C.J., Soltani, A., Good, N., Wambach,D.J. & Ayenson,M.D. (2012). Behavioral Advertising: The Offer You Cannot Refuse. *Harvard Law & Policy Review* 2012(6), pp. 273-296.

Hustinx, P.J. (2009). Protection of Personal Data On-Line: The Issue of IP Addresses. *Revue Légicom* 42(1).

Irani, D., Webb, S., Li, K., & Pu, C. (2009). *Large Online Social Footprints - An Emerging Threat.* Paper presented at the International Conference on Computational Science and Engineering, Vancouver Canada.

Jaquet-Chiffele, D.-O., Anrig, B., Benoist, E., Haenni, R., Hildebrandt, M., Kosta, E., & Lefever, K. (2008). Fidis D 2.13: *Virtual Persons and Identities.* FIDIS: Brussels.

Kafka, F. (1925). *Der Prozess.* Berlin: Die Schmiede.

Kang, J. (1998). Information Privacy in Cyberspace Transactions. *Stanford Law Review,* 50(April 1998), 1193-1294.

Karnow, C. E. A. (1994). The Encrypted Self: Fleshing out the rights of electronic personalities. *Journal of Computer and Information Law,* 13(1), 1-16.

D. Kirkpatrick (2010) *The Facebook Effect: The Inside Story of the Company That Is Connecting the World.* Virgin Books, an imprint of Ebury Publishing.

Kobrin, S. J. (2003). The Trans-Atlantic Data Privacy Dispute, Territorial Jurisdiction and Global Governance. *Knowledge@Wharton* (March 2003).

Koops, B.-J., Hildebrandt, M., & Jaquet-Chiffelle, D.-O. (2010). Bridging the Accountability Gap: Rights for New Entities in the Information Society. *Minn. J. L. Sci. & Tech.*, 11(2), 497-561.

Koops, E. J. (2011). Forgetting Footprints, Shunning Shadows. A Critical Analysis of the "Right to be Forgotten" in Big Data Practice. *ScriptEd*, 8(3), 229-256.

Koot, M.R. (2012). *Measuring and Predicting Anonymity*. Informatics Institute, PhD. University of Amsterdam, Amsterdam.

Kosta, E. (2011). *Unravelling Consent in European Data Protection Legislation; a prospective study on consent in electronic communications.* (PhD), K.U.Leuven, Leuven.

Kotler, P. (1986). The Prosumer Movement : A New Challenge for Marketers. In: R.J. Lutz (Ed.), *Advances in Consumer Research*, Volume 13, Provo, UT : Association for Consumer Research, Pages: 510-513.

Krishnamurty, B., Naryshkin, K., & Wills, C. E. (2011). *Privacy leakage vs. Protection measures: The growing disconnect.* Paper presented at the Web 2.0 Security and Privacy Workshop.

Kuner, C. (2012). The European Commission's Proposed Data Protection Regulation: A Copernican Revolution in European Data Protection Law. *Privacy & Security Law Report*, 11(6), 1-15.

Lanier, J. (2010). *You Are Not A Gadget: A manifesto.* New York: Alfred A. Knopf.

Leenes, R. (2008). Do They Know Me? Deconstructing identifiability. *University of Ottawa Law & Technology Journal*, 4(1).

Leenes, R.E. (2010). Context is everything: Sociality and privacy in Online Social Network Sites. In M. Bezzi, P. Duquenoy, S. Fischer-Hübner, M. Hansen, & G. Zhang (Eds.), *Privacy and identity management for life* (pp. 48-65). Heidelberg | Berlin | New York: Springer.

Leibniz, W. G. (1969). Discourse on Metaphysics. In L. E. Loemker (Ed.), *Leibniz: Philosophical Papers and Letters* (pp. 303-330). Dordrecht: D. Reidel Publishing Company.

Lemons, R.E. (2011). Protecting Our Digital Walls: Regulating the Privacy Policy Changes Made by Social Networking Websites, *I/S: A Journal of Law and Policy for the Information Society*, Vol. 6:3, 2011, pp. 1-26.

Leon, P. G., Cranor, L. F., McDonald, A. M., & McGuire, R. (2010). *Token Attempt: The Misrepresentation of Website Privacy Policies through the Misuse of P3P Compact Policy Tokens*. Paper presented at the WPES 2010.

Lessig, L. (1999). *Code and Other Laws of Cyberspace*. New York: Basic Books.

Levy, S. (2009). Googlenomics. *Wired*(June 2009), 108-115.

Lieshout, M. v., Kool, L., Bodea, G., Schlechter, J., & Schoonhoven, B. v. (2012). *Stimulerende en remmende factoren van Privacy by Design in Nederland*. Delft: TNO.

Lloyd, I. J. (2008). *Information Technology Law*. Oxford: Oxford University Press.

Lockwood, M. (1971). Identity and Reference. In M. K. Munitz (Ed.), *Identity and Individuation* (pp. 199-211). New York: New York University Press.

Lunefeld, P. (1999). *The Digital Dialectic*. Cambridge MA: MIT Press.

Lyon, D. (2006). The Search for Surveillance Theories. In D. Lyon (Ed.), *Theorizing Surveillance: The Panopticon and Beyond* (pp. 3-20). Devon: Willan Publishing.

Lyon, D. (2007). *Surveillance Studies: An Overview*. Cambridge: Polity Press.

Ma. M., & Agarwal, R. Through a Glass Darkly: Information Technology Design, Identity Verification, and Knowledge Contribution in Online Communities. (2007). *Information systems research : a journal of the Institute of Management Sciences*, 18(1), 42-67.

Marbus, R. C. P., Fennell - van Esch, S., & Roosendaal, A. P. C. (2009). Identiteit en openbaarheid in sociale onlineomgevingen. *Computerrecht* (2), 64-68.

Margolis, J. (1971). Difficulties for Mind-Body Identity Theories. In M. K. Munitz (Ed.), *Identity and Individuation* (pp. 213-231). New York: New York University Press.

Martin, D., Wu, H., & Alsaid, A. (2003). Hidden Surveillance by Web Sites: Web Bugs in Contemporary Use. *Communications of the ACM*, 46(12ve), 258-264.

Mattei, U. (2000). *Basic Principles of Property Law: A Comparative Legal and Economic Introduction*. London: Greenwood Press.

Mattioli, D. (2012). On Orbitz, Mac Users Steered to Pricier Hotels. *Wall Street Journal*, June 26 2012. Online available at: <http://online.wsj.com/ article/SB10001424052702304458604577488822667325882.html> (Last accessed June 27, 2012).

Mayer, J., & Narayanan, A. (2011). *Re: Protecting Consumer Privacy in an Era of Rapid Change: A Proposed Framework for Businesses and Policymakers*. Stanford: Stanford Security Laboratory, Stanford University.

Mayer-Schönberger, V. (2009). *Delete: The Virtue of Forgetting in the Digital Age*. Princeton: Princeton University Press.

McDonald, A. M., & Cranor, L. F. (2011). *A Survey of the Use of Adobe Flash Local Shared Objects to Respawn HTTP Cookies*. Pittsburgh: CyLab, Carnegie Mellon University.

McDonald, A. M., & Peha, J. M. (2011). *Track Gap: Policy Implications of User Expectations for the 'Do Not Track' Internet Privacy Feature*. Paper presented at the Telecommunications Policy Research Conference, Arlington.

McIntyre, J. J. (2011). The Number Is Me: Why Internet Protocol (IP) Adressess Should Be Protected As Personally Identifiable Information. *DePaul Law Review*, 60.

Mead, G. H. (1934). *Mind, Self, and Society (from the standpoint of a social behaviorist)*. Chicago/London: The University of Chicago Press.

Mercado Kierkegaard, S. (2005). How the cookies (almost) crumbled: Privacy & lobbyism. *Computer Law & Security Report*, 21(4), 310-322.

Metz, C. (2010). Google drops nuke on 'objective' search engine utopia, *The Register*, December 16, 2010.

Metz, C. (2012). How Facebook Knows What You Really Like. *Wired*, 24 May 2012. Online available at: <http://www.wired.com/ wiredenterprise/2012/05/facebook-open-graph/>.

Meulen, N. S. van der (2010). *Fertile Grounds: The Facilitation of Financial Identity Theft in the United States and the Netherlands*. (PhD), Tilburg University.

Moerel, L. (2012). *Binding Corporate Rules: Corporate Self-Regulation of Global Data Transfers*. Oxford University Press.

Morozov, E. (2012). En wat als Facebook u zomaar aangeeft? *NRC Handelsblad*, 28 en 29 July, pp. 22-23.

Mul, J. de, & Berg, B. van den (2011). Remote Control: Human Autonomy in the Age of Computer-Mediated Agency. In M. Hildebrandt & A. Rouvroy (Eds.), *Law, Human Agency and Autonomic Computing: The Philosophy of Law meets the Philosophy of Technology* (pp. 46-64). London: Routledge.

Murphy, S. D. (2001). U.S.-EU "Safe Harbor" Data Privacy Arrangement. *The American Journal of International Law*, 95(1), 156-159.

Nabeth, T. & Hildebrandt, M. (Eds.)(2005). *D 2.1: Inventory of topics and clusters*. FIDIS Deliverable. Brussels: FIDIS.

Nationale Ombudsman. (2009). *Herzien Openbaar Rapport, 2009/199*, 23 September 2009, online available at: <http://www.nationaleombudsman-nieuws.nl/sites/default/files/rapport2009-199_0.pdf>, (last accessed June 27, 2012).

Nettleton, E., & Llewellyn, S. (2009). ECJ Provides Further Guidance on the Ambit of Database Right. *Computer Law & Security Review*, 25, 477-481.

Nissenbaum, H. (1997). Accountability in a Computerized Society. In B. Friedman (Ed.), *Human Values and the Design of Computer Technology* (pp. 41-64). Cambridge: Cambridge University Press.

Nissenbaum, H. (2004). Privacy as Contextual Integrity. *Washington Law Review*, 79, 119-158.

Nissenbaum, H. (2010). *Privacy in Context: Technology, Policy, and the Integrity of Social Life*. Stanford: Stanford University Press.

OECD. (2007). *At a Crossroads: "personhood" and digital identity in the information society*. Directorate for Science (Ed.), STI Working Paper. Paris.

Parent, W. A. (1983). Privacy, Morality, and the Law. *Philosophy and Public Affairs*, 12(4), 269-288.

Pariser, E. (2011). *The Filter Bubble: What the internet is hiding from you.* New York: Penguin Press.

Perry, M., & Margoni, T. (2010). From Music Tracks to Google Maps: Who Owns Computer-Generated Works? *Computer Law and Security Review*, 26, 621-629.

Pfitzmann, A., & Hansen, M. (2008). *Anonymity, Unlinkability, Undetectability, Unobservability, Pseudonymity, and Identity Management - A Consolidated Proposal for Terminology.* Dresden/Kiel: TUD/ULD.

Pinckaers, J. C. S. (1996). *From Privacy Toward A New Intellectual Property Right In Persona.* The Hague: Kluwer.

Pound, R. (1922). *An Introduction to the Philosophy of Law.* New Haven: Yale University Press.

Preston, C. B., & McCann, E. W. (2011). Unwrapping Shrinkwraps, Clickwraps, and Browsewraps: How the Law Went Wrong from Horse Traders to the Law of the Horse. *BYU Journal of Public Law*, 26(1).

Pridmore, J. H. (2008). *Loyal Subjects? Consumer Surveillance in the Personal Information Economy.* (Doctor of Philosophy), Queen's University, Kingston, Ontario, Canada.

Purtova, N. (2011). *Property Rights in Personal Data: A European Perspective.* Oisterwijk: BOXPress.

Reidenberg, J. (1978). Lex Informatica: the formulation of information policy rules through technology, *Texas Law Review*, Volume 76(3), p. 553-554.

Richards, D. A. J. (1989). Rights and Autonomy. In J. Christman (Ed.), *The Inner Citadel; Essays on individual autonomy* (pp. 203-220). Oxford: Oxford University Press.

Ricoeur, P., & Blamey, K. (1992). *Oneself as another.* Chicago [etc.]: University of Chicago Press.

Riesman, D. (1950). *The Lonely Crowd: A Study of the Changing American Character.* New Haven: Yale University Press.

Ritzer, G. (2010). *Focusing on the Prosumer: On Correcting an Error in the History of Social Theory.* Heidelberg: Springer.

Ritzer, G.& Jurgenson, N. (2010). Production, Consumption, Prosumption: The nature of capitalism in the age of the digital 'prosumer'. *Journal of Consumer Culture*, March 2010 vol. 10 no. 1, pp. 13-36.

Robertson, J. (2011). AP Impact: When your criminal past isn't yours. *Daily Finance*, December 16, 2011. Online available at: <http://www.dailyfinance.com/article/ap-impact-when-your-criminal-past-isnt/2066355/> (last accessed June 27, 2012).

Robinson, N., Graux, H., Botterman, M., & Valeri, L. (2009). *Review of the European Data Protection Directive*. RAND Europe.

Roosendaal, A. (2010). *Facebook Tracks and Traces Everyone: Like This!* Retrieved from http://ssrn.com/abstract=1717563

Roosendaal, A. (2012). We Are All Connected to Facebook...by Facebook! In S. Gutwirth et al. (Ed.), *European Data protection: In Good Health?* (pp. 1-17). Heidelberg: Springer.

Roosendaal, A., & Kosta, E. (2008). A legal analysis of ICT implants. In E. Kosta & M. Gasson (Eds.), *D. 12.6: A Study on ICT Implants* (pp. 33-50): FIDIS.

Roosendaal, A., Steinbrecher, S., Leenes, R., & Buitelaar, H. (2009). *Analysis of Privacy and Identity Management Throughout Life*. PrimeLife. Internal deliverable.

Rosen, J. (2000, 30 April 2000). The Eroded Self, *The New York Times Magazine*.

Rouvroy, A., & Poullet, Y. (2009). The Right to Informational Self-Determination and the Value of Self-Development: Reassessing the Importance of Privacy for Democracy. In S. Gutwirth et al (Ed.), *Reinventing Data Protection* (pp. 45-76): Springer.

Rubinstein, I., Lee, R. D., & Schwartz, P. M. (2008). Data Mining and Internet Profiling: Emerging Regulatory and Technological Approaches. *University of Chicago Law Review*, Vol. 75, p. 261.

Sayer, P. (2010). Google's Street View Wi-Fi data included passwords, email. *InfoWorld*. Retrieved from < http://www.infoworld.com/d/networking/googles-street-view-wi-fi-data-included-passwords-email-679>.

Schermer, B. W. (2011). The limits of privacy in automated profiling and data mining. *Computer Law & Security Review*, 27, 45-52.

Schermer, B.W. & Wagemans, T. (2009). *Onze digitale schaduw*. Amsterdam: Considerati.

Schwartz, M. J. (2011). W3C Proposes Do Not Track Privacy Standard. *Information Week*, (November 14).

Schwartz, P. M. (1999). Privacy and Democracy in Cyberspace. *Vanderbilt Law Review*, 52(1609), 1609-1701.

Singer, N. (2012). You for Sale: Mapping, and Sharing, the Consumer Genome. *The New York Times*, June 16, 2012.

Soghoian, C. (2006). *The Problem of Anonymous Vanity Searches*. Retrieved from <http://ssrn.com/abstract=953673>.

Soghoian, C. (2011). The History of the Do Not Track Header. *Slight Paranoia*, (January 21, 2011). Retrieved from <http://paranoia.dubfire.net/2011/01/history-of-do-not-track-header.html>.

Solove, D. J. (2002). Conceptualizing Privacy. *California Law Review*, 90(4), 1087-1156.

Solove, D. (2003). Identity Theft, Privacy, and the Architecture of Vulnerability, *Hastings Law Journal* (2003) 54, pp. 1-46.

Solove, D. J. (2004). *The Digital Person; Technology and privacy in the information age*. New York: New York University Press.

Solove, D. J. (2006). A Taxonomy of Privacy. *University of Pennsylvania Law Review*, 154(3).

Solove, D. J. (2008). *Understanding Privacy*. Cambridge/London: Harvard University Press.

Solove, D.J. (2011). *Nothing to Hide: The False Tradeoff between Privacy and Security*. Yale University Press, New Haven & London.

Soltani, A., Canty, S., Mayo, Q., Thomas, L., & Hoofnagle, C. J. (2009). *Flash Cookies and Privacy*. SSRN eLibrary.

Solum, L. B. (1992). Legal Personhood for Artificial Intelligences. *North Carolina Law Review*, 70, 1231-1287.

Spoor, J. H., Verkade, D. W. F., & Visser, D. J. G. (2005). *Auteursrecht: Auteursrecht, naburige rechten en databankenrecht*. Deventer: Kluwer.

Stearn, J. (1998). The 10 common myths of cookies. *Computer Fraud & Security*, 1998(7), 13-15.

Stefanovic, S. (2012), *Weblining and Internet Privacy*, online available at: <http://sstefanovic.wordpress.com/2012/04/30/weblining-and-internet-privacy/>,(last visited 4 October 2012).

Steinbock, D. J. (2005). Data Matching, Data Mining, and Due Process. *Georgia Law Review*, 40(1), 1-84.

Steiner, J., & Woods, L. (2009). *EU Law* (10 ed.). Oxford: Oxford University Press.

Stepanek, M. (2000). Weblining. *Business Week*, 26-34.

Stone, C. D. (1985). Should Trees Have Standing? Revisited: How Far Will Law and Morals Reach? A Pluralist Perspective. *Southern California Law Review*, 59(1), 1-154.

Strahilevitz, L. J. (2007). *Reputation Nation: Law in an Era of Ubiquitous Personal Information*. Retrieved from http://ssrn.com/abstract=1028875

Strahilevitz, L. J. (2008). Privacy versus Antidiscrimination. *University of Chicago Law Review*, 75, 363-381.

Stroz Friedberg. (2010). *Source Code Analysis of gstumbler*. New York.

Study Group on a European Civil Code, & Research Group on EC Private Law (Acquis Group). (2009). *Principles, Definitions and Model Rules of European Private Law: Draft Common Frame of Reference* (DCFR). Munich: Sellier European Law Publishers.

Sweeney, L. (2002). k-Anonymity: A Model for Protecting Privacy. *International Journal on Uncertainity, Fuzziness and Knowledge-Based Systems*, 10(2002) 557-570.

Tene, O., & Polonetsky, J. (2011). *To Track or 'Do Not Track': Advancing Transparency and Individual Control in Online Behavioral Advertising*.

Teubner, G. (2006). Rights of Non-humans? Electronic Agents and Animals as New Actors in Politics and Law. *Journal of Law & Society*, 33(4), 497-521.

Thaler, R.H. & Sunstein, C.R. (2008). *Nudge: Improving decisions about health, wealth and happiness.* London: Penguin Books.

The Economist. (2010). Data, data everywhere: A special report on managing information. *The Economist.*

Tufekci, Z. (2008). Can You See Me Now? Audience and Disclosure Regulation in Online Social Network Sites. *Bulletin of Science, Technology & Society*, 28(1), 20-36.

Turkle, S. (1995). *Life on the Screen: Identity in the age of the Internet.* New York, N.Y., [etc.]: Simon & Schuster.

Turner, J. H., Beeghley, L., & Powers, C. H. (1998). *The Emergence of Sociological Theory.* Belmont: Wadsworth Publishing Company.

Turow, J. (2011). *The Daily You: How the New Advertising Industry Is defining Your Identity and Your Worth.* New Haven: Yale University Press.

Turow, J., Feldman, L., & Meltzer, K. (2005). *Open to Exploitation: America's Shoppers Online and Offline.* Pennsylvania: Annenberg Public Policy Center.

Tyler, R. (2012) Facebook stock sales value firm at over $100 bn, *The Telegraph* 31 March 2012, <http://www.telegraph.co.uk/technology/facebook/9177844/Facebook-stock-sales-value-firm-at-over-100bn.html>.

Vedder, A. H. (2004). KDD, Privacy, Individuality, and Fairness. In R. A. Spinello & H. T. Tavani (Eds.), *Readings in CyberEthics* (pp. 462-470). Sudbury Massachusetts: Jones and Bartlett Publishers.

Verhelst, E. (2012). *Recht doen aan privacyverklaringen: een juridische analyse van privacyverklaringen op internet.* (PhD), Tilburg University, Tilburg.

Vila, T., Greenstadt, R., & Molnar, D. (2003). *Why We Can't Be Bothered to Read Privacy Policies: Models of Privacy Economics as a Lemons Market.* Harvard University.

Wagman, L., Conitzer, V., & Taylor, C. (2010). Online Privacy and Price Discrimination. *ERID Working Paper* (Vol. 79): Duke University.

Warner, R., & Sloan, R. H. (2012). Behavioral Advertising: from One-Sided Chicken to Informational Norms. *Vanderbilt Journal of Ent. and Tech. Law*, 15. Online available at SSRN: <http://ssrn.com/abstract=2034424>.

Warren, S. D., & Brandeis, L. D. (1890). The Right to Privacy. *Harvard Law Review*, 4(5).

Wathieu, L., & Friedman, A. (2009). An Empirical Approach to Understanding Privacy Concerns. *ESMT Working Paper* (Vol. 09-001). Cambridge MA: John F. Kennedy School Harvard University.

Weil, G. L. (1963). *The European Convention on Human Rights; background, development and prospects.* Leiden: A.W. Sythoff.

Westin, A. (1967). *Privacy and Freedom.* New York: Atheneum.

Westkamp, G. (2003). *EU Database Protection for Information Uses under an Intellectual Property Scheme: Has the Time Arrived for a Flexible Assessment of the European Database Directive?* Paper presented at the Fordham University School of Law Eleventh Annual Conference, Fordham.

Whitehorn, M. (2006). The parable of the beer and diapers, *The Register.* Retrieved from http://www.theregister.co.uk/2006/08/15/beer_diapers/

Winkelhorst, R. C. (2005). Privacy en zoekmachines: vergezocht? *Privacy & Informatie*(4), 146-154.

WIPO. (2004). *WIPO Intellectual Property Handbook: Policy, Law and Use.*

Wishaw, R.M.A. (2000). *De gewaardeerde klant; privacyregels voor credit scoring.* Achtergrondstudies en Verkenningen 18, De Registratiekamer.

Witte, J.C. & Mannon, S.E. (2009). *The Internet and Social Inequalities (Contemporary Sociological Perspectives).* London: Routledge.

Wood, A. F., & Smith, M. J. (2005). *Online Communication; Linking Technology, Identity & Culture.* Mahwah: Lawrence Erlbaum Associates, Inc., Publishers.

World Economic Forum. (2012). *Rethinking Personal Data: Strengthening Trust.* Geneva: World Economic Forum.

Zarsky, T. Z. (2002-2003). "Mine Your Own Business!": Making the Case for the Implications of the Data Mining of Personal Information in the Forum of Public Opinion. *Yale Journal of Law & Technology* (2002-2003).

Zarsky, T. (2006). Online Privacy, Tailoring, and Persuasion. In K. Strandburg & D. S. Raicu (Eds.), *Privacy and Technologies of Identity - A Cross-Disciplinary Conversation* (pp. 209-224). Heidelberg: Springer.

Zimmer, D. (2005). Legal Personality. In E. Gepken-Jager, G. v. Solinge & L. Timmerman (Eds.), *VOC 1602-2002; 400 years of Company Law* (pp. 265-280). Deventer: Kluwer.

Zwick, D., & Dholakia, N. (2004). Whose Identity is it Anyway? Consumer Representation in the Age of Database Marketing. *Journal of Macromarketing*, 24(1), 31-43.

Summary

"Personal data is the new oil of the Internet and the new currency of the digital world."[704] This statement by the European Consumer Commissioner pinpoints the importance of personal data in contemporary society. Over the last decade, society has become an information society, with information and knowledge as key assets for development. Currently, we are heading towards a data society,[705] in which the collection and processing of data is at the heart of the economy.

A specific type of data that is frequently processed is personal data. Processing of personal data leads to tensions concerning control and power. Commercial organizations try to leverage data to create value, while individuals have perceptions of harm and powerlessness concerning the use and protection of their data.[706] The personal data of customers have become a major asset for companies. Together with technological developments in the field of ICT and internet services, this implies that personal data about every individual are collected, further processed, and analyzed for commercial purposes by numerous businesses.

The massive use of personal data also leads to concern among individuals. "Three out of four Europeans accept that revealing personal data is part of everyday life, but they are also worried about how companies – including search engines and social networks – use their information."[707] People are concerned about lack of control and lack of transparency. Individuals have few means to prevent their data from being processed, while at the same time they have no clear view of the purposes of the processing. The impact the processing may have on the individual is even more opaque. However, there is an impact, in particular on the privacy of the individual, in the sense of the opportunities of the individual to create his own identity free from unreasonable constraints, and on his individual autonomy.

The aim of this study is to investigate whether privacy and autonomy of individuals can be better protected by implementing the concept of the digital

---

[704] Meglena Kuneva, European Consumer Commissioner, March 2009.
[705] Van Lieshout et al. 2012, p. 20.
[706] World Economic Forum 2012.
[707] European Commission.Data Protection: Europeans share data online, but privacy concerns remain – new survey. Press release IP/11/742, Brussels, 16 June 2011, on survey results of the Eurobarometer on "Attitudes on Data Protection and Electronic Identity in the European Union": <http://ec.europa.eu/public_opinion/archives/eb_special_359_340_en.htm#359>.

persona in law. A digital persona is a digital representation of an individual in the form of data. In cases where the set cannot be directly connected to an individual, the data sets are called profiles. The use of digital personae and profiles has an effect on the rights of individuals, because these data sets are used as representations of the individual when decisions are taken that affect the individual. These effects are described from a multidisciplinary perspective, and an analysis is made of possible ways to implement the digital persona in law. The main research question that is answered in this study is the following:

Can the (legal) protection of digital personae and profiles as coherent data sets, taking into account that they are used by businesses as a basis for making decisions that affect real-world individuals, improve the protection of privacy and autonomy of the individuals represented by these digital personae?

In order to answer this question, a number of steps are taken. In Part I of this study, the theory and abstract level are described. Chapter 2 gives a description of identity and representation from different disciplinary perspectives. In particular, the sociological viewpoints of Mead and Goffman are taken as a basis for further analysis in this study. This implies that specific attention is paid to the way individuals take different roles (ways of (re)presenting themselves) related to different contexts. Subsequently, the step is taken towards representation in digital form. Here, the concepts of the digital persona and profile are introduced.

A digital persona is a representation of an individual, identifiable by the one who creates or uses the data set. The concept of the digital persona was introduced by Roger Clarke, who defined it as: "a model of an individual's public personality based on data and maintained by transactions, and intended for use as a proxy for the individual."[708] The representational capacity is a key element. It follows from the definition that functioning as a proxy for a specific individual is intended, so the representations that qualify as a digital persona are limited to those data sets which contain an identifying link to an entity. Clarke distinguishes between projected personae and imposed personae. A projected digital persona is "an image of one's self that an individual conveys to others by means of data," for instance, by creating a personal page on a social network site, whereas the imposed digital persona is "an identity projected onto a person by means of data, by outside agencies such as corporations and government agencies,"[709] for instance, a record created by a credit rating agency.

---

[708] Clarke 1994.
[709] Clarke 1994.

Another form of digital representations of individuals are profiles. They are the result of an automated process where large data sets are processed in order to compose (a set of) characteristics which can be used as a basis for decision making. A profile is a set of correlated data,[710] which is created with the use of profiling technologies, a set of technologies with as a common characteristic the use of algorithms or other techniques to create, discover or construct knowledge from huge sets of data. Profiling can be defined as "[t]he process of 'discovering' correlations between data in databases that can be used to identify and represent a human or nonhuman subject (individual or group) and/or the application of profiles (sets of correlated data) to individuate and represent a subject or to identify a subject as a member of a group or category"[711] or the creation of a representation based on automated monitoring of individual behavior. The data can be aggregated from different sources. In first instance, there is no direct connection to an entity, so individuals who may be affected later on are not necessarily aware of the data collection. When at some point in time an identifier is added to the data set, a profile can become a digital persona.

In Chapter 3, it is shown how digital personae are created in practice and for what purposes. Moreover, a third form of digital personae is introduced, namely the hybrid form. This form is nowadays the most prevalent form and combines elements from the projected and imposed persona as introduced by Clarke. The data the digital persona consists of are created or provided by the individual himself as well as by others. For instance, when opening an account in a web shop, the individual provides some data, such as name, address, and bank details. The web shop provider can enrich the data set, for instance, with information about browsing behaviour, past purchases, and specific categories of items the individual is interested in.

Part I ends with Chapter 4, showing which values and rights are at stake when using digital personae or profiles as digital representations. These are human dignity, (individual) autonomy, identity, informational self-determination, contextual integrity, and privacy. The concepts are interrelated and mutually supportive of each other. Specific rights are essential to maintain higher, more abstract values. The concepts of dignity, autonomy, identity, and privacy are closely related. On the one hand, autonomous (independent) choices have to be made in order to decide on the identity an individual wants to develop and, in relation to that, what information to share with whom and for what purposes. On the other hand, privacy, with the related main concepts of informational-self-determination and contextual integrity, is a necessary condition to facilitate this autonomy. Individual autonomy and

---

[710]   Hildebrandt & Gutwirth 2008, p. 19.
[711]   Hildebrandt & Gutwirth 2008, p. 19.

identity are directly connected to the inherent value human beings have. This inherent value is often referred to as human dignity. Human dignity is a central concept in the protection of individuals and the fundamental rights they have at an abstract level in international treaties.

In the context of the European Union, fundamental rights are now laid down in the EU Charter of Fundamental Rights. An important basis for this Charter can be found in the European Convention on Human Rights (ECHR). In the ECHR, Article 8 contains the right to respect for private and family life. In case law concerning this article, connections have been made between privacy, identity and autonomy.[712] The EU Charter starts with human dignity as a central value. In addition, it contains a specific provision on the right to privacy (Article 7) which is almost similar to Article 8 ECHR. Moreover, Article 8 of the EU Charter introduces the right to protection of personal data.

Two related key concepts that are distinguished are informational self-determination and contextual integrity. It appears that the protection of these rights and values is important in light of the personal development of the individual as an entity with an intrinsic value. In order to protect autonomy and the construction of identity, privacy is legally protected. In practice, the focus in legislation aiming at the protection of informational privacy is on data protection. The OECD has adopted guidelines on data protection which list a number of basic principles that must be respected. The principles relate to the key rights and values that need to be protected. For instance, the Collection Limitation Principle supports privacy and informational self-determination, the Purpose Specification Principle directly relates to contextual integrity, and the Individual Participation Principle supports informational self-determination, identity, and autonomy.

The principles are reflected in the EU Data Protection Directive (DPD). This Directive (95/46/EC) forms a rigid European framework on the handling and electronic processing of personal data. It defines what personal data are and what processing is allowed under which circumstances. However, there are some difficulties with regard to the terminology and its meaning. Besides, the more fundamental level of privacy protection and, in relation to that, the protection of identity and autonomy, has been moved to the background. The framework, thus, may be rigid, but mainly provides requirements and guidelines for the processing of personal data. For instance, companies need to have a legitimate ground for the processing of personal data, the processing has to be bound to a specific purpose, individuals have to be informed about the processing, and companies have to take organizational and technical

---

[712] De Hert 2008.

measures to adequately protect data. Once the requirements are met, the processing is legitimate and allowed. The difficulties in terminology and the interpretation of the requirements, however, have the result that it is often debatable whether the requirements are really met. Individuals are often unaware of the processing activities and the exact related purposes, so the framework does not provide sufficient protection of the fundamental values and rights that are presented in this Chapter.

Part II of this study concerns the practice and concrete level of the study. In Chapter 5, the use of digital personae and profiles is discussed. A technical background is provided by an analysis of web interactions. Moreover, different ways of recognizing and identifying individuals by technical means, such as cookies and user accounts, are discussed. A concrete description of how digital personae and profiles are created and used is given in three case studies. The first case study shows how Facebook collects data, enriches user profiles, and monitors internet browsing behavior of members and, sometimes, non-members. Obviously, profile information of members is collected, but also browsing behavior and activities on other websites are analyzed. Subsequently, decisions are based on this analysis, which results in steering or limiting choices for individuals. An important part of this case study consists of the tracking practices facilitated via Facebook's Like-button. The second case study concerns Google and particularly focuses on the wide range of applications and services offered by this company. The coverage resulting from the large number of implementations of their services provides Google with a very strong position in recognizing individuals and collecting information about them. Moreover, since Google launched its new privacy policy, on March 1ˢᵗ 2012, services are connected and users are automatically subscribed to different services by Google. Since the individual has no control over these subscriptions and because of the extreme difficulty not to interact with one of Google's services, individual autonomy is at stake. The third case study describes the combination of online and offline data in order to take decisions affecting individuals, for example, by credit rating agencies and banks and insurance companies that collect data. Next to that, a description is given of how companies tailor their web contents real-time, based on characteristics of the individual visitor. Also in this case, choices are steered and options are limited. If exclusion from certain services or products takes place in a structural form as a result of automated decisions, this can amount to indirect discrimination. Chapter 5 ends with an overview of implications of digital persona and profile creation and use. It appears to be very difficult for individuals to maintain control over their data being collected and analyzed. Options for choosing between services and between sharing and shielding information are reduced. This leads to conflicts with the values and rights that were described earlier.

The practical level of data protection regulation is discussed in Chapter 6. The applicability of the DPD to digital personae and profiles is assessed, including the attached rights and obligations. The use of digital personae is subject to the DPD, but for profiles this is less clear. Specifically, the issue that profiles can relatively easily become digital personae is problematic from a data protection perspective. Data controllers have to take into account whether future identification may be possible. The discussion then centers on the question of what means are likely reasonably to be used for this identification and by whom. Subsequently, an elaborate description is given of the problems that arise, even when the DPD is applicable. Firstly, there is lack of clarity and certainty with regard to the processing resulting from improper fulfillment of the information duties. The exact purposes of the processing are often unclear and only described in very generic terms. Secondly, the legitimate ground of consent is frequently used by data controllers, while this consent does not meet the requirements of 'freely given' and 'informed'. The latter relates to the information duties. Consent can often not be said to be freely given, because there is no option to choose. Thirdly, processing based on a legitimate interest of the data controller is often not preceded by a proper weighing of this interest with the interests of the data subject. A concrete problem here is the difficulty to ascribe weight to the interests that need to be balanced. The implication of these problems is that there are still conflicts with the main rights and values to be respected. Chapter 6 ends with a synthesis and the final problem definition. Two key problems are identified, namely legal uncertainty for data controllers as regards the applicability of the DPD to their processing activities, and insufficient protection of individuals resulting from lack of transparency, control, and choice.

Part III of this study is aimed at finding a solution for these problems. First, in Chapter 7, existing legal constructs are discussed in order to find out whether these can be of help in better protecting the individuals' rights in online contexts. First, the proposed General Data Protection Regulation (GDPR) that is to replace the DPD is discussed. In the proposal, some improvements as compared to the current DPD are made, but still some of the main problems remain. In specific cases, better protection is offered. For instance, more attention is paid to the individuals being affected by data processing, with the introduction of the data breach notification and the right to be forgotten, but no strong tools for individuals to have their autonomy and identity better protected are added. Moreover, the scope of applicability of relevant provisions seems to be too limited to achieve the desired effects.

Subsequently, other legal constructs are assessed on their usefulness in improving protection of individuals. These constructs are legal personality and legal status, property rights and intellectual property rights. Legal personality or a legal status for digital personae appears not to be a good solution, since the digital persona is the focus point in these constructs. In order to be helpful, digital personae would have to be active entities, which is not the case. This observation leads to the idea of looking at positions of control over the digital persona. A strong form of control is provided by the legal concept of property or, more specifically, ownership. In particular, the *erga omnes* effect is useful, because it makes the property right an absolute right, i.e., that can be invoked against anyone. With regard to digital personae, however, ownership has two important drawbacks that make it not applicable directly. Firstly, ownership concerns tangibles. The main requirement for ownership, however, is legal recognition, so this problem can be solved by recognizing digital personae as objects of property in the law. Secondly, however, ownership rights can be obtained by the creator of a thing because he creates it, which implies that digital personae often would become owned by others than the data subject. The control is, therewith, still not in the hands of the data subject.

The issue of intangibility can be solved by following the regime of intellectual property rights. Therefore, a closer look is taken at copyright, database rights, and portrait law. The most promising approach appears to be the analogous application of portrait law, i.e., the right of a person to object to the publication of his portrait or to receive a financial compensation. Nevertheless, two important issues remain. Firstly, portrait law is, in cases where the digital persona is also protected by copyright, only a limitation on the rights of the copyright holder, but it does not provide independent protection right away. Nevertheless, the opportunity to limit the rights of the user of the digital persona could provide the individual with a good instrument to exercise control. Secondly, internal use of a digital persona is not covered by portrait law, since it focuses on the making public of a portrait. However, in relation to individual autonomy, the most problematic uses of digital personae are the internal uses for taking decisions which affect the individual. The scope of protection of portrait law would need to be broadened up to cover this important part as well.

Although the existing legal concepts thus turn out not to offer a complete solution directly, an important conclusion is that the digital persona as a concept is promising. Legal implementation of the concept of the digital persona may be a means to achieve better protection of individuals' rights in online contexts. In relation to profiles, there is an extra challenge, because these relate to individuals that are not identified or identifiable. The paradoxical issue here is that, in order to achieve some control, the individual needs to be identified as being the represented individual, while remaining anonymous seems to provide better protection of privacy. To conclude, even though profiles and digital personae are closely related, the link to an identified individual appears to be a crucial point when trying to regulate the use of digital representations with a view to the rights and values of the individual that need better protection.

Finally, Chapter 8 contains a proposal for implementing the concept of the digital persona as a portrait in data protection law. Two legal regimes are combined here, which brings two important improvements for the protection of the rights of the individual. First, the burden of proof as regards the processing activities when these are based on consent is shifted to the data controller. This means that the data controller has to prove that he has obtained the informed consent from the individual for the processing for the specific purpose at stake. The data controller has an increased accountability and the individual does not have to prove that he did not give his consent. The second improvement is the recognition of the digital persona as a representation (portrait) of an individual. The link between the data set and the individual that is affected by the use of the data as a basis for decisions is emphasized. The advantage for the individual is that the result of the processing gains attention, next to the procedural requirements of the DPD. There are also options to include individual profiles under the regime by taking this approach, since comparing the profile with the individual may lead to identification (based on recognition).

Because of the forthcoming GDPR, a closer look is also taken at to what extent the described issues are covered by the proposed Regulation. At least at the practical level, the GDPR brings an improvement in the protection of individuals as opposed to the current DPD. The improvements are to a large extent in line with the protection sought for in relation to the problems described in this study. The GDPR is, thus, a welcome instrument, even though some room for improvement is still present. From the perspective of the use of digital personae and profiles and the related interests of individuals that need to be protected, some indications for improvement are provided. This includes aiming at a change in mindset by adding a Recital to the Preamble that recognizes the concepts of the digital personae and profile. This change is needed to reconnect data protection law to the concepts of privacy and autonomy of the individual. The requirements for the processing of personal data are a procedural background. Solely fulfilling these requirements, however, does make the processing legitimate, but does not enforce respect for the privacy and autonomy of the data subject. At least the theoretical value which can be achieved by embedding the concepts of digital personae and profiles in law is a worthwhile exercise and can be a source of inspiration for further development of the practical embedding of the concepts.

Embedding the concepts of the digital persona and profile in order to provide better protection of privacy and autonomy of individuals, with the final aim to better respect human dignity, seems to be well-placed for success. Practical work on the embedding needs to be done, but the theoretical analysis provided in this study proves the concept of the digital persona as such to be valuable as a legal concept. The way of implementing the concept as described above does not broaden up the interpretation of the definition of personal data, but takes a holistic approach towards complete data sets, instead of separate pieces of data. The embedding of the concept, starting from a mindset that is reflected in the Preamble of the GDPR, can bring a better protection of fundamental rights and values for the individual. Moreover, the relation between digital personae and profiles and their use is emphasized.